For Keeps

For Keeps

Marriages That Last a Lifetime

Finnegan Alford-Cooper

M.E. Sharpe
Armonk, New York
London, England

Library of Congress Cataloging-in-Publication Data

Alford-Cooper, Finnegan, 1951–
For keeps : marriages that last a lifetime / Finnegan Alford-Cooper.
p. cm.
Includes bibliographical references and index.
ISBN 0–7656–0122–2 (hardcover : alk.paper).—ISBN 0–7656–0123–0 (pbk. : alk. paper)
1. Marriage—United States—Case studies. 2. Spouses—United States—Case studies.
I. Title.
HQ536.A534 1998
306.81—dc21 97–38833
CIP

Printed in the United States of America

The paper used in this publication meets the minimum requirements of
American National Standard for Information Sciences—
Permanence of Paper for Printed Library Materials,
ANSI Z 39.48-1984.

♾

BM (c) 10   9   8   7   6   5   4   3   2   1
BM (p) 10   9   8   7   6   5   4   3   2   1

This book is dedicated to:

Clyde and Florence Matthews for the inspiration and wisdom to make this research idea a reality

My grandparents, Herman and Nell Gardner, the first couple I knew who were married fifty years

My husband, David—hoping for fifty years, too

Table of Contents

List of Tables

Preface

For the last twenty-five years the high divorce rate in the United States has been a focus of research. Much is known about breaking up a marriage, but not so much is known about making a marriage last. I decided to study marriages that last fifty or more years to see what older couples could tell me. When I began this study, I had hoped to find a recipe for successful marriage or keys to making a happy permanent relationship. I wanted to find the meanings of marriage that were significant to these couples, the ways they defined their partners and themselves within their lifetime marriages. I expected all the long-term couples to be happily married; otherwise they would have divorced, wouldn't they? As it turns out, I was wrong. I learned there are many different ways to have a long-term marriage. These lifetime couples offered some guidelines for making successful relationships, and in the right circumstances they will work. But it is more complex than that.

For various reasons many unhappy couples have remained married a lifetime, and many said they actually managed to have good lives. These couples' definitions of marriage, of family life, and of gender roles all shaped the kinds of marriages they made. And their definitions were, in turn, shaped by the larger society. When these spouses grew up and married, norms and values regarding marriage and family were different from the ones that prevail today, and that makes all the difference.

I learned more about regular people's lives during the Depression and World War II than I had expected. After dozens of interviews it became clear that these two events had been significant markers in the couples' lives. "That was the Depression years," "after the Depression," "during the war," and "after the war" were the key time markers in nearly every story they told of their early lives. As spouses explained their beliefs and values, why they married when they did, when they had their children, and how they grew up, the Depression and World War II were the centerpieces of the story. The prosperity of the 1950s and the move to the suburbs emerged as another important theme in the stories of the child-rearing years. For war-time couples, raising children during the 1960s was a struggle. The events of that decade were often used to explain why one child was more difficult than the others and, ultimately, why it is more difficult to create lasting marriages today.

This book, combining survey and interview data, focuses on couples who have been married for fifty or more years. All the names have been changed to preserve the anonymity and confidentiality of study participants. In the prologue, two couples are profiled, illustrating the range of variation in marital happiness. The first chapter explains the methodology of the research and places it in theoretical context. The couples' stories of their marriages are then presented in chronological order and within the sociohistorical context. Chapter Two examines the spouses' early years: their parents' marriages, their family backgrounds, and the effects of the Depression and World War II on their lives. Chapter Three describes how the couples met and married. In Chapter Four the child-rearing years are profiled. The interviewed couples talk about their early years of struggle, the 1950s, the move to the suburbs, and the best and worst of raising children. Chapter Five explores marital problems and conflict resolution. In Chapter Six, gender differences in the experience of long-term marriage are discussed. The profile of the Mitchells demonstrates some of these gender differences and illustrates how a less happily married couple stays together for a lifetime.

In Chapter Seven, spouses compare their lifelong marriages to the marriages of their children and of younger people in general. Spouses explain why their own marriages lasted and why many of their children's marriages did not, and they give advice on how to create a successful marriage. The profile of the Barnetts exemplifies all these guidelines to successful marriage, as well as demonstrating how personal and social resources can help a couple overcome tragedy. The profile of the Howards gives another example of a happily married couple, focusing on their adaptability, especially in the years after retirement. Chapter Eight examines several aspects of the couples' lives in the later years. These spouses, in their late sixties, seventies, and eighties, discuss the rewards and pleasures of their lives now, as well as the troubles they face. The profile of the Johnsons illustrates a happily married couple adjusting to several challenges over their lives together. Finally, Chapter Nine examines the interviewed spouses' attitudes toward widowhood, the end of their lifetime together.

Throughout the book, attention is focused on each couple's own categories of meaning, how they defined their life experiences together, and how they explain what happened to them and why. This study assumes that the participants in any social relationship are actively creating and defining the relationship, interpreting each other's behavior (i.e., giving meaning to that behavior), and reacting to those definitions. The ways these spouses defined marriage and what they expected from marriage and family life shaped their behavior within the marriage. The definitions and beliefs people have about any institution, including marriage, change over time, and vary from place to place. The meanings are subjective, and to some extent, one person can never see the world as another does.

Acknowledgments

I would like to thank Long Island University for the financial support to begin this research. In particular, I want to thank Clyde and Florence Matthews, married over fifty years and directors of the Center for Creative Retirement at Southampton College of Long Island University. Without their friendship and support this research would not have been possible.

Many individuals, groups, and organizations across Long Island helped to publicize this study. An article by Laura Muha in Long Island *Newsday* resulted in a flood of phone calls for days, and I could never have had so many participants without Ms. Muha's help. The Suffolk County Department of Aging and the Nassau County Department for Senior Citizen Affairs helped with publicity and collected names of dozens of couples married over fifty years. The Long Island Council of Churches also participated in the distribution of flyers announcing the study. Senior centers and nutrition sites all across Long Island publicized the study and collected names and addresses of volunteer couples.

My social science colleagues at Southampton were very supportive and helpful while I was conducting this research. Special thanks to John Strong, Chuck Hitchcock, Ralph Herbert, Lee Stanley, Lois Tepper, and Don Baker who kept me laughing through everything. Don, thank you for your role in turning this research into a published book. Many of my gerontology graduate students participated in various stages of this research, and their help was essential in getting the job done. Drew Girolamo deserves a special thanks for driving all over Long Island with me to interview dozens of couples, all on his own time with no compensation. Fine job, Drew.

Thanks go to my husband, David, for his tireless support of this research. Besides going along on some of the interviews, he read endless versions of papers and chapters as they were written, cooked dinner, and kept the house running when I didn't. We got a late start, but if we live long enough we'll be married fifty years.

Stetson University generously provided me with a summer research grant so that I could complete this book on time. The supportive environment here is deeply appreciated.

I want to thank all the Long Island couples who were survey participants. Your enthusiastic support for this project was essential. My deepest thanks go to the sixty couples who welcomed me and my students into their homes and told us the stories of their lives together. Meeting and getting to know all of you was one of the most important and enriching experiences of my life. Your perspectives on marriage helped me to understand what works for and against us, despite all our intentions and efforts. And your insights have helped me make a better marriage, and hopefully, others will benefit from the wisdom you shared.

Some material in this volume was first published in my article, "Commitment for a Lifetime: The Long Island Long-Term Marriage Survey," in the *Long Island Historical Journal* (Vol. 7, no. 2, Spring 1995, pp. 220–234). It is reprinted here, with some deletions and changes, by permission of the *Long Island Historical Journal*.

For Keeps

Prologue

The Mortons and the Raglins (not their real names) illustrate the enormous range of marriages that can last fifty or more years. The Mortons, typical of the happily married couples in this study, illustrate all the keys to a successful marriage. The Raglins represent the less happily married couples who are still together because of a sense of duty and commitment, a lack of alternatives, and inertia. Social skills, personality factors, and role models play a role in creating successful, enduring marriages, but so does the larger sociohistorical context.

Vignette: The Mortons

The love of putting the other first.—Mr. Morton

Mr. and Mrs. Morton grew up in the same town on Long Island. She says, "Our families were friends. We attended the same church. . . . We knew each other since we were about four or five years old." He says, "She dated in her school, and I dated in my high school and all through college, but every time I came home from college we went out." She continues, "I always had a lot of parties at my house. . . . If we needed an extra boy or something . . . I would get dates for my girl friends with him. He was always there to fill in. He wasn't my date! I had other dates. . . . Maybe we were comparing."

When he graduated from high school during the Depression, his parents could not afford to send him away to college, so he went to a local two-year college first, and worked part-time in the summer, finally graduating in 1941. When he proposed, he surprised both of them. "We went to the movies one night, September 1941. . . . I brought her home, and we were sitting in front of the house, and you might say we were smooching. . . . I just turned around and looked at her, and just asked her point blank, 'When are you going to marry me?' and I don't know what made me say that. I hadn't planned on it. It just came out!" She laughs heartily as he tells the story and adds, "I guess I said yes." He says, "We just knew we got along together . . . we had all the same values."

They married in "a big church wedding" in 1942, when they were both 21 years old. Both cited "love" and "commitment" as their reasons to marry, and thought when they married, it would last. He joined the military the same year. "Then, bingo, I was off . . . November of forty-two, I was gone . . . but we were already married by then." "But," she says, "we would probably *not* have married so quickly, if it had not been wartime."

Typical of couples in very uncertain times, the Mortons said they had few expectations when they married. She explains, "I think I just wanted to be as happy as my parents were." He wanted to be happier and had one specific expectation. "My father commuted to New York City six days a week. . . . I was gonna work in the town that I lived in. . . . I was not going to commute like my father, because I did not have the opportunity to really get to know my father. He went off about seven o'clock in the morning and he didn't get home till seven at night . . . I wanted to see my children."

During the first years of the war, he was stationed in the southern United States, and she went with him. "They kept me . . . month after month, year after year . . . as an instructor for all new recruits." He "had it up to here" because he wanted to fight. His company commander made arrangements, and after some unit training, "I was in Europe fighting the war . . . January of forty-five. . . . We went up through the . . . Battle of the Bulge." Then his unit was transferred. "I was with three different armies, and the last one was . . . Patton's Third Army, and we went over into Austria and that's where the war ended for me. They shipped us back to the States for some R&R. . . . Two days before I was supposed to go back, they dropped the atomic bomb. . . . I said, 'Don't worry, I'm not gonna go,' and I didn't." He never discussed his war experiences with his wife, and regards it as the low point in their lives. "She didn't know if I was coming back or not. I was just lucky. 'Cause some things that happened over there . . . I may not have returned. . . . I'm here, that's all that counts." Old fears crossed his face as he spoke; his voice wavered and became softer. He sat far back in his chair, hands folded tightly together as he remembered.

Their first daughter was born while he was overseas. "I wasn't alone. . . . I had my parents. . . . This was such a mixed up time for everybody in those days," she recalls. When he returned from the war, "We couldn't find a place to live. . . . There was absolutely nothing. So we did stay with my folks for a little while." He went back to school to earn a master's degree on the GI Bill and got a job. "Finally we found . . . a little summer house . . . no insulation or anything. . . . We lived there for almost three years. Then we bought this property [in 1948]. . . . In another year or so, when we decided this was where we wanted to stay, we built the house, and we've been here ever since."

When they first married she had been teaching, but "I knew when I had children I didn't want to work. . . . I wanted to bring up my children myself." The second daughter was born five years after the first. After their children were born, "It knitted us closer together," he says. "We became a family then, rather than just husband and wife. . . . It became a different kind of love. . . . It became a family love. We now had a much deeper understanding of what love was all about." They say their daughters never gave them any trouble, but they were grown before the late 1960s and 1970s. She says, "They knew what was expected of them, and we were always fair with them, and we were consistent. We had a united front." He remembers, "We would have parties here for them, because we had the downstairs and they used to bring kids here and dance. . . . But we were home and we never allowed any beer."

She says, "We've been so compatible that it's almost uncanny sometimes. . . . Not too many years ago one daughter said to us, 'You never told us it was all right to fight with each other.'" He says, "We never thought about it, because we never argued. . . . You do what you can for the other person. [She's] always first in my mind." She replies, "He's always first in mine. We always put the other one first." He sums up, "Willingness to put the other person first . . . that's number one. . . . Everything else is secondary. . . . How can you argue if you're going to put the other person first? . . . She's the light of my life." She thinks a strong religious background is also important to a successful marriage. She says "There's never a day, I think, that goes by that we don't tell each other that we love each other." He adds, "Go to bed at night with a kiss . . . wake up in the morning with a kiss."

On the Long Island Long-Term Marriage Survey they both indicated they are "very happy" in the marriage. They "always" like each other, and "always" feel understood. Each one is the other's best friend, and each says the other has grown more interesting over time. They "always" confide in each other, and both say they show affection to, laugh with, and say "I love you" to each other "every day." He and she "strongly agree" that marriage is both "long-term commitment" and "sacred obligation," and that "fidelity is essential to a successful marriage." He indicated no decline in sexual interest over time, but she did, as the result of illness.

Both come from stable families, and their parents had loving, lifelong marriages. He says of his parents, "They had a difficult marriage, I think both of our parents, because they went through the heyday of the twenties and then the bottom dropped out with the Depression and it was quite a change for them, . . . but they were like us. . . . They stuck together, and they made it through." Neither Mr. Morton's nor Mrs. Morton's parents had gone to college, but both of the them finished college and they also sent both of their daughters through college.

Mr. Morton says the best thing now is "Seeing both of our daughters graduate from college, having both daughters marry. . . . Seeing them settled, having a loving marriage like ours. . . . Having five grandchildren." Church has always been important in their lives. "We gave our children the same Christian background that our folks gave us, and we can see it going to the next generation now, which makes us feel good." At Christmas they go to visit their daughters, both of whom live in the same city a few hundred miles from the Mortons. They do not have big family reunions any more, because other family members live so far away.

She says nothing has been a real problem in the marriage, but he says they do worry about each other's health. Like most people their age, they've had some brushes with illness. He says, "Two years ago, I had a quadruple bypass. And she went through all the agonies of the damned through my operation. . . . Last fall, I went through the agonies of the damned with her because they found that she had cancer." She adds, "They say I'm completely cured."

As to the difficult times, she remembers "Low points when our parents were ill. Your mother was going through her strokes . . . and my father. . . . We were running back and forth doing what we could." He explains, "You get to be middle generation, then you know, you can have low spots on both sides, low spots because of concern for your parents . . . and low spots because you're worried about your children or grandchildren. . . . Financially, we've had no problems. . . . We were never wealthy, but we were never poor." They love to travel together, although since retiring they cannot afford a trip every year. "We still go out to eat once in a while. . . . We still are able to buy clothes. . . . We saved up seven years to buy a new car." When conflicts arise, they communicate honestly, compromise, and put each other first, doing what each other wants. They say they always resolve conflict, and neither one of them ever thought the marriage might end. No particular time was most or least happy to either one of them—all the years have been happy.

After their daughters went to college, she returned to teaching. "I was only going to teach for a few years to make it easier to send the children to college. However, I enjoyed it." She taught for fourteen years until retiring. Mr. Morton was glad to retire. "I was principal in 1967, '68, '69, '70, '71. . . . I'm talking about Jackson State, Kent State, all the troubles, SDS. . . . Didn't make education a happy place at the time. I made up my mind that when I got to be fifty-five, I was leaving this to somebody else younger. . . . I looked forward to retirement, and as a result, I never missed [working]. I miss the kids, . . . but when it got to the point when a kid could come to school looking like a ragamuffin as long as he didn't smell bad. . . . I always maintained that a student will act the way they're dressed." He tried not to take sides on the war in Vietnam, but "I served and offered my life, and they were running away. Now, it was a different situation, of course, Vietnam was never a declared war. . . . It's kind of one of those gray areas, very gray."

They are concerned about younger generations today. "I think a lot of the young people today are putting too much value on things. We were invited to a wedding. . . . What were they registered for? . . . Waterford, Limoges, Gorham. . . . They're only in their early twenties, and this is what they're asking for wedding presents? We were just asking for people to come," he sighs.

Both Mortons remain active outside the home. They both work part-time, he as a lecturer at a local museum and she as a substitute teacher. "We don't try to stay together twenty-four hours a day, and I think that is important, especially after retirement." On the survey both said that the relationship is "about the same" after retirement, and she added "always happy." She indicated they are "seldom" in each other's way, and he checked "never." They have many long-term activities, group memberships, and friends. "We volunteer. . . . We do a lot of church work. . . . We have forty-year friendships right here in town." She adds, "Fifty- and sixty-year friends who are other places." Neither one knows what they would do if they were widowed. She would love to stay in their home, but "It depends on my health." He says, "It would be an awful empty life. . . . There is only one her . . . and I got her . . . and I'm not letting go. . . . I know I got the best deal in the lot."

Summary

The Mortons exemplify the happier lifelong couples. They both indicate they are very happy in the marriage, with high levels of intimacy and affection, traditional attitudes to marriage, and no real marital problems. When conflicts occur, which is seldom, they communicate and compromise. They are compatible, they love each other, and they cite religion as an important factor in their successful marriage. The Mortons have similar family backgrounds, resulting in shared values, religious beliefs, and worldview, and they knew each other for years before marrying. From the Morton's perspective, being willing to give more than one receives and to put the partner first, along with a sense of humor, are the keys to a happy marriage.

The Mortons' lives follow the life course patterns of the wartime couples. Both were teenagers during the Depression, and they married during World War II. Like most of the interview couples, the Mortons started their marriage with few material possessions and little money. Like many of the other wartime couples, they were separated by the war. His daughter was born while he was overseas, so after the war, he rejoined a family begun in his absence. Gradually, their economic circumstances improved, they had a home built in the town where he worked, and they raised their two children. They had a traditional division of labor: Mrs. Morton took care of the home and children, while Mr. Morton worked to support them. She returned to work after the children left home. Their children were grown before the 1960s, and so, they say, they had few problems raising them. They are among the 46 percent of interviewed couples who do not have a divorced child.

The best and most rewarding aspects of their lives now are still being together, and having their children and grandchildren. They remain active in church, social, and professional organizations, and both still work part-time. They are long-term people, in their marriage, in keeping the family home, and in friends and organizations. Their major concerns, like those of most other couples at this age, are health issues, and the potential for widowhood. They have been happily married for 53 years, and they expect widowhood to be the time of their greatest social and emotional loss.

Vignette: The Raglins

It's all based on my business.—Mr. Raglin

I always do what I have to do, and that's it.
—Mrs. Raglin

The Raglins met through a mutual friend. They dated for about one year before her mother insisted that they marry or quit seeing each other. "Not any particular reason, but that's the way mothers were. . . . It was a question of either/or. He didn't necessarily want to get married, and I don't think I was that crazy about it either. But it was either stop going out together or we got married." By her account there was no romance. "I'd hardly say it was love. . . . I'm not a very emotional person, that's all, and so it just happened that way." He agrees. "I got married because her mother insisted and that's it. Not to make it a big deal. I never thought I would be married. I was forced to and I did, and that's about all."

Their parents were not happy about the situation. "All mothers want their daughters to marry doctors or lawyers or Indian chiefs. And his parents . . .

thought I was a very thin, dried-out individual. And I never was." They were married in 1930, and she says, "After that we got an apartment, and we just continued our life. . . . Then of course, my daughter was born" two years later. For her, the least happy years of the marriage were the early years of motherhood. "For the first three years, I stayed home . . . and I remember feeling extremely frustrated walking a baby carriage around. . . . Frankly, I never wanted a child. . . . I just accepted it, and I wasn't very emotional about it, but I accepted it. . . . Believe me, I have always felt I had to do the right thing at the right time and I did it. And that was it. . . . I always felt good about my child, always took care of her, read to her every night, took her everywhere. . . . I made curtains and bedspreads and cooked and did all the things I was supposed to do, so we managed to eke out an existence." He says, "She's a good mother." Having a child did not bring them closer together emotionally. She says, "I don't think that we even thought about it." He adds "There's no thinking along those lines, whether it got better or worse or anything. Nothing."

After three years she went back to work and began to attend college at night. "I became a perpetual student. . . . I went for ten years at night and got my BA. I worked during the day . . . then I took my master's." They both attribute the longevity of their marriage to their common enjoyment of his business contacts and their activities with these people. He says, "It's all based upon my business, the people whom I was in business with were very interesting people."

"He likes classical music, I have learned to like it. We've learned to play bridge, we've both enjoyed taking trips together. In that way, we both have things in common. And yet I was able to go to school at night without any hindrance, without any problem. He accepted whatever I was interested in doing alone, which was very important. So my feeling is . . . you should try to develop things that you have in common. On the other hand, if you have anything you want to do, it should be accepted."

The Raglin's survey answers indicate a low level of marital happiness and intimacy. Mrs. Raglin says that, overall, the marriage has been "unhappy," she only "sometimes" likes him as a person, and he "rarely" understands her. He says the marriage has been "somewhat happy," and he "usually" likes her as a person, but she, too, "rarely" understands him. Both of them list "willingness to compromise" as the only positive factor in their marriage. He says indecisiveness also held them together. She agrees that "marriage is a long-term commitment," as her comments indicate, but he is neutral on this issue. Neither is the other's best friend. They "rarely" confide in or laugh with each other, and she "never" shows affection or tells him she loves him. He says he "rarely" shows her affection or says "I love you."

"He'd forget your birthday, nine times out of ten your anniversary. It's almost amusing. . . . This year . . . our anniversary, I made sure we went to a good restaurant. I said 'happy anniversary.' He never even answered. . . . It's not that he doesn't care, he just doesn't think of it. So as I said, that kind of attitude has definitely changed *my* attitude, which might have improved emotionally. Just status quo." When asked if they shared values she replied, "I don't think we've even thought about it. More or less, we've done the same thing all the time, chances are we agreed, that our values were more or less the same."

Mr. Raglin says he expected "nothing exciting or anything" when he married. He has very little to say about his wife at all. He cannot identify any special or important quality that his wife has, and no particular time was most or least happy for Mr. Raglin. Asked whether they think the same things are important in life, he says, "I don't think it's ever come up." As to their sexual relationship, "Very early on, we gave up going together . . . nothing." She says the same: "As I said, as far as I'm concerned I was never very emotional. As far as he's concerned, on a personal level, I have no doubt that he was cheating; however, I guess many men are that way. . . . He was never sentimental. All he was interested in was sex as sex." Both said during the interview that they had no extramarital affairs.

Acceptance of what life has to offer is the enduring theme of the Raglin's marriage. "There was no question, once you were married, you were married. In that, there was no question. . . . My mother once said to me, . . . 'If you'd married so and so, you wouldn't have these problems.' And I told my mother that if I married somebody else, I'd have other problems. Problems are built in. And this is it, it's not a question of liking or not liking, especially when you have a child. . . . I don't think I ever thought about it. I just accepted the fact 'this is it,' and this is the way I'm going to live. . . . I just accepted it. . . . This is what I had, this is what I got, this is what I have to put up with. . . . It was just a matter of realizing that whatever I do will not be any better or worse than what I am doing. . . . It's pretty traumatic to make changes. It's easier just to [stay] status quo. As I said before, I was never emotional. I just accepted whatever life threw at me. . . . It's a question of accepting the fact, that no matter what, you make the best choices at the moment, and realize they're all choices. They could go either way. And you just learn to live with them."

They both agree that finances have been a problem over the years. She says they "never" agree on finances, but he says they "usually" agree. Beyond finances, she also indicated problems with "husband not working," and with his "annoying habits." She says they "never" agree on "aims or goals in life," but he says they "usually" agree. Not surprisingly, they do not cite "communication" as a positive factor in their marriage.

She does not think he was much of a businessman. "There was a time when he was not working, and he might have accepted a job of lesser expectations, but he refused when nobody else could get a job. . . . I always felt I had to be financially independent and do whatever I had to do. . . . I never felt that he had the financial responsibility that he should have. The fact that I became a teacher assured us of a good health plan, financial security." She also made some wise investments. "I resented that very much, . . . the fact that I did everything myself. . . . However, all in all, I accepted it, and as I said from the very beginning, problems are built in . . . so we just managed to get along."

Another problem was his lack of help around the house. "The one thing that I missed entirely . . . my one big bugaboo is that I never thought of women's lib years ago. He was not very cooperative; however, if I had been insistent . . . he might have done more. He just accepted whatever it was . . . never thought of doing anything. . . . He did nothing to help. That was accepted. I came home, I cooked, I cleaned, and my beloved husband would sit down and eat, put his *Times* up, and never even know what he was eating."

While she says they have relied on "avoidance," "compromise," and "passage of time," she also reports that they "never" resolve their conflicts. He agrees they used "avoidance" and "compromise," but he thinks they "usually" resolved their conflicts. He says that when they disagree they "Walk away. . . . When I'm troubled, I tell her. And when she's troubled, I guess she asks me; that's about all." She says, "If I had a problem, I'd stop talking and that wasn't good. I just stop talking, and he knew I would get over it. Now, somehow or other I just forget it, that's the way it is. . . . He's not much of a talker at all. . . . He rarely gives you an opinion. . . . He listens. As far as yelling is concerned, he is now getting to the point where he does. The way he talks and yells is very disturbing, and my reaction, of course, I might yell back, but it distresses me, frankly, and he wasn't always that way."

Her explanation for the current high rate of divorce illustrates her adaptation to her own unhappy marriage over the years. "The divorce rate is very high in my opinion because we don't accept the faults of others. We just expect people to be perfect, and they're not perfect. And in my opinion, the most important thing is, change what you can change, do it in a way that isn't so obvious, and things that you can't change, try to work around it. . . . I felt that I was a separate person, there were things that I wanted to do, and doing what I wanted to do has made my life much more acceptable and in general, I feel I've had a good life. . . . I don't believe that everyone should stay married. There are things . . . such as abuse, verbally, or abuse physically, no one should have to stand for, but within reason, there are arguments, and if you could find a way to defuse some of them, and if you could find a way to be yourself, and do enough things that satisfy you as an individual, you can manage to get along. I also feel very strongly that if you *do* get a divorce, you take yourself to the next marriage with the same problems that you had in the first marriage."

She discusses her own daughter, who has divorced twice and been widowed once. "She married the first person, it was a matter of religion, but that's beside the point. He wanted her to be only with him. He didn't want her to see us. We had very little to do with them anyway, but this was his way. And the second person she married . . . he was good to her. And that broke up. And then she married a man who obviously wasn't physically very well. He died. . . . And even now, she has a relationship with someone. . . . I don't really care at this time, they get along and that's all. She's sixty. My granddaughter is about twenty-eight, twenty-six, and she's having her problems, which distress us no end. In my estimation, she's very judgmental and she's never going to meet Mr. Right or Prince Charming, and she will not allow for anything else. So we have expectations that don't make sense. You're not gonna do any better as you go along, you're still gonna have problems. That's it."

Despite their relatively unhappy marriage, both claim they did not consider divorce. He says of life without her, "Never entered my mind to think of a thing like that." She says, "Frankly, I have a great fear of . . . going through the crisis of becoming a widow, things that I have to do, great fear of that. Being alone, naturally something that I know I wouldn't like, and I would just do the best I could. No problem there. I always do what I have to do and that's it. That's a big factor in my life. No matter whether I liked it or not, I do what I have to do, and I never feel guilty about it, because, there's an inner feeling of no choice, you just do what you have to do."

Both report now to be the happiest point of their marriage. To Mrs. Raglin, "The rewarding aspect is financially we are far from rich, but the feeling of independence means a great deal to me. Socially we have very good friends. We like the same things. We play golf together, we play bridge together, we enjoy music together, so it's very satisfactory, no problem. I feel that I've had a good life." Mr. Raglin says the best thing about their marriage is "My daughter. She was a good kid, she was smart. . . . Of course, my granddaughter's important, very important. . . . I'm happy about my daughter and granddaughter and that's it."

Summary

The Raglins exemplify the less happily married long-term couples. They did not love each other when they married and felt forced into marriage by family pressures. Sexual relations between them ended early in the marriage. She suspects infidelity, but he denies it. He does not hold traditional attitudes to marriage, but she does, and they have low levels of agreement on major family issues. Luckily, both had a "willingness to compromise."

Both had few expectations of married life and were resigned to do their duty to each other and their child, but without emotional attachment and involvement. They give little evidence of communicating about significant issues. After sixty years together, they are not sure whether or not they share basic values. Both spouses indicated they have used "avoidance," "compromise," and "the passage of time" to settle conflicts, which she says "never" were resolved, but he thought were "usually" resolved. He has little to say, positive or negative, about his wife. She has plenty to say about him and his annoying habits, his periods of unemployment over the years, and the financial responsibilities that she had to carry. Despite this negative portrayal of their marriage, neither wants to face widowhood. They prefer their unhappy marriage, because it still provides stability, and neither wants to be alone.

Within the continuity of a long-term marriage, they have created relatively separate, but parallel lives. Over the years, they have developed friends and activities they enjoy, some shared and some not. Their daughter and granddaughter, both of whom live in the area, are important to them. Among the interview subsample, couples who are "less happily married" are more likely than those "happily married" to have divorced children. Their daughter fits this pattern, and they worry about their granddaughter.

Chapter One

Methodology and Theoretical Perspectives

Introduction

The Long Island Long-Term Marriage Survey was conducted to determine what factors contribute to long-lasting marriage among a nonrandom sample population of couples married fifty or more years. Five hundred seventy-six couples returned completed questionnaires. Interviews with a subsample of 60 of the 576 survey couples focused on the spouses' stories of their lives together. Spouses had the chance to describe, in their own words, reasons for the longevity of their marriage, how their lives changed or remained the same over a lifetime of marriage, their theories about marital success and failure, and the meaning lifetime marriage has for them. This is the largest survey, to date, of couples married fifty or more years.

As Sharon Kaufman found in her research, "Old people formulate and reformulate personal and cultural symbols of their past to create a meaningful, coherent sense of self, and in the process they create a viable present" (1986, p. 14). These Long Island spouses, in relating their life stories, take particular symbols and experiences from their pasts and offer reasonable, coherent stories of how they came to be together in the present, and how they feel about it now. Themes emerge from these life stories, and the weaving together of themes and experiences creates the continuity of a lifetime. From Kaufman's perspective, "people crystallize certain experiences into themes," and these themes become central in their lives (p. 26). The sources of many of these themes lie in the sociocultural context. The background for these couples was the Depression and World War II. Themes of perseverance, endurance, acceptance and tolerance, hope, fidelity, family, and hard work emerge in nearly all the spouses' stories.

Methodology

During 1993–1994, flyers announcing the Long Island Long-Term Marriage Survey were mailed to virtually all nutrition sites and senior centers on Long Island, New York, asking for volunteer couples and giving an 800 telephone number to call for copies of the questionnaire. The Center for Creative Retirement at the Southampton campus of Long Island University, the Suffolk County Department of Aging, the Nassau County Department of Senior Citizen Affairs, and the Long Island Council of Churches assisted in the distribution of flyers and information about the study. In addition, local newspapers and radio stations announced the launching of the survey. Callers who responded to the publicity left their names, addresses, and telephone numbers on a message tape. A set of questionnaires (one for the wife and one for the husband) was mailed to each of these couples, with a self-addressed, stamped, return envelope. Over 1,400 couples requested copies of the questionnaire, and 576 successfully completed and returned the survey.

The questionnaire (see Appendix A) consisted of thirty items examining (1) overall marital happiness, (2) marital intimacy, (3) traditional attitudes to marriage, (4) reasons for marriage, (5) positive factors contributing to the success of the marriage, (6) agreement on eight basic family issues, (7) issues that caused problems in the marriage over the years, (8) methods of conflict resolution, and (9) changes in the marriage over time (with regard to sexuality; happiest and least happy times; whether spouses ever thought the marriage might not last, and if so, when). Each spouse also indicated year of marriage, age at marriage, religious affiliation, educational level, number of children, and current joint yearly income.

Survey spouses rated their marital happiness on a five-point scale, from "very happy" to "very unhappy." If the marriage was less than happy, spouses chose from a list of possible factors those they thought helped to hold the marriage together. In this study, marital intimacy is measured with seven questions: (1) the degree to which one likes one's spouse as a person (always to never); (2) whether one regards the spouse as best friend (yes or no); (3) the degree to which one feels the spouse understands him or her (always to never); and the frequency with which one (4) confides in (always to never), (5) shows affection to, (6) says "I love you" to, and (7) laughs with one's spouse (the last three from every day to never). Traditional attitudes toward marriage are measured by how strongly one agrees that (1) marriage is a sacred obligation and (2) marriage is a long-term commitment (very strongly agree to very strongly disagree), and by answering yes or no to the statement (3) "fidelity is essential to a successful marriage."

To achieve some comparability with other studies of long-term marriage, several survey questions were drawn directly from earlier studies. In particular, questions concerning spouse as best friend, liking one's spouse, thinking one's spouse has grown more interesting over time, defining marriage as a long-term commitment, and defining marriage as a sacred obligation were all taken from Lauer and Lauer's long-term marriage questionnaire (Lauer and Lauer 1986; Lauer, Lauer, and Kerr 1990). Questions regarding agreement on major family issues: family finances; recreation; religion; sexual activity; aims or goals in life; amount of time spent together; career decisions; division of household tasks; and how often one confides in, shows affection to, and laughs with one's spouse were taken from Spanier and Filsinger's Dyadic Adjustment Scale (1983). Questions about positive factors contributing to the success of the marriage (mutual respect, trust, good communication, children, mutual need, compatibility, and loving relationship), methods of conflict resolution (avoidance of the issue, communication, and compromise), and the happiest time of the marriage were taken from Stinnett, Carter, and Montgomery's Marital Need Satisfaction Scale (1972). Other research that stimulated survey and interview questions includes Locke and Wallace's Marital Inventory (1959); Spanier, Lewis, and Cole (1975); and Sporakowski and Houghston (1978). (See Appendix A for the complete Long Island survey.) Pearson's chi-square was used for all correlations.

Over 250 couples who were interested in follow-up interviews wrote their names, addresses, and telephone numbers on the questionnaires they returned. A random subsample of sixty of these survey couples participated in follow-up, in-depth interviews lasting from two to three hours, usually conducted in the couple's home, during 1994–1995. Forty-five of the sixty couples were interviewed together for the first half of the time, and then separately by same-sex interviewers (the researcher and graduate-student assistants). Fifteen couples were interviewed together for the entire time by the researcher and graduate assistants. Questions reviewed the spouses' lives together: how they met and married; the marriages of their parents, brothers and sisters, and children; the early years together, before and after the children were born; their expectations about marriage, then and now; the best and worst times of their married lives; day-to-day life in the later years; causes of conflict in the marriage and methods of resolving those conflicts; and the couple's advice on marriage. (See Appendix B for the interview format.) All interviews were tape-recorded, duplicated, transcribed, and archived.

The focus of this book is on the spouses' definitions and descriptions of their married lives. Whether or not the memories are, in fact, historically accurate and objectively verifiable is not the issue. What is important is, after spending a lifetime together, how did these older adults conceptualize the relationship they had, the family they created, and their lives now? How do they explain their marital longevity?

Other Research on Long-Term Marriage

Many studies of long-term marriage, including the Long Island Long-Term Marriage Survey, have found that particular interpersonal skills and characteristics and emotional commitment are significant factors in maintaining a marriage over many years. Lauer and Lauer's study of long-term marriage (1986) found that the happiest couples are friends who share lives and are compatible in interests and values. Other factors that contribute to marital longevity are commitment, agreement on life goals, laughing together, and an ability to resolve conflict. Stinnett and Sauer (1977) concluded that strong families are characterized by shared quality time, good communication, commitment to the family, some sort of religious orientation, and an ability to negotiate conflicts. Stinnett, Carter, and Montgomery (1972) also found mutual respect and trust to be characteristic of successful marriages. Results from the Long Island Long-Term Marriage Survey support all of this research.

The results of the Long Island Long-Term Marriage Survey also add support to Ade-Ridder's (1989) and Brubaker's (1985) conclusions about long-term marriage. They, too, found that mutual sharing and companionship are important for couples in long-term marriages. The present research substantiates Cole's conclusions (1984). Marriage in the later years can be an important resource for an individual's personal development over the life course. Cole discussed research data showing that happily married, partner-centered couples adjust well to retirement, and communicate and resolve conflicts in a nondestructive manner. They generally support and cushion each other against the assaults of life. The Mortons, profiled in the Prologue to this book, are an example. Cole (ibid.) also pointed out that many unhappy couples go through the marriage performing the routine instrumental tasks and activities. They fulfill their roles, but without intimate involvement with one another or the relationship. Children often become the sole focus of women, and men devote themselves to careers or avocations. Cole called these interests "safety valves," acceptable alternative attractions (ibid.). The Raglins (also profiled in the Prologue) are an example of this type, although Mrs. Raglin focused on school and work instead of children.

The Long Island Long-Term Marriage Survey provides further evidence of the importance of commitment, compatibility, love, and companionship in long-lasting marriages. Roberts's research demonstrated that independence, commitment, companionship, and caring are the most important factors in creating marital longevity (1979–1980). Rowe and Meredith's research had similar results (1982). The most important reasons for marital longevity in their sample population are love, children, companionship, commitment, compatibility, spouse's attributes, and financial security. Both commitment and companionship grow more important the longer a couple is married.

Just as Wallerstein and Blakeslee (1995) found in their study of good marriages, the more happily married Long Island couples have a "give-and-take" attitude, a willingness to sacrifice for each other. They define their marriage as a creation that has taken hard work, dedication, and commitment. Both Wallerstein and Blakeslee's study and the present study examine the effects of social change (i.e., in the economy, social values, and norms) on marriages. Unlike the Wallerstein and Blakeslee study, the Long Island Long-Term Marriage Survey found that husbands and wives had some different definitions and experiences of their marriage. Most important, husbands have more positive views of the marriage than do wives, overall.

There is no consensus on whether marital satisfaction increases, decreases, or remains the same over the marriage. Swenson, Eskew, and Kohlhepp (1981, 1989) found that expressions of love decreased over the life cycle. Herman (1994) found no age-related differences in overall marital satisfaction. In his sample, couples who report declining satisfaction most often report the sources of dissatisfaction to be sexual activity, communication, and the time spent together. The results of the Long Island survey support Herman's conclusions and suggest that expressions of love and intimacy do change, but do not necessarily decrease over the life cycle. The current research also suggests that *some aspects* of marital satisfaction may decrease during the middle child-rearing years, but this does not necessarily mean spouses are unhappy with each other or the marriage. It may simply reflect a predictable increase in role demands and less time available for the relationship, a stress overload that will diminish in time.

The Long Island Long-Term Marriage Survey is a significant contribution to marital longevity research, because, first, no other study has used such a large survey sample coupled with so many in-depth interviews. The interviews allowed the spouses to tell their life stories and to contrast their own marriages with those of younger generations, adding an intergenerational comparative component. The married couples give their perspectives on the rising divorce rate generally, and the divorces of their own children. Second, few studies of long-term marriage focus exclusively on marriage in later life. Researchers sometimes define long-term marriage as fifteen years or more, resulting in sample populations that are younger. Third, the results of this research suggest that different norms, values, and sources of social support regarding marriage may make long-term marriage more difficult to maintain now and in the future.

Theoretical Perspectives

This research relies on three major theoretical perspectives: symbolic interaction, the life course perspective, and Atchley's continuity theory (Atchley 1994, 1996). These three theoretical perspectives share three assumptions and propositions about the individual in society. First, all three theoretical perspectives examine changing definitions of the situation over time and from place to place. Every society, at any particular time, is characterized by different norms, values, and beliefs (a worldview) that specify how reality is defined and perceived by that group of people. Second, members of society are socialized to the norms, values, and beliefs of the particular culture at a specific point in time. Third, the theories assume that individuals are active participants in their social world, that there is an ongoing feedback between an individual and his or her social environment. Each has the potential to change the other, to influence subsequent definitions and behaviors. Within the larger cultural framework, norms, values, and beliefs change over time as people create new meaning and redefine situations and relationships. Husbands and wives actively create their marriages as they interact together over time within a particular sociohistorical context.

Symbolic Interaction Theory and Marital Relationships

To understand how marriage lasts a lifetime, we have to understand the meanings that spouses have given to their marital experiences, the ways in which they have defined their partners and their lives together. People define and give meaning to the world around them through interaction with others (Klein and White 1996). According to Berger and Kellner (1992), when people marry they merge biographies, so that couples not only share experiences but also share a common way of explaining those experiences. According to this theory, marriage is a unique kind of validating relationship: "the crucial nomic instrumentality in our society" ("Nomos" is a sense of order and belonging, the opposite of anomie, ibid., p. 166). Through marriage, two individuals come together, interact, and redefine themselves. Marriage is one of the most significant of the social relationships that create order and meaning in a person's life. Every individual needs his or her sense of self and place in the world to be validated by his or her significant others, so that life can "make sense." When people have no significant others to provide feedback, to share in the social construction of reality, anomie is the result (ibid.).

Berger and Kellner suggest that the best way to examine a person's relationship with others is as "an ongoing conversation," a dialectical relationship (ibid., p. 167). Each partner is offering his or her definition of the situation, and the other is reacting, responding, reshaping or reinforcing that definition, usually many times. Every conversation validates the definition of reality these spouses share. Definitions can be taken for granted and remain unquestioned, or the conversations can provide contexts for change as circumstances change. Berger and Kellner suggest that one, literally, "converses one's way through life" (ibid.). A sense of reality is maintained through conversation with significant others. This is not to say that other realities do not exist for each individual (i.e., his and her versions of the marriage).

According to Berger and Kellner, marriage creates a "nomic rupture," a rip in the sense of order and belonging for each marriage partner in all their other relationships. Marriage requires redefining the self in relation to the spouse, and to children, in-laws, and a whole host of significant others through a lifetime (ibid., p. 169). The married person sees his or her former relationships differently simply by being in a different reality-making dyad, and experiences a shift or change in his or her own identity. The couple makes new friends; new definitions of self evolve; and a new subjective reality is created through the institution of marriage, giving each partner a sense of order and belonging in the world.

People not only actively create the present. Berger and Kellner maintain that married couples can recreate and redefine their pasts in several ways (ibid.). First, sometimes a spouse's past story has been told and retold so many times that the partner knows it as well as the person who experienced the event. Many interviewed spouses retold stories of their partner's youths before they knew each other. Second, partners may not tell everything about their pasts, and thus may recreate themselves to better fit with their partners' definition of them. Third, they may learn to reinterpret their pasts from a different perspective, and thus may redefine themselves. Berger and Kellner argue that people do not recognize this nomic process, and the reality they create is perceived as "discovery" of each other and themselves. As couples talk over situations, their perceptions become real and valid to each other.

Somehow married partners have to reach some common conversation, some consensus on the definition of reality in order to continue the conversation, and thus, the relationship. When people are ambivalent or unclear, they talk it out until some common meaning can be accepted. They may agree to disagree, and this disagreement then becomes the common definition of reality. This constant conversation through which the world is defined and experienced can lead to a stable, common objective sense of reality (ibid., p. 171). Every time one's beliefs or attitudes are validated and reinforced by significant others, they become even more real, more acceptable, more "objective." The marital conversation expands into a family conversation when children are born, and with more people sharing the same definitions of reality, the family perspective on the world, and on each other, becomes even more real and valid.

The future is also defined together by marital partners. By making certain choices they forego others, and in a sense, the horizon of the future narrows. There is a "stabilization," affecting each partner's sense of present and future reality (ibid., p. 172). All things become no longer possible as one begins to actively make life choices—to marry, to have children, to choose one career over another. The perspective on the "self" grows more stable over time too. This is related to the concept of the "looking glass self," and learning to see oneself as others see us (Cooley 1922). We learn to define and experience ourselves as we think our significant others see us, define us, and experience us. We interpret other people's reactions to us, and we react on the basis of our interpretations, our definitions of the situation. After a marriage of fifty or more years, there are not only shared definitions, but a full lexicon with idioms and slang. The senses of continuity and stability and a certain character of reality are well established. However, this self-definition and the meaning given to a marriage by both partners is not necessarily positive, and stable, long-term marriages are not necessarily happy.

The family can be viewed from two different perspectives: from the inside, using the perspective of the family members themselves, and from the outside, using cultural norms and values to evaluate family members' role performances. Social roles are expectations for behavior that are associated with each social status, like wife, husband, mother, father. The status of mother has particular behavioral expectations associated with it, shaped by the norms and values of the time. Social roles make social life predictable and allow us to evaluate the effectiveness of other people's role performances. Of course, rules and roles change continually over time and vary from place to place (Klein and White 1996).

There are four basic propositions from symbolic interaction theory that can be directly applied to the study of marriage and family life (ibid.). First, when a person thinks he or she performs a role well, there is greater satisfaction in performing that role. A person who believes that he or she is successfully performing the role of husband or wife will take more satisfaction in the marital role, and will be more likely to continue playing that role.

Second, the more clearly a role is defined, and the more consensus there is about the "script" for that role, the less role strain an actor will experience. When women grow up believing that becoming a wife and mother is the path to self-fulfillment, and everyone around them supports that idea, then it is easier to perform that social role, to feel fulfilled by it, and to feel less conflict about doing it. This was more often the case with these long-married wives than with younger married women today.

Third, the more different roles a person plays, the less consensus there is about how to play the various roles. Actors will experience conflicting demands and obligations, all of which can overwhelm the average person (ibid.). For example, stay-at-home wives and mothers had fewer conflicting social roles than working mothers. Couples with many children will experience more role conflict than parents with only one or two children. Traditional breadwinner-husbands and fathers experienced fewer role conflicts than husbands today who are expected to participate in household labor and child care, and also to earn a living. Finally, the more role strain there is associated with any particular role, the more difficult it is to move into that role, and the easier it is to move out of it. Parents who had great difficulty in adjusting to the child-rearing years, and who were relieved when they launched their children, were experiencing role strain.

All of these role expectations are communicated through socialization experiences—through the lifelong, cumulative process of learning one's culture and internalizing, or learning to believe in, that culture (Berger and Luckmann 1966). The couples learned to define and believe in marriage as a lifetime commitment, and this shaped their subsequent behavior. Insofar as partners come from the same society and share ethnic, class, and religious identity, they tend to share more values, norms, attitudes, and beliefs. Once again, for these couples, more than for people who marry today, there were fewer acceptable options, so the choices were clear. Women received the most social support and socialization reinforcement to be wives and mothers, and men to be husbands, fathers, and breadwinners. However, these are ideal types. Constrained by the sociohistorical context (i.e., the Depression and World War II), each couple had to turn these expectations and ideal types into a meaningful life which they mutually defined and created. This social construction of reality by married couples takes place within a life course and a sociohistorical context.

The Life Course Perspective

Characteristic of the life course perspective is the assumption that the larger society affects the family group. Life course theorists also take a multidimensional view of time, assuming that individual family members, interactions among them, the structure of the family, family roles, norms, and so on all change over time. Not only are there external changes impinging on a family, but there are internal changes as well (Klein and White 1996). As people get older, relationships change or end, and people move through different stages of family life. These theorists also use the concept of "social process time," marking one's life by different events such as "after the war." Within families, this is "family process time," a key to explaining family change (ibid.). For example, a couple may be changed forever by some accident, so that "before the accident" and "after the accident" are the most significant markers in their lives.

A family's development over time is shaped, in part, by larger social norms which are age and stage graded (ibid., p. 127). Not only are family roles dependent on gender and age, but also there are developmental stages in a family over time, as members enter or leave the family, often with great stress. There is a generally agreed-upon sequence of stages in the family life cycle, and these stages have an expected time of occurrence and a duration, yet there is always variation. The sequence is more important than the timing. For example, cultural norms support having children some unspecified time after, not before, marriage. The family life cycle, then, is somewhat predictable, existing within an ever-changing cultural system.

In social gerontology, the life course has several different meanings. First, statistical definitions of the life course focus on statistical regularities in stage and age sequencing over the family life cycle among different age cohorts (Rindfuss 1991). Second, cultural definitions of the life course focus on what people are expected to do as they move through the various life stages. These are idealized progressions, such as the expectation that couples will not start families until they are economically able to do so, or that there are more and less ideal ages to marry, to have children, to finish school and so on (Atchley 1996).

Third, the biographical life course focuses on the paths that individuals take through the life span and how their paths are shaped by the intersection of life stage and historical era. Elder's work (1974) focuses specifically on the life course from the individual's perspective. He adds history to the analysis by taking into account time period, age, and birth cohort. Timing and sequencing norms in the family life course are shaped by the historic period, the age of the people experiencing the event, and the other norms to which each birth cohort was socialized. Thus, how the long-married couples in the present study created their marriages, how they defined their lives together, and how they evaluate those lives now were shaped by the particular historical circumstances through which they lived, and by their age and stage of the life cycle when they experienced these changes. The Depression and World War II, 1950s prosperity, the tumultuous changes of the 1960s and 1970s, and the economic downturns of the 1980s are the specific sociohistorical circumstances pertinent to this research.

Of course, real lives do not fit neatly into statistical or cultural models. There is a great deal of variation, in part because of gender, class, racial, ethnic, and regional differences. For example, the sequence of stages in the life courses of men and women differ significantly. Women often postpone or take leaves from careers or jobs to raise children, while few men do. Even when the ideals cannot be realized, they serve as guidelines (Atchley 1996, p. 138). Marriage partners must juggle ideals and expectations from the various institutions and social relationships in which they participate, to create their marriage and family.

Of particular interest in this study are the differences between the couples who married before and during the Depression era and the couples who married later. How old the spouses were during the Depression and the war made a significant difference in their lives. For example, were the couples raising their children through the Depression or were they still living at home with parents? Did the couple experience wartime separation while the husband was overseas, or were the husbands older family men who were not called into service? Was the couple among the young couples who moved to the suburbs after World War II, all about the same age raising their small children, or were they moving to the suburbs in the second wave as retirees? Did the couples raise their children before or during the 1960s?

In the 1990s, as these couples have reached their late sixties, seventies, and eighties, they have experienced many other social changes: generous veterans' benefits, the advent of Social Security, Medicare, an increasing number of private pensions, and skyrocketing property values that make their homes worth more than they could have imagined. In a sense, as Newman (1988) points out, couples who were lucky enough to have survived the war and who moved to the suburbs after World War II were in the right place at the right time. The older spouses had much different child-rearing experiences and few if any direct war experiences, and most did not have the same opportunities to accumulate the wealth and security that 1940s couples did.

Married half a century or more, these spouses grew up when there was far more consensus on the sequencing of life stages, the expectations of marriage, gender roles in the marriage, and family values. Consequently, there was less role strain despite the other stresses. Nowadays, there are many different options and there is less consensus. When large numbers of people deviate from "traditional" norms, then the change is not random; it is in response to other changes in the environment (Klein and White 1996). For example, when the cost of living rises enough and people's desires for material goods outweigh their objections to women working, then more wives will have jobs, despite the costs to families. Working wives in every decade were responding to both individual needs and sociohistorical forces propelling them into the work force. Wives can choose to have careers, to be traditional mothers, or to create some combination of the two. Husbands can work or not, share the household labor and child care or not. Another example is the changing divorce rate. As more people divorce over time, the stigma of divorce lessens, the process becomes easier, and norms regarding lifetime marriage versus divorce and serial marriage change. All these choices create more role strain, more role uncertainty, and more experimentation. The interviewed couples address these issues when they compare their own marriages to the marital histories of their children.

Continuity Theory

Central to continuity theory is the idea that people try to maintain the long-standing lifestyles, relationships, surroundings, and coping mechanisms with which they are familiar as they adapt to change (Atchley 1996). In other words, when people develop new skills, activities, and friendships, it is often within the context of the familiar. Continuity theory assumes that middle-aged and older adults have relatively stable notions of their strengths and weaknesses, their preferences, and their dislikes. They have ideas about how to adapt to life that are the result of a lifetime of learning and experience. Some people "learn" less from their experiences than do others, so they do not necessarily experience successful aging, even if they maintain continuity over a lifetime. For people who learn more about themselves and others, continuity can bring successful, more adaptive aging. We do not all adapt in the same ways, but people's long-standing personal preferences and life structure shape their later choices and adaptations (ibid., p. 170).

Atchley (ibid.) discusses several reasons why continuity and stability increase over a lifetime. First, the longer one lives, the more times one's definition of "self" is tested, so that over time, people tend to develop a very consistent image of themselves. The more times actions bring the desired results, the more confidence a person has in those actions, in those adaptive strategies, and the more often he or she will rely on them in the future.

Second, as people lose social roles over a lifetime through retirement or children moving on, there are fewer role conflicts. Third, most people age in familiar environments with long-developed definitions of the situation and ways of responding to these familiar environments.

Continuity theory can be used to understand people's adaptations to both lost and gained social roles. People spend their lives developing a "convoy of social support" (Kahn and Antonucci 1981), and spouses are among the most significant members of that convoy. As the convoy moves through life together, continuity is created through shared experiences. The convoy becomes more important over time, as one ages. Losses within the convoy significantly affect how older adults adapt to change. According to continuity theory, an identity crisis can occur if changes in the individual or the environment are sudden and very large. Then a person has to reorganize his or her theory of the "self."

This is the case with widowhood, for example, when the loss of the spouse ruptures the life structure and changes all other relationships in the person's life (Atchley 1996). After a lifetime of togetherness, the person has to learn new social roles and new ways of thinking and acting. If friends and family move away or die, there is less social support available for the widow or widower, dramatically affecting his or her adaptation to widowhood. According to Baumeister, Heatherton, and Tice (1994), the concept of willpower is central here, because widowed persons must have the will to adapt to the new situation. A few long-married spouses would rather die than face life without their partners. For them escape, or refusal to adapt, is the best choice available.

Neugarten and Hagestad (1976) and Atchley (1994) have emphasized the importance of continuity for successful adaptation and psychological health in later years, and for life satisfaction (Atchley 1996). Continuity theorists have seldom addressed the issues of long-term marriage, or the potential effects of widowhood on survivors of long-term marriage. The present work shows how continuity was created by the couples, whether or not they are particularly happy in their marriage. These couples offer unique insights into ways people can preserve a marital relationship and a coherent sense of self over the life span, as interactions and environments change and disappear.

Limitations of the Present Study

Since the couples in this study are not a random sample of couples married fifty or more years, the results do not necessarily apply to the larger population. The couples are from a limited geographic area, and have higher education and income levels than average for their cohort. Because of self-selection, unhappily married couples were probably less likely to participate in the study than were happily married couples. There are the acknowledged problems of reliability and validity when relying on subjective, retrospective reports. External validity is not an issue in this case, because the focus of the research is on eliciting these spouses' subjective interpretations and explanations of their own lives. How do they define their marriage, their time together, and their sense of self within that marriage? How has that been related, from their perspective, to the sociohistorical conditions through which they lived? Reliability of the survey instruments can be tested with replication by other researchers.

Chapter Two

Social and Historical Backgrounds

We were born during World War I, grew up during the Depression, and overcame separation and difficult times during World War II.—Mr. RL

Introduction

This chapter covers four major topics. First, the sample population is profiled and placed in the larger sociohistorical context. Next, the interviewed spouses describe the three major social and historical forces that shaped their lives: (1) their own parents and family background, (2) the Depression, and (3) World War II. Most of the interviewed spouses think that the Depression and World War II bonded them together through shared adversity, and taught them to place a high value on human relationships, cooperation, and hard work. Having overcome these obstacles, most felt they had developed adaptive skills which they continued to use throughout life. All the spouses experienced the Depression, some as children, some as young marrieds; but World War II had fewer, less severe effects on the older couples' lives.

The Sample Population in Sociohistorical Context

It was a different kind of life.—Mrs. CI

The survey population of 1,152 spouses (576 couples), all of whom live on Long Island, is a nonrandom sample of couples married fifty or more years, and is not necessarily representative of older adults in the United States. Approximately 3 percent of marriages in the United States last fifty or more years (Roberts 1979–1980; Parron, 1982). According to Mintz and Kellogg, from 1900 to 1940 the chances of a marriage lasting forty or more years increased from one in three to one in two, mostly because of increases in longevity (1988, p. 131). The average length of marriage for the Long Island couples in this study is fifty-two years (Table 2.1).

Forty-seven percent of the surveyed spouses married between the ages of twenty-two and twenty-five, and approximately 25 percent of spouses were twenty or twenty-one years old (Table 2.2). This is fairly typical of their cohort. In 1920, the median age at first marriage was twenty-one, and it rose to almost twenty-two by 1940. After 1940 it began to decline again, reaching a low of 20.3 years for women and 22.8 for men in 1950 (U.S. Bureau of the Census 1992).

Almost 98 percent of the surveyed couples have living children (Table 2.3) compared to only 80 percent of older adults, generally, in the United States (Atchley 1996). Overall, 41.9 percent of the couples have two children, and 27.2 percent have three. Catholic couples reported larger families than Protestant or Jewish couples (Table 2.4). Changes in the birthrate in the larger society during the Depression and World War II are reflected in this sample population. The number of children born declines during peak Depression years, and increases again during World War II (Table 2.5). By 1943 the birthrate in the United States was the highest it had been in twenty years (Mintz and Kellogg 1988, pp. 137, 147).

Almost half of the spouses are high school graduates, and 15 percent have less than a high school education. Another 17.8 percent completed college, and 12.5 percent have postgraduate training, making the sample better educated than the cohort in general, due to the high percentage of postgraduate education (Table 2.6). Among the surveyed couples, Jewish spouses are more likely than Catholic or Protestant spouses to have completed college and postgraduate training.

This sample population has a higher than average income for older adults in the United States. Approximately 41 percent of the surveyed spouses report current yearly earnings under $30,000, and 17.2 percent report earning $50,000 or more per year (Table 2.7). In contrast, Atchley reports that approximately 68.3 percent of persons 65 years of age and older have yearly incomes of $20,000 or less (1996, p. 30). Jewish couples surveyed in the current study tend to have higher yearly incomes than either Protestant or Catholic couples.

Forty-three percent of the spouses in this study are Catholic, 29 percent are Protestant, and 23 percent are Jewish. Both the Catholic and the Jewish religions are overrepresented compared to the United States population overall. However, the sample is more representative of New York and the Northeastern United States, where a higher percentage of Catholic and Jew-

Table 2.1

Year Married

Year	Percentage of Spouses
1929 or earlier	2.1
1930–1932	2.6
1933–1934	3.8
1935–1939	18.6
1940	10.9
1941	15.0
1942	15.6
1943	22.7
1944	8.7

Table 2.2

Age at Marriage

Age	Percentage of Spouses
Under 16	0.1
16–17	1.5
18–19	10.9
20–21	24.7
22–25	47.0
26–29	13.4
30–35	2.2
36–39	0.2

Table 2.3

Number of Children

Number	Percentage of Spouses
0	2.2
1	7.9
2	41.9
3	27.2
4	12.6
5	3.0
6	1.2
7	1.6
8	0.3
9	0.5
Missing data	1.6

Table 2.4

Number of Children by Religious Affiliation

	Percentage of Spouses		
Number	Catholic	Protestant	Jewish
1	6.9	12.1	6.2
2	37.2	40.7	59.5
3	25.7	27.8	30.8
4	18.4	14.4	3.1
5	4.3	3.2	0.4
6 or more	7.5	1.8	0.0

Table 2.5

Number of Children and Year Married

	Percentage of Spouses			
Year	1 Child	2 Children	3 Children	4+ Children
1925–1929	16.7	8.3	16.7	58.3
1930–1932	21.4	28.6	42.9	7.1
1933–1934	4.9	58.5	31.7	4.9
1935–1939	5.7	51.7	28.2	14.4
1940	7.9	53.5	22.8	15.8
1941	9.8	42.9	30.7	16.6
1942	12.1	44.3	27.6	16.0
1943	8.4	38.4	24.0	29.2
1944	0.0	34.0	39.2	26.8

Note: Table does not include childless couples.

Table 2.6

Educational Level

Education	Percentage of Spouses
Eighth grade	5.1
Less than high school	10.2
High school graduate	46.2
Some college	7.2
College graduate	17.8
Postgraduate/advanced degree	12.5
Missing data	1.0

Table 2.7

Joint Yearly Income

Yearly Income	Percentage of Spouses
Under $20,000	16.0
$20,000–29,000	25.3
$30,000–39,000	18.2
$40,000–49,000	12.1
$50,000 or more	17.2
Missing data	11.2

ish persons live (Macionis 1997; Krantz 1993). Eighty-five percent of the surveyed spouses said they married within their religion; 98 percent of Jewish spouses married within their faith, as compared to 86 percent of Catholics and 78 percent of Protestants. The recent rate of intermarriage among Jewish persons is closer to 50 percent, a significant decline in endogamy among Jews in the United States (Judd 1990).

Thus, the sample population is somewhat dissimilar from the larger population and other older adults in (1) still being married, (2) having more living children, (3) being somewhat more educated, and (4) having somewhat higher incomes, and (5) religious affiliation.

Parents of the Long-Term Married

He's a good provider, and she's a good worker.
—Mr. CA

For the most part, the childhoods and young adulthoods of the spouses studied here were times of economic struggle and uncertainty. Approximately three-fourths of the interviewed spouses stated that their parents were working class or poor. The majority of them said they are financially better off than their parents were.

> Mr. RA, married in 1926, describes his background: "My parents come from Bohemia. It's known as Czechoslovakia now. We lived . . . in New York, and Christmas time there wasn't any money around the house at all. . . . My father worked in the tobacco factory, and his pay was $7 a week. So we went to church, my mother thinks the church will help us out. This gentleman comes to the door. . . . He has a great big turkey leg in his hand, . . . and he says the church only helps people who . . . give paper money, not coins. . . . 'But there's a place called the Union Settlement. . . . You go down there and they'll give you some.' My mother goes, 'Where's Union Settlement?' In the

SOCIAL AND HISTORICAL BACKGROUNDS 33

Bohemian section, all of the cops spoke Bohemian, ... so she went to this police officer and asks him. ... He says, 'Mama, that's a long way'. ... So she went. Cold, oh boy, was it cold. She put me in the house and said, 'Sit there, don't move and when your brothers come, tell them to sit in the house.' Well, I told them they had to sit in the house. They said, 'No, we've got to go ... get wood.' Wood would float down the East River, and they had some kind of a rig with a wash line, and they'd throw a hook and reel it in. ... And we'd go to the butcher shops. Any chicken gizzards? Any necks? Any wings? 'Course they wouldn't want the gizzards or the necks. Then we'd go to the fruit stores. There was darn little fruit. ... Any fruit that's going to spoil before Monday ... could we have it? So we'd all come home with fruit on Saturday, so we didn't do too bad that way. But we did live poor."

Five of the interviewed spouses emigrated from Europe to the United States. Approximately 10 percent of the interviewed spouses' parents were first-generation immigrants who maintained many old European lifestyles and values. Even second-generation parents practiced and valued ethnic cultural ties and traditions. For example, in more traditional Jewish families, eldest children were expected to marry first. Some widowed mothers expected their sons to support them. Ethnic families tended to be geographically concentrated, with parents and adult children often working and living together and sharing leisure activities.

The CIs had very different family backgrounds in some ways, although both grew up in working-class Italian homes. She was an only child and he had seven brothers and sisters. She says, "I was a spoiled child. I never had any want in life. My mother and father always gave me what I wanted. I never went out to work." He says, "I grew up with eight kids. I took responsibilities on my shoulders. I started to work when I was only seven. I always had to work." They moved in with her parents right after marriage and lived there with them for twenty-five years, because she didn't want to leave. "My husband wanted always to get his own place. And I said no, I want to stay here with mom and papa. So he was very nice about it. He stayed."

Mr. PA's parents were brought together by unique historic circumstances. "My father ... was in the Austro Hungarian Army ... and he ran a clinic of some sort in Russia at the time. My mother was born in Russia. And he met my mother because her half-brother happened to play around with a grenade and blew off a couple of fingers. And so they took him to the clinic my father was running. And that's how they met. ... He was discharged in Hungary, he went back to Russia to get her out ... because the Revolution was taking place." They went first to Hungary for a few years, and then came to America. He says, "It was my mother wanted it. She was very unhappy in Hungary. She didn't speak the language. She had no inclination to learn the language. And her mother ... already set up in America ... sponsored her."

A few of the spouses' parents had "Old World" arranged marriages, some of which led to love and happiness while others did not. Personal fulfillment and happiness were neither goals nor expectations for these marriages. The arrangements were practical exchanges of services. Those with parents in such marriages did not emulate them, nor did they advocate arranged marriages for others.

> Mrs. AL's mother had an arranged marriage: "My mother said that she saw . . . the man that she was gonna marry through the little peep hole. . . . He was fifteen years older than mom, and mom was about fifteen at the time, . . . and she liked him. But I said, 'You went to bed with a stranger, mama?' 'That's the way it was.'"

> Both sets of the CAs' parents came from Europe. She explains, "My mother's friend said 'I know this man. He makes a good living, you know. Why don't you marry him?' They didn't know each other . . . . It was like matchmakers. So my mother met the man and she married him. She didn't know my father really. And she was young, eighteen. But it was just because somebody said, . . . 'He'll make a good provider.'" Mr. CA's mother did the same thing: "My mother came over here at age seventeen . . . in the steerage. . . . She went out and she worked as a domestic somewhere. Her parents sent her over here, they sacrificed to get her over here. . . . She meets my father. . . . He's a good provider, and she's a good worker. I don't think there was any love . . . I don't think that happened in those days. It was just a marriage of convenience. . . . I know a lot of people from that background. Maybe they didn't like each other that well. They didn't separate or divorce because there was a stigma against doing that. It was a terrible thing. They just tolerated each other and they stayed. . . . They stuck it out for the children's sake, and for their own sake."

Most of the interviewed spouses said they were raised in relatively happy, two-parent homes. They expected their lives to be much like their own parents' lives. They, too, expected to settle down, get married, and have children. Other spouses who have warm, loving marriages came from less than happy homes. They struggled with poverty and overworked parents who were stretched too thin.

> Mr. HO: "Mama was intensely emotional. Papa was intensely drunk. . . . When I came home from school if I heard 'Ramona' playing on the Victrola, that meant don't bring anybody in the house or come in yourself. . . . Mama managed to have a string of 'friends' over the years."

> Mr. NN's formative family experiences spanned two world wars. He is a refugee from Austria, whose family ultimately died in the Holocaust: "I was eighteen months [old] when my father was drafted into the Army. This is the First World War and he became a POW in Russia, that was 1914, and he

didn't come home until 1921. He was sent to Siberia and he couldn't get out of there. . . . I was nine years old when he came home. He was a stranger. . . . As far as I remember, my parents consistently fought with each other."

Mrs. NN says her parents were much the same, and they remained married for over fifty years: "There was nowhere for my mother to go, and I guess that was one of the reasons that they stayed together. . . but they argued all the time."

Mrs. PA's parents "came here in 1907 . . . steerage passengers. . . . But they raised four of us, and they stayed together. My mother worked very, very hard. She did all kind of things to keep us together. My father didn't always bring home the paycheck. My mother took in foster kids so that there was a little added income in the house. . . . They were not happy. They were two opposites. . . . My mother never learned to read or write in any language. . . . Her home and her children were just everything. My father was a good-time Charlie. He wanted to go out and have a good time, and my mother would never go."

Unhappy parents and difficult marriages left an impression on these spouses, and most said they consciously tried to avoid making these mistakes.

Mrs. NG: "I wanted my marriage to be good, because my parents had a very bad marriage, . . . and I swore . . . I'm not gonna let that happen to my kids!"

The majority did not blame their parents, and understood that having different values, norms, and expectations created conflicts in marriage. In discussing their own and others' marriages, nearly all spouses stress the importance of shared values and similar backgrounds for good marriages. Whether their parents provided good marital role models or not, most of the spouses held, as a common theme in their lives, a sense of achievement, of beginning with little, and over time building, creating, and growing into a more successful family.

Single-parent families occurred even then. By 1924 one in seven marriages in the United States ended in divorce (Mintz and Kellogg 1988). Nineteen percent of the interviewed spouses lost one or both parents before adulthood, 15 percent because of death, 4 percent because of divorce or separation.

Mr. EL: "My mother and father separated. He was a playboy, and my mother, I guess, was too busy with the children, so at some point in time, they simply separated. . . . I left home when I was thirteen, there just really wasn't enough food for all of us, and . . . my father's sister was going with a fellow from a nearby resort town, and he had a grocery store. . . . He said 'He could help me in the store, and I could help him go to school'. . . . So they took me on at thirteen, and I managed to see my mother once every two or three weeks for a few hours . . . and I stayed through college."

Mrs. NG describes her mismatched parents: "They were such different people. My mother was this very vivacious Italian girl. And she loved fun and games and she wanted people around her all the time. Where my father was . . . I guess you'd call him square, very decent, very honest, but very . . . restrictive. . . . Two different personalities. For many reasons, they were separated and then they finally got divorced! It was hell. . . ."

Mrs. EC says of her husband, "By the time he was three years old he lived with his grandma . . . like an orphan in a way. . . . Then he was fourteen years old, his grandfather put him out in a building and says you make your own living. . . . Fourteen years old! . . . He didn't even allow him to go through eighth grade."

Despite growing up in broken homes, these spouses were able to create lasting marriages. They said they grew up quickly by necessity, and they learned how to be more independent and self-reliant. Most of these spouses who had difficult childhoods felt they were stronger because of it.

The Depression

> *We learned habits of frugality that have scarred us*
> *ever since.*—Mr. AL

Millions of men were out of work for months and years during the Depression. The unemployment rate in the United States rose from 3.2 percent in 1929 to 23.6 percent (12.5 million people) in 1932. Unemployment remained above 14 percent until 1941. By 1933 people had a little over half the income they had in 1929 to buy the same things (Mintz and Kellogg 1988, p. 134). In 1932, which was the worst year of the Depression, three-fourths of all workers were part-time (ibid.). The good-provider role of men was undermined by social forces beyond their control.

For those interviewed couples who married in the 1930s, the Depression is a significant marker segmenting their lives, shaping crucial expectations and decisions about life. Economic considerations helped to determine both when they married and had children, and how many children they had. It is estimated that the Depression resulted in 800,000 postponed marriages, and in three million fewer children born in 1932 than in 1929 (ibid.). Most interviewed wives did not work outside the home, despite the economic difficulties. Gallup polls of the time indicated that 80 percent of men were opposed to women's working outside the home (ibid.). These spouses describe themselves as less materialistic and more family oriented than young people today because of their Depression experiences. Everyone they knew was as poor as they were, so they did not experience a strong sense of relative deprivation.

> The MAs married in 1936. She grew up in a family of ten children. He and six brothers and sisters were raised by his mother, who was widowed when she was thirty-three. He quit high school so he could work to help support his family. Mrs. MA says, "There were times I didn't have two nickels to rub together . . . but you know what? We were all in the same category. . . . My husband didn't make me go to work. He didn't want me to work 'cause he wanted me to be home with the children. . . . We centered our whole life on our children."

> Mrs. EC, married in 1928, describes the patchwork nature of her family's adaptation to the Depression. The Depression hit just after they built their first home, and her husband lost his job. "We went fishing, we went clamming and oystering. We did everything we could to take care of the family. And we had gardens. Everything got canned. . . . We had to move out of our house to keep from losing it. Somebody else could rent it for two years during the Depression. We worked on a farm . . . and during that time we had an orchestra. I played the piano and he played the drums, anything to make money." They played mostly at speakeasies on Long Island.

> Mrs. ME, married in 1930, makes a commonsense observation about the career she and her husband pursued: "Nineteen twenty-nine was a terrible Depression, but we were in the poultry business. People always eat. . . . I think he made like $75 a week when we got married. Our friends thought we were millionaires."
> Mr. ME did not choose poultry. "At fourteen years my father died, and . . . I had to stop going to school and I had to take over the business. . . . In those days, you know, they didn't think about education, as long as you could make money going to work." Into his seventies, he worked every day of the week from five or six in the morning to midnight. They never went hungry; she laughs, "We always had plenty of chickens."

The spouses who married during the 1940s were adolescents during the Depression, usually living at home with their parents. They helped out by giving any money they earned to their parents. Sometimes they, too, had to quit school or forego college because there was not enough money. As young people they learned how to make do with less, how to share what they had with others.

> Mr. DR, married in 1941, remarks, "I have a Depression complex. I remember my mother calling me at my father's hardware store asking me if I had fifty cents in the till to buy food. I'll never forget that. . . . She never ate, until all the kids had eaten. . . . We all said, 'Geez, we'd better take it easy, or she won't have anything to eat.'"

Mr. GR, married in 1941, was eighteen when his father died and he had to quit high school to work: "Rather than go on the dole, I went to work for the WPA swinging a sixteen-pound sledge, repairing the sewers of Harlem. . . . That was the work ethic we had in those days. To go on welfare . . . was terrible."

According to Mrs. GR, "My father was a bootlegger. He used to send the kids to New York with the booze, because they would never suspect kids of transporting it, so my brother and I . . . would go to New York carrying cans of . . . alcohol that he made. It was fearful! . . . The Depression was not a nice time, not a nice time!"

Mr. TI, married in 1943, grew up in a farming family in the Midwest. During the Depression, because of financial pressures and personal problems, his grandfather and two uncles committed suicide within one year. "Uncle Mike shot himself, Grandpa hung himself, and Uncle Joe drowned himself . . . within a nine-month period. This is 1929 and 1930." He was thirteen years old at the time.

The NAs' dating and marriage experiences were also defined by the Depression years. Mrs. NA thinks, "Thank God I grew up in the Depression, because it made us learn values, both money values and people values. . . . I think today people are so independent and you need people. . . . You still have to have friends to make life happy." Her husband dropped out of high school to work (he later returned and got his diploma). Her educational opportunities were limited, too, because of the Depression. "I had just assumed I would go to college, but . . . things got real bad financially. . . . I suddenly realized I couldn't go to college. . . . Today these kids take for granted that the money is there." They could not afford to marry until 1942.

Mr. LA, married in 1942, says, "The Depression was a time of incredible stress. . . . We had an innate urge for solidity, for something tangible." He thinks that everything motivating his wife has its source in her Depression experiences. She grew up in the heart of industrial America, where people standing in line were common, where "bums" came to her grandmother's door and got breakfast in return for beating the carpets.

Mrs. LA's mother died of a self-induced abortion in 1929. She says "We lived . . . in what I would call an ethnic neighborhood. . . . We had four very small bedrooms, one bathroom, nine people, and that was when my mother became pregnant, and did the abortion, and lost her life." Mrs. LA was six when her mother died. She has been actively involved in women's issues, including family planning, all her adult life.

Mrs. PA, married in 1941, says, "Nobody had any money. It was a much simpler lifestyle. . . . You didn't know you were supposed to miss the stuff 'cause nobody had it. . . . I never had a bicycle. . . . I had a very rich childhood. I was loved. I grew up in a very warm, huggy, kissy kind of family. I was the youngest of four kids. I wasn't deprived at all. I didn't have material things, but neither did any of my friends, so it didn't make any difference. . . . I shared the roller skates with my friend. We each skated on one skate, 'cause that's just the way it was. That's the way I grew up." After they married, she remarked, "We couldn't afford our own apartment. Many young marrieds at that time just simply moved in with mama and papa. That was the accepted thing to do, and we moved in with my parents."

Mr. CA, married in 1940, says, "We were poor, but we didn't know we were poor. . . . All our friends were in the same category. . . . We lived in a cold-water flat. . . . We had a toilet in the hall we had to share with our next-door neighbor. . . . Our parents would bring food to us every time they visited."

Whether they were coming of age or marrying and starting their own families during such economically difficult times, most of these spouses said they learned to be flexible, adaptable, ready to "make do" and try something different. They took a more general adaptive route, not specializing in only one strategy. Elder (1974) has discussed the development of adaptive strategies during the Depression years, and the later value of these learned skills and attitudes. Perhaps these spouses' greater resiliency in their early years is linked to their resiliency in adapting to long-term marriage.

World War II

> I really thought we should wait. . . . You can get
> killed in the war.—Mr. ST

Surveyed couples who married during the war years were less likely than couples who married earlier to say "the time was right" to marry, but the marriage rate increased anyway. This was because couples who had postponed marriage in the Depression could finally afford to marry, and because many couples married earlier than they had planned, fearing they would be separated forever by the war. One month after Pearl Harbor the marriage rate was 60 percent above the same month of the previous year (Mintz and Kellogg 1988, p. 153). From 1940 to 1946 there were three million more marriages than would have occurred at prewar levels (ibid., p. 154). The birthrate had been declining for twenty years before the war, but by 1943, the United States had its highest birthrate in twenty years. Between 1946 and 1965, seventy-four million babies were born: the generation named the Baby Boom (Schwartz and Scott 1994, p. 235).

The impact of World War II on interviewed couples' lives depended on whether they married before or after 1938. Thirteen of the sixty interviewed couples married between 1926 and 1938, and none of these husbands served in the military during World War II. A few of these husbands did war work, but most of the couples who married from 1926 to 1938 said the war had little effect on their lives. This was in stark contrast to the couples marrying from 1939 to 1944. Thirty-four of the forty-seven wartime husbands served in the military, and eighteen of them spent some time overseas. Eight wartime husbands did war work, two were ministers, and three were excused for other reasons. World War II is the social and historical context that affected the timing and style of these couples' weddings, how they spent their early years of marriage, and how they experienced the births of their first children.

The Home Front

> *I was a defense worker. . . . I would go to work, and I wouldn't be home for a month.*—Mr. TN

From 1940 to 1942 unemployment dropped from 15 percent to 4.7 percent. Defense plants were built all over the United States, and over fifteen million civilians moved around the country doing "war work" (Gordon and Gordon 1987). Many jobs paid much better than the military or prewar wages, but war work required long hours, sometimes seven days a week, for weeks at a time.

> Mr. EC, married in 1928, describes his experiences with war work: "Being on defense plant work, . . . I spent a lot of time away. . . . It was long days most [of] the time. I seen my children at night. . . . She'd leave them up until I got home, unless I was gonna be late. Many a night I didn't get home till two in the morning. . . . Most [of] the time it was seven days a week. I remember Thanksgiving night I came home, they saved me the drumstick."

> Mr. SE, a newly ordained minister, remarks, "I tried to get into the chaplains' corps. . . . There was a board of chaplains, . . . and they screened all the men who were going to go into the chaplaincy." A bishop wrote to him, " 'We only send our best men into the chaplaincy'. . . . It would have taken experienced men, and heaven knows, I was not! So I didn't get into the war." Instead, he covered three churches in different towns for those who did go.

A few couples actually managed to do well financially during the war, either because they were older, established, and able to take over the work of those who went to war, or because the war work they did paid well.

> Mr. CI, married in 1930, had a heart condition that exempted him from military service. "These fellows . . . had to go to service, so they had to close up their butcher shops. And the families had to put the place up for sale, and I'd buy it."

> Mr. LA, married in 1942, was deferred because he worked in essential industry. "All through World War II, one night we had mackerel, and the next

night we had hot dogs. . . . We had brownouts on Long Island because the submarines were coming up . . . but we got into the city. . . . It was before our children were born, so it was really great fun that we were able to get all about. . . . We saw everything, we went to all the plays . . . the museums. . . . We were in the city all the time."

Husbands in Service

> *I got my draft card, and what does she do with it?*
> *She hides it! Man, did I blow my stack when I found*
> *out.*—Mr. DR

In 1940 the first peacetime draft began (Gordon and Gordon 1987). Several couples married hurriedly, because they felt they had little time left. Sometimes economic considerations played a role.

> The EGs married in 1943 when he discovered his married Navy friends were getting rental allowances and clothing allowances that could make marriage affordable for them. As he tells the story, "I called (her) and said, 'How about getting married now? I may not be around for long.' "

> The WTs hurried their marriage because of the war. He says, "She really wanted to be married. . . . I said 'Look, I'm probably going overseas. Something may happen.' So she said, 'Why should that make any difference? What will we have gained if we don't get married and something happens?' "

Two wives said they hoped to get pregnant so they would always have a part of their husbands.

> Mr. GR says his wife "became a camp follower. . . . And our daughter was conceived because she wanted to have something to remember me by." She adds, "If something happened."

There were between 4 and 5 million service wives during the war, all sharing much the same worries and problems (Mintz and Kellogg 1988). The spouses who served had to put their lives on hold, giving up their former jobs, storing their possessions, and leaving their homes, not sure whether or when they would return. The civilian couples experienced wartime rationing and hardship, but they did not face the danger that military couples did.

> Mr. PG says, "I think all we wanted to do was to be able to afford to be married. . . . We didn't think that far ahead. . . . We were married in thirty-nine, Hitler went into Russia about that time, so the world was in a

turmoil. . . . I had to enlist for the draft. So we had no expectations of what was gonna happen."

Mrs. PG adds, "We figured eventually we'd get a house and raise a family, hopefully, if he lived through the war."

Mrs. MR says, "He was so afraid, you couldn't plan a future, because it looked so bleak at that time. You're talking about *war*! It sort of puts a damper on so much you'd like to do and want to do, for fear of what will happen."

As Mrs. PA tells it, "The war years. . . . They were terrible! Never knowing if your husband were going to come home or be killed."

The GEs were lucky in that he was not sent overseas, but unlucky because she could not follow him. Her widowed mother needed help running her small store. Mrs. GE says, "I grew up eating and living in the store practically. . . . Do you know what a candy store is, from six o'clock in the morning till eleven o'clock at night? . . . If you got $10 or $12 rung up in the cash register, that was a good day." She says the war "was a disaster for me. . . . The most difficult was when he had to go into the army and we had just lost the first baby. It was terrible, but we wrote to each other every day. . . . I used to cry every day. . . . It was two years he was away, but it seemed like endless. . . . It was a constant thought that he was gonna be sent overseas. That was a nightmare . . . transport boats being blown up! My two brothers were in too."

Mr. EL: "A lot of the fellows that didn't go into service made a lot of money during the war. And for a while, you felt a little bit concerned about that, because there were people in the war plants making lots of overtime. *You* were getting paid basic wages for whatever you were doing in the service."

Camp Followers

I had the luxury of seeing my wife.—Mr. EL

If the husbands remained in the United States, the wives often became "camp followers." Millions of wives and their children followed husbands as they were transferred around the United States from post to post (Schwartz and Scott 1994). Most couples rented an apartment or a furnished room off the base, and the husbands came home on weekends, sometimes more often.

At one point the YEs were stationed in Rhode Island. Mrs. YE tells the story: "We lived with a little old kerosene stove in an apartment in half a house. The other half had been washed away with a hurricane. But the guy got good rent for it. And let me tell you when it got to be twenty below zero, that kerosene stove didn't work as well as his old jacket on the bed, and an iron and a toaster alongside of us. . . . I don't think kids today would do anything like that! . . . I suppose getting married and following him was exciting, because you see, I'd never done anything like this. I'd never [been] able to see and do the things we did. . . . I could see the country."

Mr. TM recalls, "It was an adventure! We didn't have anything, we packed up our clothes in a couple of suitcases. . . . We saw the country."

Home to the Folks

> *His troop got on the train on one side, I got on the*
> *train on the other side.*—Mrs. IC

If there was no housing, if a wife was pregnant or a husband was about to ship out, then interviewed wives usually went home to their parents, occasionally to their husband's parents, even less often to their own apartments. All but one of the wives with children remained at home with parents for at least part of the time their husbands were overseas. While parents typically welcomed them into their homes, it required some adjustment. Parents both helped and interfered in child care. Families were often crowded into small houses with little privacy, increasing the tension.

> Right after Mr. PAs' son was born, he was reclassified and drafted. He left when the baby was ten weeks old. Mrs. PA: "My life changed completely at that point. We lived two blocks from my mother, and I did not want to give up my apartment. . . . My mother couldn't tolerate the idea of my being alone in an apartment with an infant, even though I was two blocks from her. She had a heart attack, and she said, 'You have to come and live with me.' And so I kept my apartment and I paid rent on that apartment for two years while my husband was in service. . . . Every time I said I was gonna go home, she had another heart attack. . . . But then when he came home, we were both so happy that we had done this, because you could not get an apartment in New York City . . . and I had the apartment. So as soon as he came home, we folded up the crib and went home."

Husbands Overseas

> *We had seen too many different things that we*
> *hadn't known about before that.*—Mr. HE

For those husbands who saw combat, much about their war experiences had remained unspoken. A few husbands had positions that required secrecy—chemical warfare, sonar, radar, and so on. Others said they never told their wives some of the frightening, bad experiences they had during the war. During the interviews a few wives heard these stories for the first time. As the men recalled those times, they relived them, shaking their heads sometimes in disbelief.

> Mr. EG was stationed with his wife, but she did not know any details of his work. He says, "Submarine service was the secret service. . . . You didn't discuss anything about subs. . . . It took twenty years before I would discuss some of the incidents."

> Mr. WT enlisted in 1942, was called up in January 1943, and the WTs married in November 1943. She traveled with him five or six weeks before he shipped overseas in January 1944. In March 1944, he was shot down, and was a prisoner of war (POW) until May 1945. He remembers, "She was a great letter writer. I got more letters, I think, than anybody else in the prison camp! I used to get them in batches."
> She remembers, "At first I cried a lot. When he was missing in action it was difficult, but once I knew he was a prisoner and his letters started to come—it took maybe two months—I felt more at ease about it. . . . He always wanted to spare us whatever the details were."
> Luckily Mr. WT was in an elite group and was treated somewhat better than most. The Russians finally liberated them. "They gave us food and entertainment, but they wouldn't let us go. . . . It took a month to get away from the Russians."

While servicemen were busy trying to survive, their wives were home leading relatively normal lives, caring for children, working at jobs, going to movies at night, and living with parents. In 1941, Rosie the Riveter became the symbol of working women in the American defense industry (Gordon and Gordon 1987). Approximately five million more women, including more wives and mothers, went to work than before the war, and servicemen's wives were three times as likely to work as other wives (Mintz and Kellogg 1988, pp. 167–168). Many women worked at jobs traditionally unavailable to them. Still, norms and values of the time stressed that a woman's first duty was to her children; this was evident in the lack of organized day care for wartime working wives (ibid.).

The majority of couples in which the husbands had gone overseas talked about writing letters every day, and about how important those letters were. Sometimes the wives had no idea where their husbands were, and had to read the war news in the paper and wonder. A few couples had worked out codes so that the wife would always know where the husband really was. Letters were lifelines between spouses, sometimes for years. Several couples in the study had kept those love letters.

> Mrs. ER says, "We used to work sometimes till nine o'clock at night, we'd

work seven days a week, but you didn't care. That was my life, just working and writing letters to him."

Mr. HE went to the South Pacific. His wife remembers, "When the fighting got heavy you got very worried, especially if you had any idea he was in the area, which I did, because we always had secret codes. . . . I moved home again. . . . Went out on Saturday nights with friends who were in the same situation I was. . . . [We'd] go to the movies, go to the diner. . . . All of us worked." And she wrote him every day.

When Mr. FT shipped out, his wife and two babies went home to live with her parents, and they wrote every day. He describes his letter-writing habits: "Even on the train when I was going cross country. Every place we stopped, I mailed a letter."

Finally, an unusual theme in some wartime couples' lives was being "saved by the bomb." Several husbands were on their way back to the war when the bomb was dropped. The war ended and they were spared.

Mrs. MT remembers, "Our daughter was born while he was overseas. . . . I lived with my parents during that time. . . . He was lucky. He was on his way to the Pacific when they dropped the bomb and they turned the ship around. . . . I get goose flesh every time we tell the story."

Mr. MT remembers the moment on board: "Suddenly we hear over the loudspeaker. . . . 'The destination of this ship is Newport News, Virginia,' at which point, all hell broke loose. People screamed and yelled."

Mr. TM: "They dropped the bomb. I was scheduled to go, and they dropped the bomb."

Returning Husbands

I guess when he finally came home, that's when our marriage got started. Of course, I already had the children.—Mrs. LD

When husbands returned home after the war, they had to adjust to ongoing families, and the families had to adjust to them. Many interviewed husbands remembered being uncertain what they would find when they rejoined their wartime brides. They felt changed, matured, and in a hurry to catch up. They had to say goodbye to wartime buddies, find a job and a place to live, and readjust to civilian family life. Add to this the stress of the housing shortage, and it is understandable why so many wartime marriages ended in divorce. The divorce rate rose during and after World War

II to one in four marriages by 1946 (Mintz and Kellogg 1988, p. 171). By comparison, the estimated divorce rate for 1979, the peak year for divorce, was one in two marriages (Schwartz and Scott 1994). Mintz and Kellogg (1988) maintain that the high postwar divorce rate was a result of hasty marriages coupled with long separations and changing gender roles. The surveyed Long Island couples managed to overcome the adversity of the war and move on with their lives together.

> Mrs. LD: "There really wasn't a marriage in the traditional sense. He was gone for so long in the beginning." He says, "When I finally got back to a normal life, the family was already established."

> Mrs. PA explains, "He was overseas for about two years, and didn't know his son when he returned. . . . [To] most of the babies from that period of time, 'Daddy' was a picture on the shelf. . . . Anybody in a uniform of any kind, it was 'Daddy'. . . . But there was a very difficult adjustment period. First of all, the men come home and there's a family, you know. And the kids, all of a sudden from having one parent, one boss saying 'no,' now there are two people there to say 'no.' And it was an adjustment period."
> Mr. PA: "They can't hold a job for you. Although you were supposed to get your job back, this was fiction."

> Overall, Mr. MR says of the war years, "Indirectly it took much more out of our lives . . . than just the time of the war, when I was in the service, because when I came out, I had to catch up with all these other people. So we were always running full tilt to catch up with things. Instead of five years, it was like ten or twelve years out of our life. . . . It wasn't till 1956 [fifteen years after we married] that we bought our own home. . . . Most people bought their home within three or four years after they got married. . . . We always seemed to be behind."

Many of the husbands who experienced combat had more difficulty.

> Mr. HE says the war years were the most difficult part of the marriage. He served thirty-one months in the Pacific in New Guinea and the Philippines. "I suspect that when we were on our way back, most of us were not quite sure . . . if we were gonna have what we left, or how it was gonna be when we tried to live together then, because we had changed."

> Mrs. NG said that when her husband returned from service he had trouble "fitting back into the home life. . . . He was a nervous wreck when he came home, plus . . . he had malaria. . . . It was hard for him to leave the buddies."
> Mr. NG says, "It was like an explosion. And I didn't know where I was going." Mrs. NG says, "I used to have nightmares all the time when he was in the heat of the war."

> Mr. ER was an aerial gunner who completed sixty-three missions. He and his wife were separated for sixteen months. He remembers that they wrote each other every day. Diminishing the impact of his fearful experiences, he says,

"She told me when I came home, I used to have nightmares. It was reliving the silly things."

The housing shortage after the war kept many young couples at home with parents, for months or years. When the young couples had children, these homes became overcrowded, creating additional tension and conflict.

Mrs. NG: "Here you have this exodus of young men coming home to their sweethearts. Everybody's starting their families. They need apartments. Now, you know the story why all the homes were built in Levittown. Anyway, money was scarce and apartments were nil, and we were going to stick it out, and live with Mom. Now my father was not there anymore. My sister, who is two years older than me, she is there with her new husband out of the Army and her first baby . . . and my kid brother was living there. Here you have two married couples, I have a baby on the way, my sister has a baby, so it was insanity, insanity. I couldn't wait to get out of there."

When the NNs first married in 1943, he was still in service, so when he came home on leave, "We stayed in my parents' apartment. . . . We didn't even have a door on our bedroom, because our bedroom was the living room. We slept on a sofa bed and that was the way we lived for two years."

Summary

This nonrandom sample of couples who have been married fifty or more years is not typical of other people their age because, first of all, they are still married. The surveyed couples also have higher incomes, higher educational levels, and more living children than average. The majority of these long-married spouses came from loving, intact families, and they represent a variety of religious, ethnic, and social class backgrounds. Nineteen percent spent at least some part of their childhoods in a single-parent family, most often because of a parent's death. A few had unhappily married parents. One or both spouses in five couples had parents with arranged marriages based on practical concerns, not romantic love. Whether these childhood families were happy or not, there was a common theme of family members working together for the good of the social group, a product of their era and the challenges it presented.

The great unity of experience for these spouses lies in the sociohistorical context: the norms and values of early twentieth-century American culture, the Great Depression, and World War II. Most spouses said they learned not to expect too much and to appreciate what they had. These couples' marriages were shaped by whether they were married before or during the Depression, or during World War II.

McCubbin (1979) has identified several successful coping strategies, all of which are exemplified by most of the couples who successfully adapted to the deprivation and stress of the Depression and World War II. First of all, they managed to maintain a sense of family. Second, they learned new skills, developing their self-reliance and self-esteem. Depression-era couples took many different kinds of jobs, whatever they had to do to get by. Third, both husbands and wives developed networks of social support. They emphasized the value of human relationships, the importance of sharing and cooperation. Fourth, they tried to remain optimistic about the future, even when faced with serious threats. Fifth, they learned about the problems facing them rather than avoiding the issues. Sixth, they used a variety of coping strategies, depending on the demands of the situation, to reduce stress. These same coping strategies contributed to their marital longevity.

Chapter Three

Meeting and Marrying

You got married when I did, you got married for keeps.
—Mrs. GR

Introduction

The courtship to matrimony phase can be divided into "meeting" and "marrying." The first part of this chapter examines how and when the surveyed couples met, what attracted them, whether they felt love at first sight, their dating behavior, and how long they knew each other before marrying. The second part of the chapter discusses their weddings, their financial security, the family support they received, and whether or not they would do it all over again.

Meeting

When and How The Couples Met

As soon as I saw her, I knew she was the one for me.
—Mr. TR

Propinquity (nearness, proximity), common physical attraction, and similar interests (compatibility) are what brought couples like these together. They lived in the same neighborhood; they knew the same people; they were at the same party; or they attended the same school, church, or synagogue. Forty-two percent of interviewed couples met this way. Ten percent of the couples have known each other since they were small children, and another 10 percent met on blind dates. Nearly one-fourth of the couples met through their friends, either by arrangement or accidentally. Brossard has isolated residential proximity as a significant factor in mate selection (1932). Proximity, especially in ethnic neighborhoods, is related to shared norms and values as well. Fifty-seven of the sixty interviewed couples and 85 percent of the surveyed couples married within their own religions.

> Mrs. RA was a telephone operator who thought she had found a girlfriend in that new voice answering the phone at the town garage. It turned out that high-pitched voice was her future husband's. Unfortunately, another telephone operator, who had been listening in on the budding romance, called the young mechanic, impersonated her coworker, and secretly dated the mechanic for weeks before confessing.

> Seventy years ago the HAs met in seventh grade. By high school they were dating. He says, "She had a couple of other boyfriends I had to get rid of. . . . I was the one with the car and I would always drive them home early and come back."

> The MTs met so young, when she was fourteen, that her parents insisted they go to different colleges and wait to marry. So they dated others, "Most of the time having the knowledge that we were number one in each other's lives."

Not all the interviewed spouses were unattached when they met their future spouses. Five spouses were dating others at the time, and two spouses were engaged to others when they met their future partners.

> Mr. EL frequently ate dinner at the restaurant where his future wife worked. They began to date five nights a week and he left on weekends. After weeks of dating, she discovered he was engaged to another girl, so she confronted him: " 'What are you gonna do about that gal you're engaged to?' . . . He almost fell off the couch!" But he chose Mrs. EL.

What Attracted the Future Spouses to Each Other

She was beautiful in my eyes.—Mr. RG

I knew that I could always count on him.
—Mrs. CN

Husbands and wives had the same reasons for choosing their partners: quality of character (i.e., they saw one another as good, kind, honest, trustworthy, and sincere), good personality, and compatibility. During the interview, 17 percent of wives mentioned their husband's good looks and their physical attraction, while, in contrast, nearly one-third of the interviewed husbands mentioned their wives' beauty and physical attraction. Twelve percent of husbands and 17 percent of wives interviewed thought their future spouses were "different" somehow, and that "difference" was very attractive.

> Mr. AL remembers, "Part of it must have been hormones, but another part was the extroverted personality she had. She was all bubbles."

> Mr. SE says, "She was very compatible. . . . And she had set a goal for herself in terms of her education . . . and I admired that quality, that 'stick-to-it-tiveness.' And I thought she was beautiful."

> Mrs. HA: "You always knew that he would be there for you . . . and your family at all times."

> Why did Mr. AE choose his wife? "I'm damned if I know. . . . She looked very beautiful. . . . She had a good mind. We enjoyed the same things, we got along, we ate the same things . . . . She wasn't hopeless or helpless."

Several spouses mentioned how fun or uplifting their partners were and how different that was from themselves and their family backgrounds.

> Mrs. SE said, "He was just one ball of fun! He just was a clown. . . . He gets along with all sorts and conditions of people. . . . I came from a very serious household. . . . It was like being lifted up, to be with him."

> The RGs knew each other as children, their families knew each other, and they lived nearby. He remembers himself as a "real skinny, ugly kid. . . . She had gorgeous black hair with long black curls. . . . When I saw her . . . I had a feeling this was the girl I was gonna marry. . . . I was always the guy in the background. But she was so lively and lovely and it just took my heart."

> The first time the RGs met, he says, "She hated me." She doesn't argue the point. "He always had 15 million friends that were running with him, and I was very independent. . . . I was like the princess of the family. . . . He wasn't a dresser, and to me, you couldn't pass my threshold unless you were dressed nice."

> She remembers telling her mother, "I don't know why, but when I go out with him, I have such a wonderful time. . . . My love for my husband grew as I knew him." Other qualities that drew her to him were "his gentleness, his kindness, his regard for his parents . . . because that's how I felt about my parents."

> The WEs met at work in 1938 when she was eighteen and he was twenty-five. She says, "There was a very deep attraction immediately. I kind of liked him, but you know, I had this commitment to this other guy. Anyway, I broke that, and we were engaged six weeks after we met." On their first date, they went up to the mountains on Labor Day to meet her brother. "We had three flat tires. We spent nine hours on the road. . . . That's when he asked me . . . would I marry him. I said, 'Yes.' . . . He was just a very quiet, considerate person. . . . I came from a very, very rambunctious household . . . a lot of noise, a lot of confusion."

Several spouses said they wanted to marry someone who was intelligent and educated.

Mrs. LA: "It was a process of natural selection. I liked the way he looked. . . . He had received his education. . . . He had a job." He had graduated from a prestigious university, adding to the attraction.

Mrs. AE: "He had a sense of humor, and he was a college graduate . . . talking about all sorts of exotic things."
Mr. AE: "I would not have married somebody who did not graduate from college."

Mrs. LS remembers, "We talked a lot . . . We each had a lot to say to each other."
Mr. LS: "She was . . . the trend setter. . . . We could sit down and discuss anything and everything."

Sometimes choice was more a matter of good luck than conscious selection. Some spouses could not say exactly why they chose this person to marry. Many now think they were too young and inexperienced to choose a life partner at that point, but sharing similar backgrounds often compensated for their lack of experience.

Mrs. PA says, "He made me feel good. I think seventeen is much too young to get married. . . . I don't know if it was love or hormones. At that age, who knows? . . . I think I was just very lucky. . . . I could easily have chosen somebody who was not as good a person."
Mr. PA agrees: "I didn't know anything about love at the time. . . . In the beginning . . . you're friends, you were comfortable, . . . and you learned."

Mr. HE thinks: "There's a lot of luck in this thing too, that we happened to meet each other."
Mrs. HE agrees. "We were very fortunate because our backgrounds were a lot alike, we were the same religion . . . same kind of family. . . . We expected certain things."

Mrs. EE: "When you're young like that, you really don't analyze these things."

Love at First Sight

I wanted to have a good time. He just wanted to get married.—Mrs. NA

I went home with sore lips.—Mr. EE

Five interviewed couples mutually experienced love at first sight. Eleven husbands felt that way, although their feelings were not reciprocated at first.

One wife fell in love at first sight, whereas her future husband took a little longer. Overall, the women were more cautious.

Mrs. FL: "He picked me up . . . on Ocean Parkway. . . . I was sitting on a bench with a friend." After one date, he proposed. "He says to me, 'I'm gonna marry you.' I said to him, 'You're crazy! You don't even know who I am!' . . ." She remembers his saying to her, " 'I always knew that when I . . . met the one . . . I would know right away, and you're the one.' . . . I said, 'I could never love you.' . . . Famous last words. . . .'' At first she still dated other fellows, but, "He used to follow me . . . on dates. . . . He would stand and cry. . . . He was a stalker and I married him." She laughs.

Mrs. WT: "Actually [my husband] was going out with my girlfriend, . . . and one day I . . . got on to the trolley, and he was on the trolley, . . . and a wind came along and blew up my skirt, you know like Marilyn Monroe. And I got off, but he called me right afterwards." The other girlfriend obviously was forgotten, for Mr. WT remembers, "She was the first and only girl that I really went with."

When the TIs met at summer religious camp in Wisconsin, it was love at first sight for him, but not for her. The day they met, Mr. TI said to her, "Do you know how to make gravy . . . because anybody I marry oughta know how to make gravy." Mrs. TI remembers, "I wasn't very interested in him." That Thanksgiving he proposed to his future wife, "sitting on a cultivator tongue out in the snow . . . I'm a farmer, so that was very romantic."

The MEs met in 1928. She says, "I never thought I'd ever see him again, because I was very popular . . . very pretty, slender and tall. But his mother always told me that when he came home from his vacation, he had told her he met the girl he was going to marry. . . . I was very impressed [with him], although I had gone out with some wealthier boys than him. I wasn't going to go with any poor guy, what was the sense?" When they met, she was seventeen and he was eighteen. She continues, "I was the prettiest girl he ever went out with . . . and the richest."

Mr. TR remembers they were on a blind date, but not with each other: "When she came out the door . . . I thought to myself, 'I got the wrong one'. . . . I didn't waste any time. I called her the next day and got a date. . . . I just liked everything about her."

The YEs met while she was a registered nurse, caring for Mr. YE's mother. "One Sunday morning . . . I looked down the hall and I saw this streak of white lightning coming down the hall in his Navy uniform, and I almost dropped a bucket of water! . . . I didn't let him go after that."

Mr. GR fell in love at first sight, but his future wife did not. She says, "He'd say to me all the time, 'Do you love me?' and I'd say, 'No.' One time I hesitated and he said, 'OK, you're starting!' "

Dating

> *I had a car. . . . In those days not many people had*
> *cars, so I was "it"!*—Mr. ME

The practice of dating began during the 1920s, primarily among middle- and upper-class youth who had the time and the money (Schwartz and Scott 1994). This emergence of dating was part of a change involving more personal choice and less parental involvement in mate selection. The idea was to go out with many different people, and compare. Comparison led to competition: having a car, the right clothes, and money to spend. This changed during the Depression, when there was less money to spend on dating (Waller 1937). Couples in the 1930s and 1940s engaged in more group dating than nowadays. Young people of both sexes met at clubs and parks, went on picnics, and had parties at each others' houses. They had little if any privacy, and since almost no one had cars, they walked and used public transportation. Movies were a major form of entertainment, as were church activities and parties.

> Mrs. CN began dating her future husband when she was fifteen. "Then it wasn't like going together is now!" she laughs. "I mean my mother allowed me to go to the movies on a Sunday afternoon, and we said good-bye at the gate."

> Mrs. PA explains, "People didn't date [in the '30s]. . . . First of all, you didn't have any money. Nobody had a car, . . . so you kinda hung out in each others' houses. . . . You were always in somebody's house, and mama was always home to supervise. You went to ice cream parlors, the candy store and got a soda."
> "Dutch treat," Mr. PA remembers, was a sign of those times.

> Mrs. AL recalls, "We went to the . . . concerts . . . at City College. We didn't have the quarter [to pay] to sit on the pillow instead of the hard concrete. . . . We used to take the trolley car . . . but we'd walk over the bridges. . . . On the Triborough Bridge, he kissed me. And I loved it! . . . but I thought I was committing a sin. . . . I told the priest that I had been kissed and I enjoyed it. . . . And then when we were on the George Washington Bridge walking, I kissed him! I didn't feel guilty at all. I just enjoyed it." He adds with a smile and a wink, "We covered all the bridges."

Premarital Sex

> *You're lucky you got a kiss goodnight.*—Mr. NA

There was less premarital sex in the 1930s and the 1940s than today, and more women married as virgins. However, some research suggests that premarital sex was not that uncommon. Lewis Terman's research early in this century found that 90 percent of surveyed women who were born before 1890 were virgins at marriage, but only 32 percent of women born after 1910 had no premarital sex; Alfred Kinsey found much the same thing, and says the big change occurred among women born after 1900 (see Mintz and Kellogg 1988, p. 112). Over two-thirds of the interviewed wives stated they were virgins, and none of the sixty interviewed couples lived together before they were married.

> Mr. NA: "There were certain girls. . . . Very few fellows really bothered with girls that were 'that way.' . . . They'd go out with them. . . . Drop them like a hot potato after that. . . . We didn't have cars at that time either. You used to take trolley cars and buses and subways."
> Mrs. NA smiles, "And you had the vestibule."

> The ERs spent their winter honeymoon at a farm in upstate New York. Mr. ER remembers, "We had a book that your sister loaned us on sex; we didn't know anything, . . . and we were reading this book."
> Mrs. ER continues, "In those days, people didn't sleep together before they got married."
> Mr. ER agrees, "Yeah, no experimenting." She says proudly, "We were the first for each other, and the only one of our whole lives."

Length of Courtship

> *We were in a Depression. We couldn't get married for five years.*—Mr. AL

> *It was wartime and he was going to be shipping out.*
> —Mrs. LD

The timing of marriages for these couples was more influenced by social norms than by personal desires. As is typical of the times, the couples in the study married relatively young by today's standards.

> Mrs. WE, married in 1940, says, "Girls never got married later than twenty-one."

> Mrs. PA, married in 1941 at age seventeen, says, "Early marriages were the thing then. Everybody got married very early, very young."

Since premarital sex was less common, marriage was the avenue to legitimate sexual relationships.

Mrs. NA explains, "At that time, men were more serious than women. . . . A man wanted to get married. That was one way he would get . . . what he wanted."

Occasionally, educational goals played a role in timing of marriage, particularly for middle-class couples.

Mrs. TI: "I thought I had to finish college. It was just one of the things you did. You went to college. You got married afterwards."

From the perspective of the life course theory, the significant difference between coming of age in the Depression and coming of age during World War II is that the Depression caused people to postpone marriage, while the war hastened the decision to marry. Thirty-five percent of the couples said they had to wait until they could afford to marry, mostly as a result of the Depression, and nearly 40 percent said the timing of their marriage was based specifically on war events—being inducted, shipping overseas, or coming home on leave.

The interviewed spouses typically knew each other quite a long time before they married, which most of them think contributed to their marital success. None of them married in less than six months from meeting; however, many fell in love and became engaged in a much shorter time span. Twenty-eight percent of couples married within the first two years after meeting (13 percent within the first year), and 27 percent waited two to three years to marry. Seventeen percent waited three to four years, and 28 percent waited five or more years to marry. Those who waited the longest most often cited as reasons waiting until the young woman was old enough (12 percent) and until they had enough money to marry. One-sixth of the couples had family issues propelling them into marriage—unhappy home lives, pushy parents, dying parents. Two of the sixty couples married because of pregnancy.

The CNs waited to marry until she was twenty-one, as her mother wanted. He says, "She had to twist my arm [to get married]. It was the Depression years, and we both came from a family that didn't have too much. It was taking on a job, an extra job" [to get married].

The LDs married in 1941 because of the war. He says, "You never knew where you were going or if you would be alive the next morning."

The ELs married in 1943. "I think the war accelerated everything, because we all knew you only have a few months and you're gone."

The war and family illness determined the timing of the RGs marriage in 1942. Mr. RG explains, "We were married just right after war was declared. . . . My father, who was the rabbi, performed the marriage ceremony. We were the last couple he married before he died."

She remembers, "We don't know what's gonna happen. We might as well get married . . . because the times were very precarious."

Mrs. SO explains, "It took World War II to make me realize how much I did love him because . . . he was always the dearest friend I ever had. He was always there for me. It was like my eyes being opened how much I loved him and how much I missed him. . . . I didn't want him to go and not leave me something of his, such as a baby, so if anything happened, I would always have a part of him with me." They married shortly after Pearl Harbor in February 1942.

The NNs had been dating for two years. When Mr. NN, who was already a soldier, wrote to say he didn't know whether he'd still be around in June, she wrote back, "How would you like to get married this weekend?"

Couples who married during the war years were somewhat more likely than Depression-era couples to cite "commitment" as a reason to marry (less than 25 percent of those marrying in 1932 or earlier versus 36 to 42 percent during 1940–1944). On the questionnaire, surveyed spouses could check any or all of the reasons for marriage that applied to them, and could write additional comments. Ninety-four percent of the surveyed spouses checked "love for future spouse." Additional written reasons were: "family pressures," "to grow up," "to become a man," and "it was expected" (Table 3.1). Protestants were more likely than Catholic or Jewish persons to indicate "commitment" as a reason for marriage (44 percent versus 30 percent of Catholics and Jews). Catholics and Protestants were more likely than Jews to indicate "desire for children" as a reason to marry (31 percent versus 28 percent of Protestants and 14 percent of Jews).

Marrying

We had a very simple wedding.
—Unidentified surveyed spouse

The timing and the style of the wedding were shaped largely by social class norms, ethnic traditions, and either the Depression or World War II. The majority of couples had next to nothing when they married, but nearly all had at least some family support of their marriage.

Table 3.1

Reasons to Marry

Reasons	Percentage of Spouses
Commitment to my future spouse	94
Love for my future spouse	34
The time was right to marry	27
To have children	26
Duty, obligation to others	1

Weddings

> *My mother had an extra ring. I couldn't afford to buy one in those days.*—Mr. HA

During the Depression, people could not afford to marry or they could afford only small weddings, often without honeymoons. During World War II, wedding plans were hastily made, and sometimes family and friends couldn't attend because of rationing and rushed plans. Most spouses remembered how common it was to have small, simple, informal weddings. Many couples have only one or two posed wedding portraits, and some have no pictures from their wedding. Only one-third of the couples interviewed said they had some kind of honeymoon, mostly in the New York area, usually for a few days. Wedding gifts were simple and inexpensive. No one had lists of requested gifts or elaborate bridal showers.

> Mrs. HE: "You got a toaster, you got a nice iron, . . . but those were not the days of big gifts."

Nearly two-thirds of the sixty interviewed couples married in a church, a synagogue, a rectory, or a rabbi's study. Four married at home, and five eloped. Five couples had both civil and religious ceremonies, including some of those who eloped. The rest married in catering halls, hotels, and "marriage mills," or had civil services. The two couples who were already expecting babies when they married were among those who eloped.

> The CIs, married over sixty years, married when she was seventeen. "Something happened, as usual. . . . She got pregnant. . . . I says, 'We can't tell our parents. We're gonna get married, and then we'll tell our parents. . . . So we eloped. . . . The judge married us. . . . We came home. . . . Our parents say,

'You're not married! . . . You have to get married in church,' so we had to."
Ever since, the couple has had two wedding dates to celebrate.

The RAs married sixty years ago, soon after her father died. "We just got ready on Monday morning and told my mother we were going to be married before the day was over, and that was it . . . no family. . . . My niece lived in [a nearby town] . . . and we went to her house and had supper and that was our wedding. . . . His mother didn't know it. So he went home and I went home."

Mrs. ER recalls that when Mr. ER finally got leave, "I had one week. . . . We were able to get a dress. . . . My mother went all around to all the neighbors, and got all their ration coupons that they would give away, and they bought hams and turkeys and we had a home reception."

The WTs also had a quickly arranged wartime wedding. Mrs. WT says, "We had a real Jewish wedding. . . . We had like . . . three days' notice that he was coming, but we got a place, and we had a regular rabbi and a regular dinner, and everybody came."

Mrs. WE: "I wanted to be dressed as a bride and I was. . . . It was very simple, what we could afford, what everybody in our circumstances, in our neighborhood was doing."

One of the social class distinctions of the time was whether or not a couple had a "football wedding." Working-class couples often had "football weddings" with sandwiches and beer, in a casual home setting, usually with just close friends and family.

The MAs had a football wedding, with ham, cheese, and salami sandwiches. "They asked what kind of sandwich did you want and they threw it at you," he laughs, with his hand in the air as if to catch the sandwich.

Whether the couple had a long-postponed Depression-era wedding or a hastily arranged wartime wedding, the marriage did not always begin as planned.

Mrs. NG: "I'm at home, missing my sweetheart, and I decided it was very glamorous for a young girl to be married, and live on the base. . . . I said, 'Come home, we're gonna get married.' "
He remembers it as an ultimatum: "Within one week, she got her gown and we had the wedding, . . . and [a] one-week honeymoon in New York City."
Mrs. NG laughs, "My next contact was a telegram: 'Sorry. Leaving. Going overseas.' " And that's the last she saw of him for two years.

The HEs married during the hurricane of 1938. That evening, as they left for the wedding, the street was flooded and she had to be carried to a car. Afterward, when they went to the photographer, the bride's dress was so badly wrinkled, "She stood me with my dress over the ironing board and ironed the dress before she would take a picture!"

Mrs. EE had an eye infection the day of the wedding: "That's how I was married, walking down the aisle with this pink patch." Her mother was in a wheelchair with a broken leg. They were married by a municipal court judge who whispered to Mr. EE before the wedding, 'Son, you can still change your mind.'"

Mr. TI recalls their nontraditional wedding: "We were married outdoors. Fifty years ago you didn't write your own ceremony, so we wrote our own ceremony. And we . . . had the altar outside." One of his two best men "came in full uniform, and then [my wife] came out of the house completely veiled, and the veil caught on the . . . rock garden." Her family had moved to a new town after she left for college, and her minister father invited both of his congregations to her wedding, so, she says, "We ended up having quite a few people at the wedding, none of whom I knew."

Financial Security and Family Support

> *When you're in love, you could care less about stability.*—Mrs. CA

> *Her mother gave us the biggest gift, $75.*—Mr. WD

One-third of the interviewed couples said they were not financially secure when they married. One-half said they managed to get by with either husband or both husband and wife working. Few of them had any savings, and they lived from paycheck to paycheck. Only ten of the sixty couples said they were relatively secure economically. Two couples were robbed of everything during their honeymoons.

The WEs spent their January honeymoon at a hotel near West Point and had a wonderful time as the only guests (it was normally a summer resort). When they came home they found that their apartment had been robbed, and "Every single thing that we had saved for had been stolen . . . . We just had the clothes we had taken with us."

Most of the couples had a great deal of family support and help when they married. Nearly all the spouses' parents attended their weddings. Parents helped financially; provided housing, food, and advice; and helped with child care later.

> Mrs. EE remembers what her mother said when she decided to marry her soldier husband: "With my head, I would not let you go, with a war going on, but with my heart, I know how you feel." Her parents took her across the country by train so she could marry Mr. EE.

> Mrs. RG's mother had taken out an insurance policy for 25 cents a week when her daughter was born. She had accumulated $800 in the policy and gave that to her daughter. "The money I was gonna spend on a wedding, I will give to you." The couple went to New York for a one-day honeymoon, and then moved in with his family, because her family's home didn't have any room for them.

> Mrs. NA was an only child whose father had died. She says, "We were going to ask my mother to live with us. . . . [But my mother] said, 'You know, you have the home here. Why don't you just move in?' And so we just took over the whole house." Mrs. NA's mother lived with them until she died, seventeen years later.

Twenty percent of the interviewed couples faced some initial disapproval from one or both sides of the family. The reasons for such disapproval included their ages (too young) or their different religions, ethnic backgrounds, or social classes. A few disapproving parents feared the loss of their children's affection and/or incomes.

> Mrs. SE's parents objected to her husband's profession: "My father . . . really tried to put everything that he could in my way."

> Mrs. MT: "She was a tough person to have for a mother-in-law. . . . She really was very angry at me, because I took her son away from her."

Regrets?

> *If we knew what was gonna be in the future, we*
> *probably wouldn't get married.*—Mrs. TA

Spouses in fifty-two of the sixty interviewed couples said, without hesitation, that they would do it all again. Those who hesitated or said they would not do it again explained that they were too young, they were not really in love, or they had not known enough about their partner or married life to make the choice. Less happy interviewed couples show some different patterns in meeting and marrying. The strong attraction to each other seemed to blind them to personality and background differences, which led to future conflicts. In almost all cases, the wife is less happy than the husband. Three of the less happy interviewed couples married in the 1930s, one because of pregnancy and one because of family pressures even though they were not in love. The third couple disagreed about the husband's career choice, and this created continuing problems.

Eight of the less happy couples married in the 1940s. They cited as reasons to marry family pressures, rushed wartime decisions, and expectations to be married by that age. Yet all of them waited at least a year from meeting to marrying, some waited as long as seven years, and most expressed some feelings of love for their partner. The causes of their unhappiness are diverse, but usually involve unfulfilled expectations: the spouse was less ambitious, less honest, more temperamental, or more demanding than the other realized. Cole's research on long-term marriage revealed similar patterns. He says that less happy marriages tend to be the result of unrealistic and/or inflexible expectations (1984, p. 64).

Summary

The major social factors influencing how the interviewed couples met are social class, religious and ethnic norms and values, propinquity, and luck. Both spouses mentioned the same qualities, overall, when they described their attraction, but men more than women mentioned physical beauty as part of the initial attraction, and women more often focused on personal character—whether the man was reliable and dependable, kind and good. More husbands than wives fell in love at first sight.

In those days dating was simpler than it is now, more group oriented, and much less costly. Dating was constrained by finances, lack of privacy, and parental influence. Few of the couples in this study had access to cars or other situations that afforded privacy, limiting opportunities for premarital sex. In fact, the majority of spouses said they had no sexual experience with anyone before marriage. All the couples interviewed knew each other at least six months before they married, and most of them knew each other between one and two years. Long dating and engagement periods gave them a chance to get to know each other.

Both class and generational differences are evident. Working-class couples more often held football weddings and moved in with parents. Middle- and upper-class couples could still have more formal weddings, and sometimes got their own apartments. Both couples marrying in the 1930s or earlier and those marrying during the war years faced economic limitations, which meant that weddings were simple, gifts were small, and honeymoons were short. Couples in the Depression tended to postpone marriage, but World War II weddings were often organized in haste, limited by rationing, and flexible in arrangements.

Both Depression and World War II couples typically began marriage with little money and few possessions. Families overall were very supportive of these couples, providing what assistance they could. Despite these early difficulties, the vast majority of the survey couples would do it all again.

Chapter Four

Having Children

I don't think that anybody's prepared for marriage or parenting.—Mr. PA

Introduction

Almost 98 percent of the surveyed couples have children. The desire for children and family planning, how lives changed when couples became a family, the effects of 1950s prosperity and the migration to the suburbs, and the best and worst of the child-rearing years are the subjects of this chapter. The paradox of having children, according to these couples, is the work and conflict generated by child rearing, matched by the joy and rewards of seeing those children grown.

Desire for Children and Family Planning

We just had the children and thought about it later.
—Mrs. SK

Twenty-six percent of the surveyed spouses said that one of the reasons they married was to have children. The higher the educational attainment and yearly income, the less often "desire for children" was cited as a reason for marriage. Catholic and Protestant spouses were more likely than Jewish spouses to say a desire for children was a reason for marriage (Table 4.1).

> Mrs. ER says, "The second one was a surprise.... Our only prevention was rhythm, ... but we weren't really upset.... We both wanted a family very much."

When couples planned their families and delayed having children, they

64

Table 4.1

"Desire for Children" as Reason to Marry by Demographic Variables

Variable	Percentage of Spouses
Joint yearly income	
Under $20,000	30.0
50,000 or more	15.0
Educational level	
Eighth grade	41.0
Less than high school	31.9
High school graduate	24.8
Some college	25.6
College graduate	22.5
Postgraduate/advanced	19.6
Religious affiliation	
Catholic	31.0
Protestant	28.0
Jewish	14.0

did it to save money, to finish their educations, to build their relationship together first, and because of the uncertainties of the war.

> The TMs waited almost seven years to have a child. She says, "It was a case of being practical. . . . We couldn't afford to have a child and so we waited. . . . As soon as he finished his residency, and got established in a position, we went ahead and had the first child." The four-year gap between their first and second children was, again, for practical reasons: "He was studying for his medical boards, and didn't think he wanted a baby screaming around while he was studying."

> Mr. EG says, "We waited until 1946." "We didn't have children until after everything was over," she explains.

> Mrs. LA: "When I was nineteen the first thing I did was go to a Planned Parenthood clinic and get birth control. . . . It was a solid four years before we accepted parental responsibility."

In a few cases, outside events motivated couples to have children, some early and others later on in the marriage.

> Mrs. PA: "We were married three years. I was twenty years old. I worked. We would not have started a family at that point, but my older sister died very young. . . . My mother was in very, very bad mental condition . . . threatening suicide, and the love of my mother's life was babies. . . . We both felt that it would help pull my mother over a very difficult period, and it did . . . . I saw my mother . . . go from a person who talked about going up on the roof and

jumping off, to a person who could pick up this infant and look at him and smile and sing him lullabies."

Mrs. GR: "I was thirty-seven years old when I had him. I was finished after the first two, and then my friend had a baby, and I had such a strong yen, and I had to convince him [my husband] that we should have another child before it's too late."

The PGs already had three children. She says, "Then, all of a sudden a couple of our friends lost their children, and we decided to have another one seven years later."

A few couples had difficulty conceiving or had problems during the pregnancy and delivery.

Mrs. CA: "We would have had more children, if God had allowed us to have more children, because we didn't want to stop at four, but we had to."

Mrs. NN: "We were married two years before I decided I was ready to have a child, and I just couldn't conceive, but finally . . . I did conceive, and this wonderful child came just before I was thirty."
    Mr. NN recalls, "She had breech in both cases and the doctor . . . pulled me aside and said, 'Enough is enough, no more.'"

From Couple to Family

> *Having children makes a whole new world.*
> —Mr. NN

Interviewed spouses discussed how the first child changed their relationship, what their early child-rearing years were like, what their division of labor was, how the family made time and space, and what rules they established to govern themselves. They also explained whether and how 1950s prosperity affected them and whether they were part of the migration to the suburbs.

First Children

> *It didn't change our marriage. We just had an extra person around the house.*—Mr. MT

Mr. MT is in the minority, because most spouses thought their lives changed dramatically. Finding enough time to do all the work and still be a married couple was the biggest challenge. Most spouses said they had less time to give each other attention and affection. Role conflicts emerged as mothers tried to satisfy the needs of both children and husbands. Many spouses said that becoming parents forced them to grow up.

> Mr. PG, married in 1939, did not choose parenting as the best time of life: "Once you have a child, the thing between a husband and a wife changes. . . . There's a whole change of roles, and I wasn't too happy with it in the beginning."

> Mrs. SE says having their first child was "the most wonderful thing in the world. . . . Also I think, when you have that union between two people, and all of a sudden, by your own doing there's a third, and I think, a mother-wife is torn between her child and her husband's needs. So it naturally, it takes a little adjusting."

> Mrs. YE: "I kinda think it was growing up. . . . I mean, all of a sudden we had responsibility. . . . Before that we were lighthearted. If we stayed out half the night it was all right. . . . We weren't too sure of babysitters, . . . so we just plain gave up, and it was quite a shock to us. . . . I think we settled right down."

> The AEs were the only couple who adopted children—four siblings, aged two, four, six, and eight. "Well, it was gonna tear the heck out of our life. We'd been married fifteen years without children . . . and four would probably be a little easier, because you wouldn't be worrying about one of them all the time, and if one died, or something like that, you wouldn't be as heart broken."
>
> Mrs. AE says, "I find babies kind of boring. . . . It was perfect. . . . They were not pitiful pups. . . . I don't think we would have taken on four pitiful pups. . . . We had to grow up. We were mom, pop, and the kids."

The Early Child-Rearing Years: The Family Grows

> *I think that was the hardest part, when I had two teentsy ones.*—Mrs. SE

In the interviews, nearly all the couples said they struggled financially when they began their families. While financial resources were limited, their pleasure in the marriage and in the births of their children usually outweighed the troubles they faced.

> Mrs. FL: "I remember once a brother of mine paid our rent, and he had to buy shoes for my children, yet we always had food on the table. . . . We lived in a neighborhood that was mostly Italian and Jewish. . . . The Italian peddler . . . would stop outside the house, and I would buy a basket of damaged fruit, 'cause I couldn't afford to buy it by the pound. My children used to call it 'used fruit.' "

Mrs. NG: "We loved our babies! . . . It's a tremendous hardship, there's no two ways about it. . . . I have three babies. . . . It's only a one-bedroom apartment, so we had our bed in the living room."

Mr. NG remembers missing time with his sons: "I was still working two jobs." When he had to work instead of play ball with his son, he says, "I coulda cried."

As their five children grew older, Mrs. TA remembers, "When you have that many kids, you don't have enough money to give them what they want. We'd have to sit down and talk, and figure out how to tell 'em."

Child rearing imposed new needs and more work. Television was becoming popular in the 1950s, as were many household "labor-saving" appliances. Most of the couples could not afford everything they wanted, so they set priorities, and they emphasized paying with cash, not credit, both then and now.

Mrs. TN's choice was a television set. "In the building we lived in, we were the only ones with TV, and sometimes we'd have fifteen, twenty kids sitting in front of our TV set." On the other hand, Mr. TN points out, "She had to use a washing board until 1947, 1948."

The PAs chose a washer: "We were young marrieds living in a three-room apartment in the Bronx on the fourth floor, [a] walk-up, with two little kids . . . . I was scrubbing clothes with a washboard because . . . a washing machine in the basement . . . meant lugging clothes up and down four flights of steps." They bought a washer. "My next-door neighbor, whom I'm still friends with, bought a TV, and so we went in her house to watch TV, and she did her laundry in my apartment." This is not so different from the times when, as a child, she had shared her roller skates with a friend.

Many spouses said they turned inward, focusing more on their family.

Mrs. LS: "We got more and more into just doing things with the children."

Additional children, coupled with existing financial uncertainty, created problems for some couples.

Mrs. PA remembers when she discovered she was pregnant with her third child. "This was not a planned pregnancy, . . . which did a real number on my head, because the other kids were planned. . . . I thought I was too old to have kids." Her husband was trying to get a business going. "We didn't even know if we could afford this house. . . . I had a premature baby, and the first year of her life she screamed. . . . They were extremely difficult years. . . . When she stopped screaming, I guess I stopped crying."

Mrs. NG conceived the NG's fourth and last child nearly ten years after the third child was born. "I was very, very miserable. . . . I went to a young priest." She told the priest, "I can't stand him. . . . I gotta get outta this marriage! . . . He said to me, 'If you want love, you have to give love'. . . . So that night I went home, and I prepared his favorite meal with the candlelight, and I did everything . . . gritting my teeth, but I did it. And nine months later . . ."

Family Time

> When I came home from work . . . we all sat down at
> the table together.—Mr. RG

Almost all the interviewed couples said they tried to make sure they created specific time to be with the children. The ritual of the family dinner was handed down from their own parents. Several couples noted the disappearance of family dinners in the younger generations, because fewer wives are home to prepare meals, and family members have competing activities.

Mr. MA, married in 1936, says, "In our time nobody sat at the dinner table till we were all there together, as a family unit, my kids, my wife, every night, together at the dinner table . . . where the kids could explode and explain their problems."

Mrs. CA, married in 1940, says, "When we had dinner we always had it together, with the children. . . . We all sat around the table, and we did that all our lives."

When everyday time was limited, some families tried to maximize vacations.

The WEs camped up and down the East Coast. Mrs. WE says, "We were a camping family. And we did it because it was a very frenetic life, raising three kids with school and cub scouts and girl scouts and boy scouts and 4H and dancing classes. . . . Everybody was very busy. We had a very active social life. We decided that we had to have time with our kids, so we bought a tent and we bought a station wagon, and we would go away every weekend . . . . We camped until our sons got married, and they brought their wives camping with us, too."

For ten years, the LSs camped by the ocean during the summer. Mr. LS came out on weekends, and his wife and children and the dog were alone during the week, unless friends joined them. He remembers, "[We were] right on the water. . . . [The] kids never wore bathing suits. . . . We were sleeping on the ground."

Mrs. LS recalls, "It was a lot of work. . . . What you enjoyed about it was the freedom for yourself and for your children. . . . We had a little rowboat. . . .

We went to the laundromat." He adds, "We had to bring in our water, our ice.
. . . The boys, every one of them, discuss it as the highest point of their lives."

Family Rules

We had to present a united front.—Mrs. TM

Despite the mother's dominance of household and child-rearing activities
and everyday decisions at home, most of the spouses defined the husband as
the "official" head of the household. Mothers had informal power in the
father's absence, but fathers held the title of authority. Typically, one parent
was more the disciplinarian; this was usually the father, but not always.

> Mr. CA: "I was probably more of a hard taskmaster. . . . She was a little more
> lenient."
>   She agrees: "I was the one who always stuck up for them. Of course, the
> father always expects [his] sons to be better than him. Meanwhile, some of
> them have to be a little worse."

> Mr. GE says, "She was the disciplinarian." And she adds, "He would come
> home with a Hershey bar in each pocket for the kids."

Parents had to learn how to discipline and raise their children as a team.
Most agreed to present a united front, rarely challenging each other's parenting in front of the children.

> Mrs. TM: "He used to say, 'Go ask your mother,' and I would always say, 'What
> did your father say?' because . . . we wouldn't let one play against the other."

> Mr. MA: "We had a secret, my wife and I. . . . Anytime the children . . .
> want[ed] to go anyplace, they would ask their mother. If she did not want
> them to go, she said, 'Ask your father.' When she said, 'Ask your father,'
> that meant automatically no. . . . She'd say, 'It's all right with me, but you
> gotta ask your father first.' That was our signal. She didn't want them to go,
> but I took the blame. And that worked for fifteen, maybe twenty years."

This frequently translated into an agreement not to fight in front of the
children at all. A few spouses remembered how their parents had fought in
front of them, and this avoidance of visible conflict was a conscious choice
to be different. The NNs and the RAs illustrate the role early socialization
experiences play in shaping future behavior.

> Mr. NN had volatile parents who fought constantly. He describes his mar-
> riage: "Both of us were determined we're never going to argue in front of the

children, and this is why they thought that's all there is to it, it's 'honey' and 'dearie' and everything is love and it isn't. When they finally discovered we do have what we call 'intellectual discussions,' then . . . all of a sudden they woke up. So from me to you, don't pretend that you don't argue with your wife. . . . We both had parents who did not get along too well, and when you have role models like that, there's a tendency to go the other way."

Mrs. NN agrees. "I paid a price. . . . I ended up going to therapy." She found her early socialization had suppressed her assertiveness. "It was more important for me to have peace in the family."

The RAs, married in 1926, came from different backgrounds. Her parents had never argued, while his folks "used to scrap pretty bad . . . physical." She says, "We tried never to have a squabble in front of the kids and tried to straighten out whatever it was at night when we were alone. We still do. The kids can come in, and we might be fighting like blue blazes, but they never know it."

In retrospect, some thought this approach was not the best idea, because it gave their children a false impression of marriage.

Mrs. LS: "We did not believe in arguing in front of our children, which might have been a mistake. They're supposed to see how you are, at least you read that now. . . . I don't know, my parents argued in front of me."

Mrs. CN: "He and I never argued . . . in front of the children. That was bad, I think, in a way, because they thought everything was perfect."

1950s Economic Prosperity

We never expected to have all the things we have now.
—Mr. CA

The Good Life

We were a typical postwar family of mother, father, and one child in an apartment complex. . . . It was a great life. . . . We were all about the same age, all about the same experience.—Mr. EL

All doing the same things, belonging to the same groups.—Mrs. EL

By the 1950s the nation was experiencing prosperity after twenty years of struggling through economic depression and war. The fertility rate in the

United States rose 50 percent between 1940 and 1957 (Mintz and Kellogg 1988, p. 179). During the 1950s more children were born closer together and earlier in the marriage than in the previous generation, an exception to general historical trends since the nineteenth century. The rate of divorce was lower than in previous decades, and it remained low until the 1960s. The 1920s "companionate" concept of marriage, emphasizing friendship, emotional intimacy, and sexual satisfaction with each other, was finally realized in the 1950s (ibid.).

Mintz and Kellogg (ibid.) interpret this focus on marriage and procreation as a reaction to the extremes of the Depression and war years. The improved economy made it possible for many families to do well, to think beyond survival issues. Couples who grew up with nothing during the Depression wanted to do more for their children, and this sentiment was continually expressed by interviewed couples. Popular media such as magazines, books, and television portrayed marriage and family as the path to fulfillment, and most interviewed couples shared those sentiments.

Life was not perfect for couples in the 1950s. Mothers of the 1950s were expected to focus their lives on their home and children. Many interviewed wives said they experienced frustration, isolated in the home with limited adult companionship. Women who had worked outside the home, especially during the war years, had tasted economic independence, responsibility outside the home, and an identity beyond "wife and mother," and now, these opportunities had diminished.

The absent father often discussed in interviews was typical of the time. Many popular magazines and books of the 1950s discussed the increasingly limited role of father. Instead of being the patriarch, he was the breadwinner and little else (ibid.). Job-related stress became a major health concern during the 1950s, experienced by both blue- and white-collar workers (ibid.). Many interviewed husbands felt exhausted by the demands of work and commuting, and had little energy left to interact with their family. Several husbands who earned low salaries said they felt inadequate, and that is how some wives described them. But the strong economy meant that most couples' economic situation improved over time.

> The HEs had their first child, a son, in 1948, five years after they married, and she quit work. "We had to struggle for a while. And that was when he started to play weekend jobs with the guitar. He had a day job, which he ultimately had for fifty years. . . . But in those other years . . . he played the guitar weekends." In 1955 they had a daughter. She continues, "It was different . . . because economically we were better situated."

Mrs. GE describes a particular memory that sums up the good life of the 1950s for her: "I realized how much I had . . . a new Dodge. . . . We had a house, we had two wonderful kids, my mother was with us, . . . and we had enough money to buy whatever we wanted, and that day I felt that really I had nothing in the world to complain about. I always think of that day, I was driving and mom was next to me, and I'm thinking, 'Isn't this perfect?' " On the other hand, this was not among the happiest times for Mrs. GE's husband: "He was with his father and brother and sister in an office supply business. That was a very difficult time for him, he got ulcers. His brother and father were very demanding."

Migration to the Suburbs

> *I was in heaven. I never knew what it was to live in*
> *your own home.*—Mrs. TT

The relocation to the suburbs was a major national change, a part of the economic prosperity of the 1950s. The growth of the suburbs depended, in part, on postwar low-interest home loans for veterans, and was fed by the housing shortage that forced so many couples to live with parents. In 1949 Levittown and the Long Island suburban boom were born (Gordon and Gordon 1987). Couples left extended families in the city to live farther away, in the first home that many of these couples had owned, often committing husbands to lengthy commutes. The private home with a yard, outside the city, became the American dream, the ideal place to raise children (Mintz and Kellogg 1988; Gordon and Gordon 1987).

The WTs, married in 1943, had two children when they moved to the suburbs. "We came out to Long Island in 1953. . . . We bought a very modest house . . . and lived there for thirty-two years." Before they moved, she says, "We didn't know anybody who owned a house."

Mrs. LA, married in 1940, says, "I remember when the second child came, it was kinda tough, like wonder how you're gonna pay your bills. . . . We didn't know how much was coming in every week. . . . He's made enough to support us. . . . We had the four kids. We never lived in luxury, but we had everything we wanted. . . . When we first got married . . . we had a three-room apartment, and the children came. Then we had a . . . five-room apartment. Apartments got a little bit too small. We wanted a dog . . . so we had to have a house." They lived thirty years in that house.

Mrs. NN, married in 1943, says, "When the second child was born we started to look for a house. She was nine months old when we came in here. We've been here for forty-three years. . . . We had money in the bank because we had lived with my parents for so long."

The ERs, married in 1943, left her parents' home for their new bungalow on Long Island. Mrs. ER says, "Everybody was about our age . . . with all little children, so it was nice for our children growing up that way." The couple lived in that house for thirty years, adding on six rooms and a fireplace.

The WEs, married in 1940, moved to Long Island in 1951. She explains, "Then our whole life changed. There was all young people, same circumstances financially. We had a nice little house, and we had a very nice social life there. It was all, you know, similar circumstances."

Most interviewed couples emphasized that their suburban neighbors were much like them: wartime couples about the same age, raising children about the same age. Financial stability for many of the Depression-era couples came in their later years, as did the suburban migration. Their children were usually grown and did not share the more prosperous times with their parents. Occasionally, couples had children spread many years apart; these couples said that older children are sometimes jealous of younger siblings, who have more possessions and more freedom than they had.

The TNs, married in 1938, had nine children, divided in some sense into three different families. She says, "My oldest is 54; . . . [the youngest] is 32 . . . . Some of my bigger kids resented the last three because they felt the little ones are getting more. . . . We used to go camping and money was tight; . . . then . . . these three went all over, on a cruise."

The FTs remember the leaner years raising their two girls. The girls are eleven and twelve years older, respectively, than their brother, who was "a surprise." Mrs. FT says, "My son is the one who always had the toys, because when my daughters was little, who could afford 'em? . . . He was spoiled . . . . tanks, robot men, you name it, whatever came out we bought him."

Problems Raising the Children

That's your immortality . . . the children give you wonderful grandchildren.—Mrs. PA

Mostly they give you heartburn. . . . Listen, anything has bitter and sweet.—Mr. PA

Twenty-one percent of the 1,152 spouses surveyed said that raising the children had created marital problems for them. Raising children was the fourth most common issue, after finances (29 percent) and ill health and relatives (both 24 percent). Approximately 20 percent of spouses who married in 1932 or earlier reported problems in raising children. The percentage declines to 11.8 percent for spouses marrying between 1935 and 1939, and then increases every year of the war to a high of 32 percent of those marrying in 1944 (Table 4.2). Wives reported this problem more frequently than did husbands. For example, among husbands and wives who married in 1943, 32 percent of wives versus 20 percent of husbands said that raising children was a problem. When spouses had problems raising children, they were also more likely to report problems with sexual relations, spouse's annoying habits, wife working, relatives, ($p < .05$) and finances ($p < .001$).

When spouses reported problems with raising the children, they more often reported lower levels of marital happiness ($p < .001$) and lower levels of most measures of marital intimacy ($p < .05$). The more children in a family, the more often spouses said they had problems with finances and with raising the children ($p < .05$).

> Mrs. ER says, "When we were first married . . . I had to bathe two little boys and take care of the baby, and after they were in bed, I had to do the dishes by hand. He would come home and want to go to bed, and I didn't feel like it."

> Mr. PG: "When we lived in the other house I used to get Sunday afternoon headaches. . . . Sometimes [it took] two hours before the darned thing would go away." After the kids left home, "I never had one since." Mrs. PG also had migraines when the children were little. She adds, "With four kids you're exhausted too. . . . Once in a while, I'd get so tired, too tired for sex."

Discipline problems, particularly in adolescence, were the most common complaint of parents.

> Mrs. WE thought the hardest thing about raising children was "teaching them values. . . . Teaching them that they should not be influenced by kids who had other values. . . . We didn't agree with a lot of things, and we would expect them to respect our point of view." He adds, "Whatever they do, never condemn, see? But we just have to point out, because we were older, we had more experience, and we explained that to them."

> Mr. YE remembers the litany of problems: "We had our arguments about our daughter. . . . She'd stay out late. She was going out with fellows that were a little racy, they kinda reminded me of me, but that's part of growing up. . . . There was alcohol once in a while. . . . The youngest one [a son] got in trouble . . . racing his cars."

Table 4.2

Problem with Raising Children by Year Married

Year Married	Percentage of Spouses
1929 or earlier	20.8
1930–1932	20.0
1933–1934	16.3
1935–1939	11.8
1940	16.1
1941	21.9
1942	24.7
1943	26.3
1944	32.0

> Mr. EL: "Most of our disagreements have been over ... disciplining chil-
> dren. . . . I was more of a disciplinarian, but I like to point to the successes in
> the children."
>
> Mrs. EL: "I probably did a lot of covering up for the kids, or if they
> wanted anything they would go through me and I would then tackle him."

Raising one child did not always give couples the right skills for raising
another child. Each child is unique, as the TMs discovered.

> Mrs. TM says their oldest daughter "Never gave us any problems. . . . She
> was a goody-goody in school." The second daughter "had terrific temper
> tantrums. . . . You'd put her to bed, and she'd wake up and she'd scream
> bloody murder. [My husband] used to get up sometimes and go out, drive,
> ride for an hour. . . . That's why we bought a television, so we could put her
> in her room and let her scream. . . . After a while we realized she didn't need
> sleep . . . so when she'd wake up at eleven or twelve o'clock at night and
> start to scream, what we did was put her in her playpen and put a little light
> on and then go back to bed and go back to sleep. Then she was happy. . . .
> Number three was hardest to handle. . . . She decided she wanted to drop out
> of school. . . . I signed the papers. . . . She passed all her Regents', she was a
> national merit finalist, and she didn't graduate from high school. . . . She's an
> attorney now."

The larger price of the child-rearing years was summed up by Mr.
DR.

> I felt you lose freedom, you gotta come home at night and you can't go to the
> movies unless you get a babysitter. . . . One day I came home [and] I said,
> "This is it! I want a divorce!" and I was kidding. She said, "You
> can have a divorce. Take the kids with you."

Letting one's children grow up and move on was seen as one of the hardest parts of raising them.

> Mrs. EG says, "That was my life, taking care of the children. . . . The hardest time in my life, I think, was when the kids left, because they went to college, and they never came back to live."

> Mrs. PA: "I think the most difficult thing is separating from one's children, from losing control, from having them grow up to the point where you can't stop them from doing things that you feel maybe are wrong or detrimental or are gonna make them unhappy. And you lose this control and then you just have to sit back and pray a lot that whatever you put into them . . . is enough to get them through these periods. The other stuff . . . the measles . . . the falls, and the broken arms and legs . . . all that's routine. But the really difficult part is seeing them grow up and grow away from you, and yet that's what you want."

Couples married in the 1940s, more than Depression couples, raised children during the 1960s and frequently had problems. The hippie movement, drugs, sex, and questioning of authority are all mentioned.

> The MTs were married in 1941. Mr. MT says, "We had a very stormy time with our son for awhile . . . went through the whole thing in the '60s. . . . He was saving the world."

> Mr. ER: "He was a child of the '60s so . . . we were tested greatly."

> Mrs. AE, married in 1943, says the "teens were miserable of course, but they are with any children. . . . And we had six years of the drug scene. . . . One child decided it [drug scene] was too stupid for words, one went for alcohol, and one had to go all the way. . . . After they left the house, . . . we never knew for sure sometimes where they were."

> Mr. WT says the best part of having children was "when they moved out." His wife agrees, with a laugh: "Somebody said when my first son was born, from this minute, you'll never have another minute's peace in your life. . . . The older one was a hippie. . . . We did have arguments." They both think that their son was "radicalized" when a friend of his was shot and killed at Kent State.

The Best and Worst of the Child-Rearing Years

Kids are always giving you joy and a lot of grief.
—Mrs. AL

This section examines (1) how children contribute to the success of a marriage, (2) the best aspects of raising children, and (3) how the death or near death of children transformed the marriage.

Children as a Positive Factor in the Marriage

> *We never realized what a joy they would be.*
> —Mr. EL

Fifty-seven percent of the surveyed couples said that their children were one of the positive factors contributing to the success of their marriage. Most interviewed couples regarded child rearing as one of the happiest, most meaningful experiences of their lives. When children are a positive factor in a marriage, many other aspects of the marriage are reportedly working well too. Yet, spouses who reported that children are a positive factor in their marriage were also likely to report that raising children was a problem, illustrating the paradox of having children. One day, the children will be grown, and the burden of child rearing is lifted. Then spouses can enjoy the people their children have become and see the cycle start again.

> Mr. MA says the best period of marriage "was simply watching my children being born and growing up." The most difficult period of the marriage from his perspective was the same time: "Trying to provide them with the right clothes, the right food. Always struggling. I never knew a can of beer. We couldn't afford it."

> Mr. GR: "We have a very close relationship with them. . . . That's the rewards that you get for all the years you spent together living and growing and working."

Child Rearing: The Happiest Years of Marriage

> *It was a very fulfilled life.*—Mrs. PA

Spouses differed widely in what they regarded as the best parts of raising children, from preferring when they were small children to seeing them as happily married adults now.

> Mr. NN says the happiest time of their marriage was "when we got children. . . . They're both great girls, the way they raise their kids, I see my wife all over again, because my daughters, whether they liked it or not, they took their mother as a role model." Of his grandsons, he says, "I'm leaving something when I'm gone, for the rest of the world to see what I was like."

> Mr. WT says the best part of having children is "seeing them grown, and settled, and happily married." Illustrating that a mother's worries never end, Mrs. WT adds, "You always keep your fingers crossed."

The PGs do not agree about the best part of child rearing. Mr. PG says, "I don't think there was a good part. . . . There was constant turmoil in the house."

Mrs. PG: "When the kids finally grew up, I hated it. That's why I went to work." Mrs. PG was one of the few wives interviewed who felt she suffered from the "empty nest," but Mr. PG was happiest when the children left home.

Just as earlier results indicated that the lower the yearly income, the more often a desire for children was cited as a reason to marry, also the lower the income, the more often spouses said that they were happiest after the children were born. Thirty-one percent of the spouses who earn $20,000 or less said child rearing was the happiest time of their marriage, but only 16 percent of those earning $30,000 or more report raising the children as the best time of the marriage.

The LEs have always been relatively poor. They raised their two sons in a two-and-a-half-room apartment, in which they lived for over thirty-five years. She says the best years were "when I had my two children. . . . I only worked part-time because I wanted to make sure I was home for my children at all times. . . . I loved cooking and baking. I always was a homebody."

Overall, 22 percent of the survey spouses indicated that their marriage was happiest after their children were born. However, attitudes toward children show a small but significant shift over time. The later in time a couple married, the less likely they were to choose as the happiest years those "after the children were born."

Mrs. EC, married in 1928, recalls, "We were both young with our children . . . . My oldest daughter always thought of me more like a sister first off than a mother. We did everything with them. . . . We took them sleigh riding, we joined a grange. . . . I never went anywhere, only to church. . . . I played jump rope . . . I went fishing with them. . . . I've done everything for the boys the same as my husband. . . . I made sure my boys would go with their father fishing, hunting, [and that they] had baseball, Boy Scouts. The girls had sewing and crocheting and knitting, [joined] 4H, learned to cook. When my children were growing up they had to walk to school. It didn't hurt them. . . . They made friends on the way. We lived in a beautiful era."

Couples who married during the peak years of the Depression (1930–1932) were less likely than couples marrying earlier or later to say their happiest years were after the children were born. Of the spouses who married between 1933 and 1934, 37.2 percent said the happiest years of their marriage were after the children were born. From then on, the percentage declines to a low of 16.5 percent among those who married in 1944 (Table 4.3). Not only were wartime spouses less likely to choose the child-rearing years as the best years. More of them chose "after the children left home" as the best years of the marriage. From 1930 on, there is a small increase in the

Table 4.3

Year Married and Happiest Years

Year Married	Percentage of Spouses Happiest After Children Were Born	Percentage of Spouses Happiest After Children Left Home
1929 or earlier	26.1	4.3
1930–1932	16.7	0.0
1933–1934	37.2	2.3
1935–1939	26.3	2.0
1940	22.6	2.4
1941	17.5	2.3
1942	18.0	2.9
1943	21.0	4.4
1944	16.5	8.2

number of surveyed spouses who reported that their happiest years were after the children left home (Table 4.3).

There are several possible reasons for these two changes over time. First, Depression-era couples often struggled financially, making child rearing more difficult. Second, wartime separation left many women to raise their young children alone. Couples could not share these early child-rearing years. Third, the reintegration of the father after the war into an ongoing family unit was often stressful for everyone. Fourth, the wartime spouses, who reported more problems in raising children, especially during the 1960s, sometimes felt relief when their children were grown. After the children left home, they were free of many responsibilities. Finally, many couples said they became more spontaneous. If they were financially stable and healthy, they traveled more together and had more time for relaxation and enjoyment.

> Mr. ER, married in 1943, remembers when the children left home: "It was like a rejuvenation. . . . We still had our health. . . . We'd go on trips, vacations; we both had nice salaries coming in and the kids were gone off on their own. . . . These were the prime years." (The ERs were in their late forties when their children left home.)

Family Tragedies

> *That was a terrible part of our lives, thirteen months in Vietnam.*—Mr. CA

Sometimes death takes a child, although less often today than in the past. Sometimes death just comes close. In the interviews, the death or near death of a child was always defined as the worst thing that had happened in the couple's lives. The impression of these tragedies was still fresh in these older faces decades after the events occurred. Forever after, their lives were divided into two periods: before the tragedy and after.

> The RAs nearly lost their middle son. She explains, her voice hoarse, tears rolling down her cheeks: "A car of city people who'd never been [here] before had come out ... riding around, seeing the sights.... The driver turned her head.... She wasn't watching what she was doing ... and she just turned and come right into the yard and mowed my little boy down.... Smashed up his head, didn't know whether there was brain damage or not. He was in the ... hospital for two, three, four weeks.... I'd go up to visit him, and I'd never know whether I was going to find him alive or not. You'd walk into the room, and you had to stand there and look at him to see whether he was breathing or not.... He couldn't talk after this all happened.... After a while, he kind of snapped out of it.... Today he is fine."

> One of the LSs' sons was seriously injured in a car accident. Mrs. LS is visibly angry while telling the story, and she sighs frequently. "He is a paraplegic, but he is very capable.... The most physical of all of our sons, and he ended up the least able."

Eight interviewed couples had experienced the loss of one or more children, including miscarriages and stillbirths. When children died, the spouses felt they had lost a part of their past, as well as a potential future. The void in their lives was permanent.

> Mrs. FL experienced both a miscarriage and the death of an adult child. "I had a miscarriage in the fourth month. It was a boy. It was a horror, but you come through it." She had three more sons, but her third son died "at thirty-three ... of a cerebral hemorrhage," two years after a serious motorcycle accident. The stress of her son's death created problems in the FL's marriage. She says, "We were pulling apart.... We went to a psychologist, and she had the stupidity to tell me to divorce him." Next they tried a bereavement group, which gradually helped them readjust. Nevertheless, she says the loss is always with her. "It's never the same, it's like losing a limb."

> The YEs lost their middle child, their first son, in the Vietnam War, just one week after Mr. YE retired. She says, "It was very, very difficult because this number one boy was the apple of my husband's eye.... My husband was very upset, because he wanted his other son to come out of the service immediately and he didn't want to do that." She notes, "I think our marriage was even more solid than ever.... It just seemed to glue us right together."

> The CIs, married in 1930, lost two children. Their first child died at birth. Mr. CI remembers, "We went down to the morgue and seen [sic] him ... signed him out and we walked out, and that was the end of that." And she interjects,

"That's the first heartbreak." Mr. CI continues, "Anyway, the second boy was born, and we lived with her parents. They brought him up; we used to go out at night." She adds, "We never missed our youth, because my parents saw to it that we didn't miss it." Mr. CI continues, "One day [our son] comes in; he says he doesn't feel well: 'My head hurts.' . . . He went into a coma . . . for two weeks, and he had a fever over 110. The doctor got us on the side and says, 'Pray that God takes him.' So we prayed."

Mrs. CI: "We buried him on his seventh birthday. . . . This is what taught us that you should treasure children. . . . He had tubercular meningitis . . . out of the clear blue sky." Both are crying as they relive a past almost five decades old. She remembers, "I didn't want more children. . . . A year to the day, our daughter was born. . . . She is a joy. All my children are joys."

Hill (1958) has called the loss of a family member a "crisis of dismemberment." He compares the family to a physical body which has lost a limb and now must function in different ways. Schiff (1977) and Tietz, McSherry, and Britt (1977) found that separation and divorce occur in approximately 70 to 90 percent of all families in which a child dies. The personal resources and social supports of the couples in this study helped them adapt to their losses. The void could not be filled, but they managed to go on with their lives.

Summary

Nearly all the interviewed spouses described their early years as times of struggle. As they adapted to financial demands, heavy workloads, and new family roles, they simply had less time to be together as a couple. Most of the interviewed couples had a traditional division of labor. The breadwinner-fathers usually were the official heads of the households, but the housewife-mothers typically handled most of the day-to-day family decisions. The couples learned how to discipline their children and how to present a united front. With all their conflicting role demands, parents had to find ways to create family time, but the interviewed couples said that nowadays family time is "a thing of the past."

The affluence of the 1950s gave many of these couples the luxury to focus on more than survival. Of course, working-class and poor families were still struggling to pay the bills and put food on the table. The 1950s nuclear family was also increasingly separated from the larger extended family with the migration to suburbs. The suburban neighborhoods were a peer-oriented culture compared to the family networks they left behind in the city. The Depression-era couples experienced the postwar economic upturn at a different stage in their lives. The Depression couples interviewed already lived on Long Island in small towns and rural areas, or they remained in the city until they retired, and so their experience of suburban living was very different from that of young wartime families.

Over half of the surveyed spouses cited children as a positive factor contributing to their marital success, and 22 percent of surveyed spouses said the happiest years of their marriages were after the children were born. Not all spouses, of course, regarded the child-rearing years as the best time of the marriage. Among all surveyed spouses, 3 percent were happiest *before* the children were born, 7 percent were least happy *after* the children were born, and 3 percent were happiest after children *left home*. The later the year of marriage, the less often spouses reported the child-rearing years as the happiest years, and the more likely they were to say that after the children left home was the happiest time in the marriage.

The paradox of child rearing is the huge investment it requires in time, money, and energy, and the tremendous risk involved, as contrasted to the tremendous rewards that most of the couples experienced. When children left home, much of the stress and tension subsided, and most of the interviewed couples refocused on their relationship, enjoying the life they created together. This may help to explain why some studies find a curvilinear pattern of marital happiness, from the initial happy years to declining happiness in the child-rearing years, followed by an increase in marital happiness in the later years (Medley 1977; Blood and Wolfe 1960; Clark and Wallin 1965). The worst fear for one's children is to lose them. When a child died, it was a family tragedy that forever changed the couple and led, in nearly every case included in this survey, to a renewed appreciation of family life.

Chapter Five

Conflict and Resolution

We both wanted this marriage to work, and whatever it took, we were gonna do it.—Mr. GE

You buckle yourselves together, and you endure the hard times.—Mr. EC

Introduction

The HEs, an upper-middle-class couple happily married a little over fifty years, live in an immaculate home in a upscale condominium complex for seniors. Throughout most of their lives together, they have participated in many outside activities, and Mrs. HE worked outside the home as well. They describe themselves as independent, self-reliant individuals. After fifty years of marriage, both spouses recognize the importance of controlling their tempers. They communicate, compromise, and sometimes let time pass before they discuss an issue.

> Mrs. HE: "We talk about it, unless we both feel it would be better to let it lie. And then we do that too, you know. And we'll talk about other things, and then we'll come back to it. . . . I would have been the one who yelled and screamed if anybody did. He's quiet in these things, and that was very frustrating. If we did have an argument, he wouldn't argue," she laughs. "So, no, he would say how he felt, and if I disagreed very strongly and started in, he would say things like 'Well, maybe we ought to talk about it later,' or 'I have to go out now to a meeting,' or something like that, and you know, that would finish it off. But you learn, you learn after a while, for heaven's sake." She laughs again. "I was kinda sulky but I outgrew that. . . . I learned that this is a kind of a childish way to try and resolve something, by sulking. . . . We learned."
>
> Mr. HE says, "We've had some conflicts over some different points of view and sometimes some heated ones, OK? Heated to the extent where one of us would leave the house . . . or one of us would go upstairs. But I think

we knew a long time ago that these things were not supposed to last too long. . . . She's very good, she will not bring it up again, and I will try not to bring it up again . . . until maybe a couple of days later . . . when everything's cooled down and maybe we'll decide to let it go. . . . I don't have to win them all. And I don't think she does either. . . . We try to work it somehow so we don't get really antagonistic with one another. . . . I think I hold it in sometimes because I'm afraid we're gonna have a big fight about it. But then eventually it comes out. Perhaps I wait until I have the opportune moment. . . . We both argue the same way. We usually have a point of view which is maybe foreign to the other person, but we keep talking about it. Sometimes we find middle ground. Sometimes we find that one of us or both of us can give a little bit. . . . Nothing carries over for a long period of time. . . . I think our values are pretty much the same. And I think maybe mine have changed over the years to better match hers."

The HEs represent a typical happily married couple, exhibiting the most common methods of conflict resolution—communication and compromise, avoidance of recriminations and harsh language, and growth over time in managing conflicts in their marriage. They both agree that they "usually" resolve their conflicts.

The JTs, an upper-middle-class couple who describe themselves as somewhat happily married, live in a large two-story home. Throughout their lives he has been away from home, working long hours at his business. She has worked too and is now involved in several volunteer activities. When problems occur they tend to avoid issues, rely on the passage of time, and do what the other wants. She has difficulty in communicating with him, making compromise less possible.

Mrs. JT: "He was not my ideal husband. When I married him I thought he was, but living with him, his nature is too volatile. . . . He has gotta be in control. . . . In the past he could never say 'I'm sorry.' " He has never hit her, but he has been physically violent with two sons on a few occasions. "I promise myself, talk low because I think maybe it'll do more . . . because if he fights back, you know, answers back, I want to die. . . . I felt like a divorce many times. I'd love to leave. Where would I go?" The second of three times Mrs. JT overdosed on pills, the doctor asked her why and she said, "He makes me feel this small."

Mr. JT sees their marriage differently: "I really don't know. All our problems always resolve themselves, somehow. It's mysterious how it works. We have no procedure. . . . I am the sulker. . . . Nine out of ten arguments, I clam up . . . and that's it. . . . She yells at me. I generally sulk, and that protects me. . . . Then she could argue till the cows come home. I listen. I don't argue back. She knows she's not gaining points by continuing to argue. . . . It's a dead issue. I'll sulk for a couple of days, we won't talk, then all of a sudden it moves back again, and everything is fine. That's generally how we ride out a storm, because I'm the silent one. . . . I had one violent act in our marriage.

She had a big shelf unit that she had all her gorgeous antiques on, and I was sitting at the table, . . . and she bugged me with something, and bugged me and bugged me until I picked up one of the chairs and I very carefully aimed at that closet and threw the chair and smashed all the antiques." He says it happened right after they married, and he's never done anything like that since. "That was a lesson to me."

Sometimes special thoughtfulness can outweigh many problems. She says, "We were married twenty-five years, he didn't send me a card, didn't even say happy anniversary. I was so distraught. . . . He was working and there was no loving. . . . Every time I needed money, I had to ask him. . . . We went out that evening for this dinner dance that I wasn't looking forward to, I wasn't even talking to him. . . . We get there, and it was a surprise party for us that he had planned all the time. . . . I would have divorced him, and here he had this planned!"

This couple seems to be in two different marriages. From her perspective, she is married to a man who has her walking on eggshells with the remains of her self-esteem. He sees himself as married to a woman who can annoy him so much that he has to sulk or explode. Mr. JT said they had no procedure for settling arguments. The problems just work out. From her perspective, the problems do not work out. She simply lives with them. Despite the serious conflicts they have had in the past, they say they love and depend on each other.

The HEs and the JTs illustrate the two extremes of conflict resolution among the couples in this study: the happily married communicating compromisers, and the less happily married couples who tend to avoid communication, wait for problems to pass, and do what the other spouse wants.

Integrating both survey and interview data, this chapter focuses on three major areas. First, how the sources of conflict and methods of conflict resolution are correlated with overall marital quality. Second, how changes in marital problems and conflict resolution over the family life cycle affect the marriage, and particularly, when and why some spouses thought the marriage might not last. Third, marital problems and methods of conflict resolution of the Depression-era and wartime couples are compared, relating particular social and historical events to sources of their marital conflict and its resolution.

Conflict and Marital Quality

Sources of Conflict and the Marital Relationship

The most common problems reported by the 1,152 surveyed spouses are finances (29 percent), relatives (24 percent), ill health (24 percent), raising the children (21 percent), and the spouse's annoying habits (everything from snoring to alcoholism, 17 percent) (see Table 5.1). Some of these problems have a greater impact on the quality of the marriage than others.

Problems with Spouse's Annoying Habits, The Sexual Relationship, and Raising the Children

> *Some people get out of bed as soon as they've had sex, and have a cigarette. That used to bother the daylights out of me!*—Mrs. SE

Problems with the sexual relationship, the spouse's annoying habits, and raising the children are negatively correlated with overall marital happiness ($p <$ .001) and most measures of marital intimacy ($p < .001$, $p < .001$, and $p < .05$, respectively). Wives are significantly more likely than husbands to indicate that their spouse's annoying habits have been a problem ($p < .001$). Spouses who agreed less strongly that marriage is a sacred obligation or a long-term commitment more often indicated problems with the sexual relationship ($p < .05$) and with the spouse's annoying habits ($p < .001$). Spouses who reported problems over sex were also less likely to say that fidelity is essential to a successful marriage ($p < .001$) and more likely to report infidelity ($p < .001$).

> Mrs. CN: "There were sexual problems at times . . . when you just don't feel like it. Nowadays, if the man approached the woman, she could call rape. I mean in those days there was never such a thing as that."
>
> Mr. CN says, "The major thing is I'm a sexual person . . . so that was probably one of the conflicts. . . . Her whole life and faith is in the Catholic religion. . . . She never wanted me to use contraceptive, right, that was forbidden."
>
> Mrs. EL: "Raising the kids, we didn't get along in that department, except when it came down to the very serious, serious things, then we were together." They had five children, so this problem lasted for some time.
>
> He was picky about little things: Mrs. EL says, "The house could be a mess all day, but a half hour before dad came home, we all got busy and put stuff away." She doesn't tell him everything because "he just gets so uptight." This goes for things the kids did, little aches and pains, and small accidents. For her, intimacy does not call for total honesty.

Infidelity

> *If you ask me retrospectively, the best thing one can do to avoid divorce, avoid extramarital affairs.*
> —An unidentified surveyed husband

Infidelity is seldom reported, but when it occurs, spouses indicate lower levels of marital happiness ($p < .001$) and intimacy ($p < .01$). Spouses who

Table 5.1

Issues That Created Problems

Problem Issue	Percentage of Spouses
Finances	29
Relatives	24
Illness	24
Raising the children	21
Spouse's annoying habits	17
Sexual relations	10
Husband not working	3
Wife working	3
Infidelity	2

reported infidelity agreed less strongly that marriage is a sacred obligation ($p < .001$), less often indicated that fidelity is essential to a successful marriage ($p < .001$), and less often reported trust as a positive factor ($p < .01$). Finally, 83 percent of those reporting infidelity as a problem in the marriage are women, mostly reporting infidelity on the part of their husbands.

> An unidentified surveyed husband wrote, "There were times in our marriage when I didn't think it would last due to my problems with alcohol and other women. However, my wife had faith in me even though we were separated and I was out of work. In reality if it weren't for her faith, love, and trust, the marriage probably would have ended."

> Mr. TA says his infidelity early in his marriage was not an important relationship: "It was available." But when Mrs. TA found out, she nearly left him: "I think she came close when she found out. . . . She just decided she wasn't gonna be that easy." He says it "took a while" to restore the trust. "She was hurt and I know it."

> Mrs. BD decided not to be so easy either: "More than once I would have divorced. . . . We were separated once. He had his love affair, and was not faithful. . . . it was during the time that the baby we lost was born . . . we had a couple of children by then."

> Mr. BD adds, "It certainly belongs in our equation. . . . It was quite serious."

> She guesses the affair happened because "it was the war. Girls were available." He agrees: "We worked in the same building." And she adds, "I had a couple of kids and was a homebody. I mean, it's a classic scene."

> Mr. BD says of his affair, "From the male point of view, there was real pleasure there, but it wasn't worth it. . . . That was one thing I learned I will never do again. I wasn't even clever or devious." When she found out, he moved home with his parents and continued the affair. She got a job at a defense industry, so she had to move and let his elderly aunts care for their two children. She thinks he was trying to get her to be financially independent of him, although he disagrees.

She explains, "Initially you're hurt, so terribly hurt at first. . . . That person is mine, and to think that person could do that to you is a very, very hurtful thing, very hurtful. And it's a while to get over that. You don't hate . . . when you're hurting. It's when the hurt starts to wear off, that you begin to get lots of hatred of this and hatred of that, in my experience anyway. I went to work, and I knew that this was still going on. . . . My life was really pretty rotten for a while. . . . I figured, I'll be damned. This babe wants what I got, she wants my husband, and she wants my life, and she's not gonna get it. . . . So I had to consent, convince myself that I wanted the same husband again in order to even bother. I just decided I was not keeping up that kind of a life. I left the job, and I took my two children, and I moved back to the house, and I said, 'Do what you please about it. We're staying here.' Now he did not move back in immediately by any means. But he got in the habit of stopping around once in awhile, until I told him I didn't want to see this. . . . We can't have a hello and goodbye kind of a friendship." The affair ended after about one year. "He came back and broke off his affair, which I'm sure was not easy for him either, and we tried. . . . Religion is a big thing with me, . . . and I *vowed*. . . . I don't commit myself to you. You vow to stay with this person. That has a different meaning to me." Mr. BD thinks that today's young women would not be as deeply hurt or as surprised as his wife was, because times have changed, and it is not so uncommon now. She disagrees, and says it is a matter of gender. "A feminine thing. . . . I don't think the age or the group has much to do with it."

The BDs' story demonstrates some of the effects of infidelity on a marriage. She is somewhat happy in the marriage, while he reports being happy. She usually likes him, but feels he only sometimes understands her. He is not her best friend. She reports low levels of intimacy, rarely confiding in him or laughing with him, only sometimes saying she loves him. The only methods of conflict resolution she indicated were doing what her spouse wanted, counseling, and temporary separation. He has a more optimistic view of the marriage. He says she is his best friend, he always likes her, and he feels that she usually understands him. He reports higher levels of intimacy than she does, and says they have communicated honestly, compromised, and relied on the passage of time to resolve conflicts.

A combination of crises makes divorce more likely. With the loss of a child and infidelity, the odds against this couple were enormous, yet they were able to adapt to the stressors and remain married. Hill's ABCX model (1958) and McCubbin and Patterson's Double ABCX model (1983) can be used to analyze this couple's situation. In this model, A refers to the stressor and the changes it brings, B refers to the resources the family brings to the event, C is the family's definition of the event, and X is the resulting vulnerability to that crisis.

Both personal timing—in their own life cycle, after a baby dies, a time of marital difficulty—and social timing—during the war, when opportunities for infidelity were available—contributed to their marital crisis. A pileup of stressors led to a temporary separation (A). Mr. BD returned to his parents' home, and Mrs. BD, who could more easily find a job because of the war, went to work (B). She described the process of recognizing, reacting to, and adapting to infidelity in the marriage; the decisions she had to make; and the role financial independence played. She had to cope with her fear, with anger at her husband, and with the tremendous sense of pain and loss she felt. Her strong religious faith helped to sustain her. She had already defined the marriage as a lifetime commitment when she took her wedding vows, but she had to decide whether she wanted him back in order to make the effort (C). Once she decided, which was not right away, she quit her job and moved back to their home. She told him she would take him back only on her terms, and he came home. The stressors created major changes in their lives, but each partner found the strengths and resources to cope, and both defined the situation in such a way that reconciliation was possible (X). The pain and distrust were not erased, but the marriage continued.

Problems with Ill Health, Finances, and Relatives

> *One doesn't feel well, the other one objects to not being able to do things. It spirals into an argument.*
> —Mr. FL

Other factors that negatively affect marital happiness are problems over finances and illness ($p < .05$). Interview data suggest that spouses are not blamed for illness, because it is largely out of their control, but the problem can still generate conflict. Partners who had financial problems more often reported problems with the husband not working ($p < .001$), the wife working ($p < .01$), raising the children ($p < .001$), and the spouse's annoying habits ($p < .05$). Each set of stressors brings its own set of hardships (Hill, 1958). Working wives bring in welcome additional income, but the husband may have ambivalent feelings about seeing his wife in the role of breadwinner. Meanwhile, raising the children is more difficult for working mothers, who have less time available for the children. The more problems couples have to face, the greater the demands on their financial, emotional, and social resources (ibid.); and the more vulnerable they are to crisis.

As Mrs. ME joked, "When money's gone, love flies out the window."

Spouses who reported problems with relatives more often relied on compromise and passage of time to resolve conflicts than did spouses without this problem ($p < .05$). Spouses who had problems with relatives more often indicated problems with the sexual relationship, and with raising the children ($p < .05$).

> Mrs. GR: "My father, his mother, they were the biggest problems in our lives."

> The YEs reported little intimacy during the time her mother lived with them. From their perspective, the tensions her mother's presence created between them affected nearly every aspect of their marriage. Mrs. YE: "She lived here for thirteen years. . . . That was the one time our marriage was on the verge of anything, because my mother and my husband just did not hit it off. . . . She was very domineering. . . . Probably if I hadn't been working and he [hadn't been] working the long hours he did at the automobile place, that probably was what saved us. At least, we had that apart." Mr. YE agrees that her mother brought them to the brink of divorce. He gave Mrs. YE an ultimatum, and her mother moved.

Marital Problems and Family Background

> *We're two easygoing people.*—Mrs. ME

A few of the interviewed couples said they never argued. They never had any major problems, and never encountered situations on which they profoundly differed. They experienced only minor disagreements, mostly over silly things. These partners emphasized their common backgrounds and their shared values and beliefs.

> Mr. DR: "We're similar in most of the problems, most of the feelings. . . . That's the beauty of being brought up in the same town, we have the same values."

> Mr. ME: "We're married sixty-four years. We've never had an argument. We never went to bed being mad at each other. . . . The only time we argued was when I worked too hard. Then she started to holler at me. . . . I'm a happily married man."

> In contrast, Mrs. TI explains how differing family backgrounds led to clashes in her marriage. Mrs. TI grew up in a family "that is Midwestern, very stoic." To get attention growing up, she had to "practically throw temper tantrums." In contrast, Mr. TI had a great deal of tragedy in his family background and was extremely uncomfortable with conflict. "He has

an impossible time handling anyone that's not really, really happy. . . . You can't even be neutral, you gotta be happy." For her part, "I learned very soon that I couldn't have these temper tantrums. . . . He couldn't fight back, because it's so forbidding for him, so he'd just leave. . . . It was just 100 percent flight for him, and so he'd leave the house. . . . I learned very fast, like to walk on eggs. I'm still careful how I say anything."

Methods of Conflict Resolution and the Marital Relationship

Compromise and honest communication are the most commonly reported methods of conflict resolution (reported by 69 percent and 65 percent, respectively, of 1,152 surveyed spouses). Twenty-five percent of spouses said they do what the other spouse wants, and 17 percent indicated that their spouses do what they want. Twenty-three percent reported relying on the passage of time, 9 percent report avoiding discussion of problems, 4 percent reported counseling, and 1 percent had a temporary separation (Table 5.2).

Honest Communication and Compromise

We're communicators.—Mrs. LA

Both compromise and honest communication are positively correlated with marital happiness ($p < .001$), most measures of marital intimacy ($p < .001$), and all eight positive factors that contribute to successful marriage ($p < .01$). Honest communication is correlated with agreement that marriage is both a long-term commitment and a sacred obligation ($p < .001$).

> Mr. RG thinks, "With every problem you overcome in a marriage, your marriage grows stronger. . . . Communication is so important. . . . If it's possible, our love got stronger. . . . Not only love, but our respect for each other. . . . Even if we're angry, we control ourselves. . . . There's a mutual respect." They don't harbor grudges. "It's over, forget it. . . . We look forward, not backward."

> The TRs set a standard for their decisions that embodies the notion of compromise. Mrs. TR says, "We decided that if either one or the other was not completely satisfied, . . . we wouldn't do anything."

> Mrs. MT: "Both of us always felt that our relationship was primary, and that it was absolutely essential to keep this thing going the best way we could!" (All the while she says this, she taps the table hard with her finger, emphasizing each word.) "And if we were disagreeing, then we would have to find a way to deal with it, because we weren't going to let ourselves split up over something, or anything really!"

Table 5.2

Methods of Conflict Resolution

Methods	Percentage of Spouses
Compromise	69
Honest communication	65
I did what my spouse wanted.	25
Passage of time	23
My spouse did what I wanted.	17
We avoided discussing problems.	9
Counseling	4
Temporary separation	1

Ground rules for settling conflicts and making decisions helped to keep conflict less personal and more focused on the issues.

Mrs. EG: "I never criticize him the way he would get mad. . . . In a subtle way I try to change things."

Mr. PG has learned that criticism brings immediate challenge: "If I criticized something she did wrong, she'd make me do it, so I didn't criticize." She laughs, "One day [he] was criticizing me, and I looked at him, and I said 'You go to hell!'" He laughs, "I stepped over the line."

Mrs. LA's rule is "Never by tears or threat of sexual politics" during quarrels. Both of the LAs believe in open communication and tolerance, which shows in their styles of conflict resolution. Both are willing to talk things out and to listen to one another. As for the arguments they do have, she says, "If I have something . . . causing me a problem, . . . when I present it to him he listens very patiently. . . . He doesn't say, 'OK, now I'm going to do something different,' but I can see that he does do something different. Which says to me . . . he values what I say. . . . We've learned from each other when we have disagreements, the techniques that we each use, so if he presents me with a response, then I feed him back the same kind of response so that we have a kind of a level playing field, so it's not all hyperemotional. It's pragmatic, it's practical, it's good communication. It's clear, it's thorough, it covers all the bases, so we're communicators!"

Spouses who agree on a definition of marriage and on the most important family issues find it easier to communicate and compromise. The open communication of these couples allows compromise and enhances the closeness they feel. As shown the beginning of this chapter, the HEs exemplify this.

Avoiding Discussion and the Passage of Time

> *You have a little argument, you just walk in two directions for a while.*—Mr. ST

Spouses who avoid discussion of problems are also significantly more likely to rely on the passage of time to resolve conflict ($p < .001$), and significantly less likely to use either honest communication or compromise ($p < .001$). Avoidance and passage of time as methods of conflict resolution are negatively correlated with marital happiness ($p < .001$), with most measures of marital intimacy ($p < .001$), and with agreement that marriage is a sacred obligation ($p < .001$). Interviewed spouses suggest that avoidance is sometimes used when further discussion is pointless, or because of embarrassment and discomfort.

> Mr. PA describes their arguments: "The first thing she starts doing is screaming, and . . . I scream back, both of us, right away, 'You started it!' 'No, you started it!' Then we cool down and we arbitrate. . . . She thinks it over. . . . If I have something on my mind, then I'll discuss it, but I have to be judicious when I open up the discussion. . . . I know what the reaction ahead of time is gonna be, so I keep putting it off as long as possible."

> Mr. WT: "I found it hard to talk about sex. . . . Now I can talk. . . . I found it very hard to talk about what I wanted or what I desired, and perhaps she didn't sense it, so it was sort of hanging in the air at times, but I would never open up. . . . If I had my life to live over again, I would be more open with her, . . . but times change and the mores change."

Avoidance is also referred to as "the silent treatment" by interviewed spouses. The "silent treatment" means refusing to speak to one's partner, refusing to discuss the problem, going to another part of the house, pretending the problem doesn't exist, and/or storming out of the house to prevent further discussion. Interviewed wives more often said they use the silent treatment (avoid the issue), while many husbands said they lose their tempers, walk out, and come back later (avoid the issue and rely on the passage of time). Both approaches are attempts to control the situation, because they stop any further communication until the avoider decides to speak or come home. With no communication, the problem may not be resolved, but no one loses the argument either.

> The MAs disagreed while they were planting a tree in their yard. She says, "Well, he had a pitchfork and he went after me like this [jabbing at her]. And I looked at him, and I said, 'Don't you dare.' You know what I did? I came in

the house, I packed up and I went to my niece. . . . I stayed with her. . . . I wouldn't argue with him. Come back like nothing happened."

By leaving for a few days, she asserted her independence. By not discussing it when she returned, in her view, she had restored balance. The CIs do the same thing.

Mr. CI asserts, "I holler!" and Mrs. CI retorts, "I holler back!" Mr. CI explains, "When I know I can't win, I walk out." Then she worries and cries until he returns. "I get scared," she says. He says, after he comes home, "When we go to bed, I kiss her goodnight, and that's it. It's all over. We forgive and forget. . . . That's it. Don't bring the same subject up again. Forget it."

Mr. EE demonstrates why the silent treatment is sometimes an effective strategy. It does stop the quarreling. Mr. EE: "She gives me what I call the silent treatment. . . . She just doesn't answer me, and it makes me more angry, but what can I do? I can't fight with myself."

Another pattern is for one spouse, usually the wife, to remain silent until the other spouse or both of them decide to end the quarrel by apologizing or doing something romantic.

Mrs. WE recalls a recent argument. "We had a very, very bad argument three weeks ago, . . . and for three days I was really nasty, I wouldn't speak to him. He came back with one rose, and he says, 'Will you forgive me?' . . . and I started to laugh. How could you not do it?"

Mrs. ER says, "I didn't talk to him. That was my way of arguing. I didn't talk for a couple of days. Then all of a sudden he'd come over and put his arms around me. He could always end it. But I would never give in."

Relying on the passage of time can be a positively adaptive approach in three ways. First, spouses who define marriage as a lifetime commitment can rely on time to resolve conflicts, because they have the rest of their lives.

Mrs. AZ says, "We took our vows more seriously and never entertained the thought of leaving the marriage. We, therefore, let time heal our differences."

Mrs. WT says, "When you look at fifty years, . . . so you figure you had twenty years that weren't so great, and with it all there were still good times."

Second, allowing time to pass means that you simply tough out a problem until it goes away. For example, a couple may be able to tolerate differences in disciplining children, because they know the children will grow up and leave home one day. They may put up with in-laws, because in-laws too are only temporary.

> Mr. PG: "She and I usually don't argue. . . . We would sulk. . . . Lots of times you're better off shutting up. . . . Withdrawing, that's what she and I did. . . . Eventually it's going to work itself out."
> Mrs. PG remembers that showing tempers was so rare in their home that "Twice in our marriage we yelled at each other and the kids were sure we got a divorce."

Third, relying on the passage of time also means learning how to time a disagreement, to wait for a calmer, more appropriate moment to discuss difficult issues. Among the interviewed couples, it was very common for spouses to take "cool off" periods so they did not say or do something they would regret.

> Mr. MR says, "It requires constant vigilance. . . . All too easily arguments can escalate. . . . They feed upon themselves. . . . One or both of us just quiets down, get in separate parts of the house maybe . . . till we can quiet down a little bit, and maybe even come back together, and just ignore what went on before, because most of the time . . . we have the biggest arguments about . . . the most trivial things."

Doing What My Spouse Wants

> *I accommodated myself more to her at the time.*
> —Mr. WT

Spouses who indicated they do what their spouses want to resolve conflict reported lower levels of marital happiness ($p < .01$), agreed less on major family issues ($p < .05$), and less often cited compromise as a positive factor in the marriage ($p < .05$). Based on the principle of least interest (Waller and Hill 1951), both spouses are not equally interested in maintaining the relationship, and the balance may shift over time. However, the needier person in the relationship has less control and more motivation to maintain the relationship, so he or she does what the other person wants. When spouses say they frequently give in, doing what the other wants, hostility, frustration, and resentment are often the results.

> Mr. NG has weighed the costs of conflict to himself and has chosen a conflict style that reflects those costs. He feels that, mostly, he just gives in and does what she wants. "We'll sit down and discuss it, but she'll always end up by being right. And I'll say 'Yes, but . . .' [and she'll say], 'Did you hear what I just said?' And rather than get into a deep cursing argument, I'll walk away

... although down deep I feel why don't I tell her that she's. . . ." He breaks off, banging his hand on his chair arm repeatedly and then continues, "Rather than making a fuss, because she'll walk away. She'll walk out of the house. 'To hell with you! Make your own dinner.' So rather than have that, . . . I bite my tongue, and I say, 'Yes, I'm sorry.' "

Doing what the other spouse wants does not always mean surrender. Spouses who checked "I did what my spouse wanted" were also more likely to check "spouse did what I wanted" ($p < .001$). This is a means of exchange rather than compromise. Each partner has a turn at getting what he or she wants, "winning" the argument. Communication occurs, but it is not necessary beyond determining whose turn it is. If the turn taking is relatively equal, no one complains. Several spouses talked about doing what their partner wants when they realize it means more to the spouse than to themselves. In those cases, the partners are communicating well enough to make their wishes clear, and there is enough caring between them that those wishes matter.

> Mr. MR: "We used to argue them out until we got tired of arguing. . . . I think we compromised in the sense that, on certain occasions I gave in, on certain occasions she gave in. You can't really compromise. . . . One or the other has to give in."

> Mr. TM says, "We have different opinions, but we argue in similar ways. . . . Sometimes I go along with her, and sometimes she goes along with me. . . . Sometimes, something means more to her than to me, so I give in, and sometimes, something means more to me. . . . It's not a system really, it just works out that way."

> Mr. AL illustrates the interaction of communication, compromise, and doing what the spouse wants: "We discuss it frankly and openly. . . . If it can be resolved, we resolve it together. If it can't, because her opinion differs from mine, then either I capitulate or she does. Depends on how important it is. If it's a matter of great principle, I might stick to my guns."

Counseling and Temporary Separation

I wanted to work out my problems.—Mrs. TI

Very few surveyed spouses reported seeking counseling and temporarily separating. These two methods of conflict resolution are negatively associated with marital happiness ($p < .01$, $p < .001$, respectively), defining one's spouse as best friend ($p < .001$ for both), confiding in one's spouse ($p < .05$ and $p < .001$, respectively), and agreeing that marriage is a sacred obligation ($p < .001$ for both). The severity of the problems that force couples into counseling or a separation had a serious or lengthy enough impact that the relationships are difficult to rebuild. Spouses who experienced infidelity were more likely to report temporary separation ($p < .001$).

Other Issues in Conflict Resolution

> *Don't let the sun set upon your wrath.*—Mr. WE

Many interviewed couples mentioned the informal rule they have made of not going to bed angry, effectively setting a limit on how long conflicts could last without some resolution.

> Mr. GR says, "Early on I made it a rule, and she knew it, that we would never go to bed mad, . . . and anything that occurred during the day would be resolved by that night." Mrs. GR laughs, "And always when we made up, we had sex."

> Mrs. NN says, "We withdraw, we cut it. . . . We promised each other we would never go to bed angry, and we have gone to bed angry, but not often."

Physical aggression was rarely mentioned, even though it is estimated that between 25 percent and 33 percent of all women in the United States have been battered at least once (Schwartz and Scott 1994). Among interviewed couples there were three incidents of violence against children and two instances of violence between spouses reported.

> The YEs usually yelled at each other when they were angry, but once it went further. Mr. YE: "I never raised my hand to her. I threw a plate at her one time and it sailed like a Frisbee, and it just bounced off, and she threw a pot of chow mein that she was cooking at me."

> The MAs have different and mutually accommodating styles of arguing. She says, "I just walk away, 'cause he goes off the wall, like a lunatic. . . . I shut up. . . . I don't want to antagonize him. No, I would never talk, because I can't get a word through. . . . He goes nuts, he goes bananas! Sometimes I say to myself, what the hell, it's not worth it."
> Mr. MA mostly agrees with this assessment: "We've had some serious ones. . . . What I have to do is control myself, because I go off the deep end. I grab a couple of beers, or hop in the car and take a ride, or get a pack of cigarettes and start smoking and when I get back it's all over. . . . She backs down all the time. I don't back down, I'm a sonofabitch! I don't back down! . . . I go upstairs, I have a TV in the room. I shut my door. . . . She always backs down. If I don't like it, I go bananas! I would pick up this table and I wouldn't care if I broke everything you saw in there. Believe me, I go

bananas! ... I get the hell out before I do it. I never laid a finger on that woman in fifty-seven years, because I know I have a temper. . . . I fight like hell with her!"

Overall Conflict Resolution

> *I blow quickly, and I get over it quickly. I don't hold a grudge . . . maybe ten minutes is a long time.*
> —Mr. HA

Ninety percent of surveyed spouses said they always or usually resolve their conflicts, and only 2 percent reported they rarely or never resolve them. Overall marital happiness ($p < .001$), all measures of marital intimacy ($p < .001$), agreeing that marriage is both a sacred obligation and a long-term commitment ($p < .001$), and agreeing that 'fidelity is essential to a successful marriage ($p < .05$) are positively correlated with frequent conflict resolution. Protestant and Catholic husbands are more likely than their wives to report always resolving conflicts (55 percent versus 38 percent and 48 percent versus 37 percent, respectively), but there is no significant difference among Jewish couples.

Mrs. EL says, "We might be mad for a while, but we got over it quickly . . . without even realizing you were getting over it."

Mrs. CN: "We usually look at each other, it was just a look, and then you'd cuddle and kiss and that was over. Sometimes we'd never talk it out, but you forget about it. . . . Suppose I never see him again?"

Changes over the Life Cycle in Marital Conflict and Resolution

> *We believe marriage is the best school for our growth. Wouldn't it be stupid to drop out when it got hard?*—Mrs. TI

Sources of Conflict and Methods of Resolution

> *As young people it was sexual. . . . As we matured, it was definitely money.*—Mrs. NG

> *I gave up arguing. . . . Now in our mellow years, I don't care anymore.*—Mr. MA

Different life stages brought different challenges to the couples. Most interviewed spouses explained that both their problems and their styles of arguing evolved as they matured. At first, they were young and inexperienced, and they did not know each other as well as they would later.

> Mrs. TI: "It started out with lots of problems due to our immaturity, and got better and better. . . . In the beginning when I was not happy, divorce was not an option. Later, when I started working on myself, with a little professional help, I saw our problems as part of our learning experience, and took it as a challenge. I think we both did. . . . We believe marriage is the best school for our growth. Wouldn't it be stupid to drop out when it got hard? . . . We both had psychological problems which really clashed, but we have both, with much effort, largely overcome them."

> How Mrs. NG handled conflicts changed over time: "I would yell more than he does. . . . As you mature, you don't even yell. You just walk away, you don't bother. I've stated my main complaints and there's nothing you can do about them. . . . You can't change a person's personality."

Almost all the spouses in the study mentioned discovering each other's boundaries and limits of behavior, which also changed over time. Flexibility and learning contributed to better adaptation.

As previously discussed, a few couples had a traumatic event, such as a child's death, that changed their lives completely. After that loss, all their disagreements paled in comparison.

> When the YEs' oldest son was killed in Vietnam, this tragedy changed the way they handled conflicts. In the past, their arguments had often lasted for days. After their son was killed, Mrs. YE said, "We seemed to understand each other more, and if we have our disagreements . . . it's so easy to turn around and realize that you said your part and I said mine, and there isn't any darkness hanging over us . . . that awful feeling I used to have . . . Will we ever come to the end of this argument? . . . Today it's very, very easy to just simplify it." Their loss brought them closer together, and no disagreement they had could compare to it.

Over the course of their lives together, a few husbands realized, usually in the later years, that their habits had been destructive to the relationship, and that they had neglected their wives' needs.

> Mr. TR, who became sober at age eighty, concedes, "For a while I drank too much." His wife had been telling him so for years, as she recalls: "By then, I was just . . . being cranky. . . . He wouldn't answer me. . . . One morning we were laying [sic] in bed . . . and I told him everything he had ever done that he shouldn't have done to me, and we got it all straightened out. . . . I told him something he did when he'd had too much to drink, . . . and he said, ... 'I'm not going to drink anymore. That's it.' And it's been it . . . but we didn't have a bad life during all this time, . . . except that since then, it's been so much nicer."

> Mrs. TM says, "He was a very active alcoholic up until about two and a half years ago and then he just stopped. All by himself. Things have calmed down a lot. . . . We didn't spend quite as much time together in the evenings as we do now. . . . It makes a big difference. . . . He didn't drink all the time. It was by spells. . . . The good times outnumber the bad. . . . I never considered divorce. A couple of times I thought, 'Maybe I should get an apartment,' . . . but always as a temporary arrangement."
>
> He admits, "I had a drinking problem . . . for about seven or eight years . . . I didn't like the job . . . I was just frustrated."

Many spouses learned ways of defining the situation that led to more agreement, or at least less discord, and over time, circumstances changed. Both partners in happier marriages learned how to openly discuss problems without angry recriminations, and to develop a mutual tolerance of each other's differences. This was not the case among the less happily married interviewed couples. Nearly all the interviewed spouses said there is much less to argue about in the later years. Many of the problems that divided them are moot, or they have learned to live with them. The children are grown, and usually both spouses are retired, so there are fewer conflicting roles. Their problems are small in comparison to the appreciation they have for still being together.

> Mr. ER says he and his wife used different methods of conflict resolution, depending on "situation and timing over the years. We are now in the mellow years. Most conflicts are behind us." Of their earlier years he says, "We had fights, we had screaming . . . [now] I think what we do is, rather than stir things up, I think we don't say things, and just let it go away. You can start a fight very easily. . . . Why bother? I think at this age you're realizing it's so stupid. Tomorrow's another good day, and we'll get to it. I think she adjusts to me with my foibles, and I guess I do the same thing."
>
> Mr. EL: "She's more apt to defend her position now than she was ten years ago. So I guess we're more on an even keel. It used to be, she tells me this, she would just go along with what I had expressed." He says during conflicts he yells less than he did in the past—he, too, has changed. "Present your case, give reasons, accept her reasons, see how different they are, and see what similarities there are, and try to put them together."

Thinking the Marriage Might Not Last

> *I was beginning to think that maybe it was time for us to split up.*—Mrs. PA

Twenty-one percent of the spouses surveyed indicated that, at some point, they thought their marriages might not last. Of those spouses, half of them reported that this point occurred midway through the marriage, 29 percent said it occurred early in the marriage, 18 percent said it occurred in the later years, and 3 percent gave various answers (i.e., "now and then," "sometimes") or left the question blank. When spouses reported thinking the marriage might not last, they reported lower levels of marital intimacy, and less strong agreement on traditional attitudes to marriage ($p < .05$). Catholic wives were slightly more likely than their husbands to think the marriage might not last (23 percent versus 15 percent), but there were no gender differences on this question among Jewish and Protestant couples.

> Mrs. WE says of her husband, "Sometimes he can be very trying. . . . He can be very difficult. . . . There are lots of deep divisions, and lots of deep disagreements and they can get very, very nasty sometimes. . . . At one point, we had so many arguments, even down to financially, we were stripped. . . . I said, this is crazy, I can't live on just half of what we have. . . . I better reconsider, . . . and where am I gonna go? Why should I leave all this? Then you realize the stupidity. It's pride, it's stubbornness. . . . It's not a lack of feeling for each other. You let all these other things get in the way."

> The NGs' biggest argument followed his decision (which he made without discussing it with her) not to take a job with a raise because it involved some traveling. They had been struggling financially for years, she remembers. "I was livid. . . . We had an argument and I stormed out of the house expecting him to come after me. . . . I drove to the ocean. . . . It was a very, very serious time. I cried myself sick. I knew I had to come home. . . . I couldn't get in. I ring [sic] the doorbell. He came to the door laughing. . . . He laughed it away, which killed me. I'm sure that took a good month, to get over that. He did not realize the depth of how that hurt me. There's an insensitivity there! He never got it. . . . At that point when I went to the beach . . . I literally hated him."
>   Mr. NG offers a different view of this incident: "She was just frustrated. . . . The children and too much work around the house . . . it was getting too much for her. . . . It just went away. . . . We never sat down and talked about it." He does not mention the job decision, indicating, perhaps, that he did not understand why she almost left him. He goes on, "The children help keep you together. . . . You're almost ready for divorce, you have two or three children. . . . 'No, we can't. Let's kiss and make up.' "

> Mrs. AE, who is somewhat happy in her marriage, says, "His tone of voice is a downright insult a good deal of the time." They both say they yell "at the top of our lungs." She says, "We never did break that habit after we got the kids. We were so used to privacy, of squaring off. . . . If they heard, that's the way it is." Asked if they tried "time-outs" or "cooling-off" periods, he said, "Not very often, unfortunately. You repeat like stuck records." In his view, "It usually gets straightened out in the next half hour or something." She interjects, "I don't agree, but . . . the heat goes out of it." When asked if they ever considered separation, they laughed. He said, "No, couldn't afford it,"

and she adds, "That was the bottom line. . . . By the time you buy a house, you've made that kind of joint investment. You are as much a business as you are a personal relationship." Are they comfortable saying what's on their minds? He says, "I guess so. We talk often enough, seriously." She counters, "Yes . . . no . . . sometimes . . . depending on the topic."

Survey data indicate that spouses who married at very young ages, from sixteen to twenty-one, more often thought that the marriage might not last than did those who married after age twenty-one ($p < .05$). Spouses earning under $20,000 and over $50,000 more often reported thinking the marriage might fail than did couples with incomes in the middle range. Financial problems can erode a relationship over time, and having higher incomes can give spouses more options. While those with least money have fewest options, education adds options too. The higher the educational level, the more often spouses reported thinking the marriage might not last ($p < .01$). Catholic spouses were least likely to think the marriage might not last (19 percent), while 28 percent of both Protestant and Jewish spouses thought the marriage might fail. It is likely that Catholic spouses were more constrained by religious beliefs condemning divorce than were Protestant and Jewish spouses.

Changes over Time in Marital Conflicts and Resolution

> *We proved the theory that you can't have two men in the same house. . . . We lasted eighteen months.*
> —Mr. ER

> *He's gotten mellow as he's gotten older.*—Mrs. TA

This section will examine the effects of the Depression and World War II on five problem areas: relatives, husband not working, sexual relations, raising the children, and overall conflict resolution.

First, 25 percent of spouses who married between 1933 and 1939 reported problems with relatives. During the Depression many couples were forced to live with parents, often in cramped quarters. Only 14 percent of spouses who married in 1940 reported problems with relatives. This may suggest that more of these couples were able to find their own apartments. For those spouses who married between 1941 and 1944, problems with relatives grew more common again. Thirty-two percent of couples who married in 1942 reported problems with relatives. Not only did this cohort of wives often live with their parents while their husbands were overseas, but after the war, because of the housing shortage, some of the couples had to live with parents for months or years until they could find a place of their own.

Second, Depression-era spouses were far more likely than wartime spouses to report problems over husbands not working, no doubt because of widespread unemployment ($p < .001$). When men lost their jobs during the Depression they were typically out of work for months, or even years. Third, the later in time that couples married, the lower their levels of overall conflict resolution, so that couples who married in the Depression years reported a higher level of conflict resolution than do wartime couples ($p < .05$). Reasons for this are unclear.

Fourth, as discussed in Chapter Four, wartime couples reported more problems in raising their children and showed an increase in the percentage of spouses who say the happiest years were after the children left home. Finally, wartime spouses more often report problems with the sexual relationship than do Depression-era spouses ($p < .05$). By the 1940s there was more information available about sexuality and more premarital sex (Mintz and Kellogg 1988; Schwartz and Scott 1994). Many spouses said they talked more openly with others, comparing their sexual relationships. New expectations could lead to new disappointments.

> While Mrs. FL was too embarrassed to discuss their sexual relationship with her husband, she was able to talk to her sisters. She says, "In these days, you would look into it, but I didn't want to embarrass him. But I used to tell my two sisters. They would say 'I'd never put up with it,' and I thought to myself, . . . 'Maybe they're more sexual than I am.' "

Summary

Survey and interview data indicate that some problems are more damaging to a marriage than others. Problems with infidelity, sexual relations, and spouse's annoying habits are negatively correlated with marital happiness, marital intimacy, and traditional attitudes toward marriage. Issues such as finances and raising the children can be very serious, but are not so damaging to overall marital quality.

Honest communication and compromise are the methods of conflict resolution associated with greater marital happiness. Spouses who rely on these methods emphasize that they work through the difficulties together. In contrast, spouses who rely on avoidance and passage of time tend to report less happy marriages, lower levels of marital intimacy, and less agreement on major issues. Avoidance was often described by spouses as "the silent treatment," and sometimes it was effective in ending a quarrel without creating a loser. Relying on the passage of time to resolve conflicts has three meanings. First, lifetime commitment gives couples unlimited time to resolve problems. Second, the passage of time can also mean enduring a problem that may or may not improve with time. Third, the passage of time can refer to time-outs during which spouses calm down before discussing their problems.

Doing what the spouse wants can lead to an imbalance when one partner usually or always does what the other wants. But this strategy can also be effective if spouses take turns having their way. When no compromise is possible, taking turns means that each partner can have what he or she wants at least sometimes. Women are more likely than men to report avoidance and passage of time as methods of conflict resolution, and women cite lower levels of conflict resolution throughout the marriage than do men.

Marital problems and their resolution also change over the life cycle. The majority of interview couples said they had little if any reason to have conflicts in their later years. Problems had been resolved or accepted long ago. Husbands and wives adapted to and accepted unhappy marriages, because they would rather do that than divorce. Most of the less happy spouses stopped fighting and directed their energies elsewhere. Over time, a key life lesson for these long-married couples is that you cannot change another person.

Finally, there were differences between Depression-era and World War II couples in both problems and means of conflict resolution. The Depression led to more problems about the husband's not working, and World War II was associated with more problems about raising the children and the sexual relationship. Wartime couples reported lower levels of overall conflict resolution than spouses who married earlier.

Chapter Six

His or Her Marriage

*They used to always say that a marriage is 80
percent woman and 20 percent man.*—Mrs. EC

She's the pillar of the house.—Mr. ME

Introduction

This chapter combines survey and interview data to examine gender differences in two areas: (1) marital happiness and (2) division of labor. The
interviews allowed the spouses to describe both gender roles to which they
were socialized and how these roles evolved during their lifetime.

Gender Differences in Marital Happiness

*I think we hurt easier than a man does. They're able
to take things easy.*—Mrs. EC

Surveyed husbands have a more positive view of their marriages and reported fewer disagreements than did wives. Wives were more likely to
report being happy or somewhat happy in their marriage, while husbands
were more likely to report being very happy ($p < .05$) (Table 6.1). Husbands more often reported being always understood and always liking their
partners, while wives were more likely to report usually being understood
and usually liking their spouses ($p < .001$). Ninety-five percent of spouses
said their partner is their best friend, but nearly two-thirds of those who said
no to this question are wives. Only three of the eight problem areas are
significantly correlated with gender: Wives were more likely than husbands
to report that spouse's annoying habits ($p < .001$), raising children ($p < .01$),
and infidelity ($p < .001$) have been problems.

Overall, wives were also more likely to rely on avoidance and the passage

Table 6.1

Marital Happiness by Sex

	Percentage of spouses				
	Very Happy	Happy	Somewhat Happy	Unhappy	Very Unhappy
Females	51.4	39.4	8.6	0.4	0.2
Males	59.7	35.1	4.6	0.4	0.2

of time to resolve conflicts ($p < .01$), and they reported a lower frequency of conflict resolution than did husbands ($p < .01$). Wives are more likely to think their marriages might not last ($p < .01$). While only 6 percent of all spouses said that their marriages were least happy in the later years, almost twice as many wives as husbands said this (63 percent versus 38 percent). Wives more often said their sexual interest declined over time ($p < .001$). In particular, Protestant and Catholic wives more often reported a decline in sexual interest over time than did their respective husbands ($p < .05$), but the difference between Jewish husbands and wives is insignificant.

None of the husbands interviewed said the reason they were still married was economic dependence on the wife, but several less happily married wives offered this reason. According to interviewed spouses, the main reason women of their time did not leave less than happy marriages was lack of educational and work opportunities.

> Mrs. WT: "Women are more liberated now. They're not afraid to be alone. [When we were first married, women] didn't drive cars. They didn't know how things functioned. . . . And it wasn't expected of you years ago. Years ago they were more dependent on a spouse for their livelihood. I mean, unless you had some kind of a skill." She considered divorce when they experienced serious financial problems, although Mr. WT did not. "But my mother and my father, I realized after a while they didn't want me, 'cause I had two small children. . . . They said, 'You're gonna live with it.' I was unhappy for years, I really was, but I couldn't see a way out of it." Once, after a serious quarrel with her husband, she drove to the ocean, where she sat for hours trying to decide what to do. With no one to take her in, she thought, "I'll take a room in a motel, right? I opened my pocketbook, and I had, like a dollar and a half. Now, today's woman would have her charge cards!"

Gender Differences in Division of Labor

Division of Labor in the Home

He was gone, and I raised 'em!—Mrs. TI

> Mr. CA: "We really didn't plan ahead. But we did recognize our responsibilities. I recognized my responsibility as the head of the household, that I had to supply

the needs of my family. [My wife] recognized her responsibilities as taking care of the children and taking care of the household things. She knew that I had to go out to work. Sometimes I worked odd hours. . . . Sometimes I'd be working during the daytime. I'd come home for dinner . . . then run out . . . and maybe not be home until midnight, because I made calls in the evening mostly. . . . I don't think we set rules that way. . . . We recognized our responsibilities."

The CAs didn't plan it that way, but socialized from childhood to these gender roles and norms, they "recognized" their responsibilities in the family. They accepted it as "right, normal, and natural" that she would be the homemaker and he would be the breadwinner, and that both would sacrifice for the sake of the family, defining it as "the right thing to do." Most interviewed couples had a traditional division of labor, at least when the children were younger. Although many wives never worked outside the home, nearly all of those who had been working quit their jobs when they began to have children.

> Mrs. PA: "I was totally into motherhood, completely into motherhood. I was never career minded, and women of my generation were always raised to be mothers. That was your goal in life. . . . Everything was family oriented. And so I felt very fulfilled. . . . And we were all very close. You know, everybody lived within a few block radius in this little neighborhood, and we were together all the time. My sister with her little one, and me with mine."

> When the PGs moved to Long Island, he had to commute to New York City. Mrs. PG says, "At that point, women weren't working. That was the thing to do. . . . He took care of the business and I took care of the home and the children."
> He adds, "I suppose we had definite roles to play."

> The NGs always struggled with money, but still she chose to give up her job when their last child came. "When I got pregnant . . . I had a nice secretarial job. . . . I could have just taken a maternity leave. . . . Why didn't I do it? I had nobody to help me with that baby. And I did not want to put a stranger with my baby."

Both the STs and the EGs had two small children within two years of each other. Neither wife had help from her husband in caring for the home and children. The two couples are from the same socioeconomic background and lived in similar suburban situations, but they defined their situations in radically different ways.

> Mrs. ST: "I had two children right away, and it was like I thought it was a nightmare, because they both had to be diapered and they both had to be in the carriage, and I didn't have much help. . . . He went to work, came home, and ate. I was with the kids. . . . I never had any free time."

Mrs. EG: "We . . . had a great time. I'd have all my work done by ten o'clock in the morning, have them dressed . . . put them in a big carriage, and went out for a walk, two, three hours a day." He adds "And I'd get home and look forward to an hour playtime with them before dinner."

The role of "housewife" as described by these wives was active, not passive. Wives made decisions, often handled the family finances, planned social events, managed correspondence, met with teachers, and took children to lessons. They devoted themselves to the development and maintenance of their families.

Mr. ER: "The wives would get together as soon as the men come home from work at five o'clock, we'd all go down to the beach. . . . We'd have a cook-out . . . so that erased the whole miserable day. . . . I was a shop steward and union delegate. I not only had my problems, I had all of their problems, so you come home with all that load, and if I have to hear a whole bunch of stuff about the kids. . . . She didn't do that to me."

Mrs. PA: "I think the fact that we have made such good strong friendships has helped us in our marriage to stay together. I think you need a good strong support group. You can't just rely on each other all the time. You really need other people in your life. . . . But I think that's helped a lot . . . the fact that we have a lot of good strong friendships. [My husband] has always insisted, and I think he's right, that if he was left to his own devices, he would not have friends. He would be very content to sit in the house and read. He would not go out and make friendships. . . . But I think maybe in most marriages, it's the woman who does the social things, and makes the social engagements, and invites people to your home."

Both FTs describe Mrs. FT in terms of her role performance, how well she "did" wife and mother. She made the home for everyone, stayed sexually attractive and appealing, and never had to work outside the home.

Mr. FT: "She was a good wife. . . . You could eat off the floors the way she cleans. And then she cleans again."
Mrs. FT: "I never had to work. . . . I raised the kids, you know. . . . I liked to be a homemaker."
Mr. FT: "She had enough work to do at home. . . . I always found a nice meal on the table when I came home. It was nice. And after we eat we sit and hold hands."
Mrs. FT: "A woman wants a lot of affection, she wants to know she's important in the man's life. . . . I always pretended when he came home from work, I dolled up like I was going on a date. I always did that. . . . Women let themselves go, and they don't care how they look, but I was always fussy."

The interviewed couples typically defined the husband as head of the household, but that did not mean he made all the decisions, controlled all the finances, or earned all the money. Head of household is a title, a status often given to the husband because he is the breadwinner, the public spokesperson for the family.

A few husbands knew the dilemma of the good-provider role—it was satisfying while they were successful, but if they were not able to fill the role because of illness, bad luck, retirement, or lack of ambition, then they questioned their self-worth and felt guilty. One of the basic propositions of symbolic interaction theories is that the less successful a person is in performing his or her role, the less satisfying that role is. Most of the less successful breadwinners interviewed were relieved to retire.

Breadwinners, laden with the financial responsibility for the family, had little time to be with that family, sometimes working six days a week and into the evenings. At what point a dedicated breadwinner crosses the line from hard worker to "workaholic" is hard to measure. A few husbands recognized it in themselves, and several wives described their husbands as workaholics.

> Mr. FL: "I used to go to work at seven at night . . . and work till seven in the morning, right through the night. I was ambitious. I wanted to start a business. . . . I rented the store. I put in a little woodworking equipment. . . . I would go home, sleep for a couple of hours, rush to the store, and from there I would go to work, but it was an almost around-the-clock thing."
>
> The FLs had two sons, twenty-one months apart. According to Mrs. FL, "I had to be both a mother and a father to them. . . . He never played ball with them, never showed them how to use a tool."
>
> Mr. SE: "I have always been a workaholic. I probably neglected our first child. If I had to go back and redo some things in my life, that is one thing I would want to undo."
>
> Mrs. NN: "He went to work at ten of seven and he came home ten of seven . . . . On the weekends he was glad to play with the kids." He adds, "I knew so little about my children, being gone twelve hours a day, and by the time I came home from New York City I was tired."
>
> The EEs had two daughters, sixteen months apart. He explains, "I worked from early in the morning till late at night six days a week. . . . I really didn't raise the children. I used to leave in the morning, they were sleeping, and when I came home at night they were sleeping."
>
> Mr. CN: "She was the big one to mold the kids. . . . Working was my whole life."

A few spouses said the husband's absence contributed to the success of their marriage.

> Mrs. EL, mother of five, remembers, "He was gone all week to work [in

another city]. . . . He would come home on Saturday afternoon, and I would go to work Saturday night . . . and go back to work on Sunday, and he'd go back on Monday morning. . . . I think one of the reasons the marriage has worked so well is that he hasn't been home a lot. . . . You're on your own for a while, and then you're so glad to see them come back and they're so glad to be back, and then everybody's so glad for them to leave, so it balances beautifully."

Mr. HE: "Someone asked us one day . . . why we had done so well together, and the answer obviously was, I was never home." She agrees: "It's easy to get along that way."

Having devoted themselves to a lifetime of working, men frequently did not develop hobbies or other interests, so that after retiring they had nothing to fill the time or replace the sense of power and interest.

Mrs. PA: "I think to this day there are times when it's a blow to his ego that he's not earning money, that he's not being productive."

When wives took a position of economic dependence on their husbands, they had to accept the consequences of that dependence.

After the LAs married in 1943, they moved nineteen times for his job, which was very disruptive to her and the children, but not to him. "My wife says that the times that we were moved [by the corporation] were the most stressful times. I can candidly say that my head was so much in my business that to me it was routine. It's not that big a deal, really."

Mrs. TI: "I think it takes at least two people to make one successful person. And I ended up being a background to him."

When Mothers Went to Work

> Women didn't think about careers at that period of time.—Mrs. PA

Women who married in the 1920s and 1930s had less work experience before marriage and were less likely to work after marriage than were wartime wives. World War II was a shock wave that swept women into the work force, so that almost half of all women in the United States had a job at some time during the war (Mintz and Kellogg 1988, p. 161). During the 1950s there was a decline in the numbers of working women, but by 1960, one-third of all wives and 25 percent of middle-class wives were working outside the home, compared to 7 percent of middle-class wives just after World War II (ibid., p. 199).

Women's work experiences gave them new freedom and independence. They earned extra money, found new avenues for personal achievement and success, and developed new interests beyond the home. Most wives worked in clerical, sales, and service jobs that were flexible enough to adapt to their children's schedules. Only a few of the interviewed wives had careers, usually as teachers, nurses, and social workers. Even when mothers went back to work, almost all defined their children and husbands as first priority, before the job. Women who had been socialized to their housewife role since they were children, as had their breadwinner-husbands, were now forced to choose between responsibilities at work and at home.

> Mrs. RA, married in 1926, worked outside the home for a while because of economic necessity. When the oldest child was "a baby, I went back to the telephone office and my mother . . . took him home with her. . . . I lived in the telephone office. . . . I was the night agent . . . and I worked from nine o'clock at night to seven o'clock in the morning. . . . I must have been pregnant with (the second child) when I gave that up."

> Mrs. RG, married in 1942, worked outside the home when the children were older. At first she worked from ten in the morning until two in the afternoon so she could see them off to school and be there when they got home, and then later she worked from nine to three. "When they opened up the door, I was home. . . . Now that my daughter is going back to work, oh, I'm so thrilled. I always said to her, the worst thing for a woman is, when she has the children, that she becomes nothing but a hausfrau. Very bad."

> Mrs. TM, married in 1943, worked when her children were older—the eldest a senior in high school, the middle in junior high, and the youngest aged six. "My hours and hers [the youngest child's] were about the same. I got home the same time she did as a rule, . . . and my mother was retired by then."

> Mr. EL, married in 1943, remembers his wife's job options: "Her work career . . . would have been different if not for children. When children are involved, then you seek those kinds of jobs that go with the school year, or she was a waitress for a while because she could do that at night after I got home."

Only three wives interviewed said they relied on a regularly paid employee for child care while they were at work.

> Mrs. WE, married in 1940, had the WE's first child, a son, in 1945. When he was eighteen months old she started a business with another ex-serviceman's wife. "I had full-time housekeepers for my kids, because I wanted to work. [My husband] always encouraged me to do that."

Working wives augmented insufficient family incomes, earned additional money to buy extras and luxuries, saved money for their children's college educations and occasionally provided pensions after retirement.

> Mr. WT, married in 1943, comments, "I went through a terrible bankruptcy. . . . It looked like we would never crawl out of debt. . . . [My wife] went right back to work. . . . I started from the bottom all over again. . . . I had a day shift, and she had a night shift. . . . We had one car."

He says, "There was always one of us home." For five years Mr. WT took care of his children at night, after work, while his wife went to her job. "I used to advance the clock so I could get them into bed earlier. . . . I'd pull down the shades and tell them, 'It's seven o'clock. It's time for you to be in bed.' It might have been only five o'clock, but it got them out of my hair so that I would have a little peace and quiet on my own."

Mrs. ER, married in 1943, knew why she wanted to work: "In 1961, I took a weekend job . . . to save money for college. I'd start out weekends because [our daughter] was about nine and I didn't want to leave her alone during the week, so I would work four to twelve on weekends and then he would watch them. . . . So they had no loans [going to college]." She had a plan, she achieved her goal, and she enjoyed the satisfaction of that accomplishment.

Mrs. YE's father drilled into her that she had to marry someone who could support her, but she said, "Whoever was going to support me, we were going to do it together. Mrs. YE, married in 1942, was a nurse. "That bought our refrigerators and things like that. . . . As soon as the little fellow was old enough to stay with his grandmother, . . . I went right back to work . . . three to eleven. . . . One thing I would have changed; . . . if I had been working days . . . I would have been home when the children came home. . . . I should have been taking part in after-school activities." Mr. YE cooked dinner and put the children to bed every night.

Mrs. AL, married in 1940, was a teacher. She describes her career: "I was gonna work for a year, and I lasted twenty-five years. I loved it. I loved every bit of it. It was not easy. . . . He didn't like it in the beginning, but he saw that I enjoyed it."

Mrs. HE, married in 1943, says, "I worked . . . for eighteen years. I have a lot of things that I'm involved with, so when we would come home at the end of the day, . . . we had so many things to tell each other."

For many wives, their excursion into the working world was essential to their personal growth and happiness in their marriage. At the same time, working wives were taken as evidence of a husband who did not earn enough money.

Mrs. PA describes the crisis that led her to find work outside the home: "My youngest . . . I guess she was about ten years old. . . . I found myself screaming my head off at her, because she left a finger mark on the wall. And it kind of brought me up short and I said [to myself], 'I think it's time for you to sit down and reevaluate what's important.' I wasn't running a house, the house was running me. I told [my husband], 'I'm gonna go back to work. I'm gonna go get a job, because my life has closed in on me to the point where I've lost my sense of values. I have to get out of this house! I have to be with other adults, and get my head straightened out!' And he was very, very upset at the idea that I wanted to go to work. His reaction was to put his hand in his pocket, and he said, 'Here's money. What is it you want to buy? Go buy it.' And I tried to explain to him that it had nothing to do with money. It was a blow to his ego. Because you have to remember, we both grew up in an era when wives did not work.... We talked a lot about it at first, we fought about it, you know, and we yelled at each other, and then we both calmed down and I said, 'All I can talk about is when I washed the floor last or the best buy in the supermarket.' I felt stupid. I was beginning to feel as though my brains were drying up.... And when I made him understand that, he was not thrilled, but he agreed that if that's what I wanted to do, then he would support me in whatever way he could.... I didn't go to work until after she left for school, and I came home before she arrived.... It all fell into place, and it worked. And I was very happy doing that. I was very happy working .... Then I became a person in my own right.... I began to feel like I was doing something that was all for me.... The twenty years I worked, I worked for me. And I made my own friends, and I made a life outside of my home and my children, and when I went out in adult company I had something to contribute to the conversation.... I grew through those years. I grew as a person.... My head started to expand. I started to go to school.... I went to college with women that I worked with, all of whom had degrees and were just the kind of people who loved the mental stimulation of learning .... We used to go in to NYU and the New School, ... and we took all kinds of classes. And I loved it. And worlds opened up to me that I did not know existed.... I always felt like I was the least talented person in the whole world, and suddenly I could do something that other people looked at and said, 'Gee, that's good.' ... I guess I gained a lot of confidence in myself, confidence I had lost over the years. Because when you're seventeen, you know everything, you're brilliant. And then as you grow into your life, you're suddenly not so brilliant.... Sometimes I felt like I was completely lost, like the 'me' was gone, absolutely gone."

Mrs. PA describes what many couples experienced when wives wanted to go to work. Husbands feared that they might be considered inadequate breadwinners and that they might be neglected. At first, they did not understand their wives' need to expand their roles. Mrs. PA points to the need for outside stimulation so many wives felt. The role of wife and mother had overwhelmed Mrs. PA's sense of self. The couple combined honest communication, passage of time, and compromise to resolve the conflict, and then she went to work, fitting the job around the children's schedule and the household tasks.

When Mrs. PG returned to work after the children left home, there was conflict at first. She says, "Oh, he minded! ... They would call when they needed people, and he used to scream at me, 'You don't need to run.'"

He counters, "First off, when she worked at night, that means I didn't get fed. I had to go out to eat." They compromised. He came to the mall where she worked, and they ate out together.

Mrs. SE sees the evolution of women's roles over three generations in her family.

> Mrs. SE's father was "old fashioned." "He never went near the kitchen. He sat at the table and he was served. And my mother had a linen tablecloth, a centerpiece, candles; and everything was absolutely perfect at the table for her husband. When he wasn't there, which wasn't very often, . . . we just sat around and had something very informal in front of the radio; then there was no television. But when my father was there, he was the king, so you see I grew up with that. And [my husband] was my king for a long time, but then something happened that I decided I had to be me. So it was, maybe it was happening in the rest of the world too, I don't know. . . . My mother was really a slave to my father, let's put it that way. He was a European kind of husband, his wife was a servant really, as well as his bedmate. . . . When our younger son was older, I think he was four, I got myself a job in a nursery school. . . . I started then to make my own life because this husband was going to be doing his thing all the time. . . . I didn't 'have' to go to work, you see, it was a fulfillment. . . . I just wasn't satisfied to do nothing. . . . Then this opportunity came along . . . outside the house! Get up and get dressed. Put your earrings on and go out in the world. . . . I had to do something that was me! . . . I think you young people have that all solved now, because you see, all three of our children, all three of our daughters and daughters-in-law are career wives, and our two sons and our son-in-law have accepted that just without any question, and they fill in . . . where they must, doing the cooking, doing the shopping, doing the housecleaning, all of that. That wasn't so in my era. . . . [My husband] didn't ever buy a loaf of bread. I'm not disparaging that. I'm just saying that was the lifestyle. Just as my father never did any of that!"

Nowadays, women are increasingly seeking careers instead of jobs, a change that demands of both sexes huge investments of time. The pay may be quite high, but the cost in personal time for marriage and family life is also high. Many older spouses attributed the marital problems of the younger generation to dual-career families, but they do not condemn them. They worry about their latchkey grandchildren, but they understand the pressures on their children. For most young people on Long Island today, buying a home as comfortable and large as the one their parents have, the home in which they grew up, is unlikely without two incomes (Newman 1988). Many spouses see the situation in their own families, and a few see no solution, except to "want less."

> Mrs. PA: "So many young people seem to feel that they have to keep up with the Joneses. There are too many young families with latchkey kids where the mothers have to go to work. 'Have to,' a term you have to define. You 'have to' if your expectations are such that your child must have every toy that comes out on the market, that your child has to have the latest computer, that your child has to have riding lessons and has to have tennis lessons and has

to have this and that. . . . If those are your expectations, then you're gonna have to go to work, because the chances are your husband is not gonna be able to provide all this in today's economy. And I think that's one of the things that has to be rethought."

Mrs. NA did not want to work full time and would not if she was a young mother today. "I always wanted to be here when they came home from school. That was very, very important to me. . . . I think the worst thing you can do, is have a child and work full-time. . . . I worked through my married life, a lot. So I'm not taking that away from anyone. But these people that . . . want the good life. . . . You have no time to clean your house unless you're lucky enough to have a cleaning woman, which they all want. Now, in the morning, you wake up, you gotta get ready for work, he's gotta get ready for work, and we gotta get the baby out to the babysitter. It's sleeting. . . . He goes out to start the car. . . . The baby is crying. . . . You need this before you go to work? . . . Naturally by the time you get into the car, the three of you, he's not talking to you, and you're not talking to him, and the baby's still crying, and this is how you head to work. Then when you come home, you're tired, he's tired. Who's gonna cook dinner? The baby's crying."

Mrs. GR says, "It's wonderful today that girls have been taught to take care of themselves. When I got married, they weren't."

These older wives were socialized to put their families first. A career plus a family could mean a collision of roles, but a flexible job fell just within the old role boundary. Today's young women face more complicated decisions.

Summary

Overall, surveyed husbands have a more optimistic view of their marriages than their wives do. They report higher levels of marital satisfaction and intimacy than do wives. Field and Weishaus (1984) and Stinnett, Carter, and Montgomery (1970) found similar gender differences in their studies of long-term marriage and marital satisfaction. In the present study, husbands less often report thinking the marriage might fail at some point, and less often report declines in sexual interest over time. Wives more often than husbands report withholding information, avoiding the topic, and waiting on the passage of time to resolve conflicts.

Husbands may have more positive views of their marriage because it is one of their few intimate relationships. Some research has found that husbands have difficulty becoming intimate with anyone other than their wives (Schwartz and Scott 1994). Interviewed husbands had some of the same responses as Nordstrom's subjects (1986). For these men, marriage and family life kept them from being alone, gave them a reason to live, and gave them someone upon whom they could depend. Like Nordstrom's subjects, many of the Long Island husbands expressed satisfaction with their role as breadwinner, providing for their family—it meant they were successful in their primary social role.

These spouses usually had a traditional division of labor, with breadwinner-husbands and stay-at-home mothers. While nearly all interviewed wives stayed home with young children, the wartime wives were more likely than Depression-era wives to have worked before and after marriage. If they worked while their children were in school, they usually arranged their work hours around the children's schedules. These wives more often had a series of jobs in sales, service, or clerical positions rather than professional careers. Spouses said the main reason women tended to stay in unhappy marriages was because of their limited educational and work opportunities, which left them unable to support themselves and their children.

Vignette: The Mitchells

We go in two directions now.—Mr. Mitchell

The Mitchells met when she was eighteen and he was nineteen. Mr. Mitchell says of his wife, "She was a dazzling girl . . . a very popular girl. . . . She was a stunning lady, an immaculate dresser, and it's one of those things, that chemistry does . . . I guess when you're so crazy about a girl, you . . . think it's gonna work." Both describe it as love at first sight. She says, "I think it's a chemical reaction, isn't it? He was different than the other fellows I went out with. It just happened." Later, they discovered neither person is what the other expected.

After Mr. Mitchell had been introduced to his future wife, "Each evening, for four consecutive evenings, I encountered her on my way home. First time she was going to her aunt's and I said hello. . . . We stopped for a few minutes. . . . The next night we passed each other again, and . . . I thought it was a coincidence until years later I found, apparently, it was a typical feminine trick." She says she knew when he got off work and was purposely running into him.

He says he had little experience in dating other women. He was very shy. "I always, all my life, doubted my ability to do things as well as the other guy. . . . I never had confidence. . . . I never felt I was adequate, like they were making a mistake promoting me." In part, he blames his mother: "The . . . theory is you praise your child, you spoil the child. . . . But in doing that, you don't support your children where they have faith in themselves, 'cause I did not have it. I got it from sports. I became proficient in sports, and then you raise your feeling about yourself, you feel I'm not the worst guy, I'm as good as anybody else. . . . Sports did that for me."

He and his father were against the marriage for different reasons. "My father, to his dying day, always blamed her for ruining my career as a ball player." He was more concerned about the war. "I didn't want to marry . . . because I didn't think I'd come back, because lots of people die in infantry." But she prevailed, and they married. She checked "love" as the reason to marry, and he checked "commitment." They had a private ceremony with a justice of the peace in 1943, and then when she was pregnant they wed in the church in 1944 during one of his fourteen-day furloughs. "I got my dress off the racks at Macy's." she recalls. He says he made all the plans with the church, but "I made no other plans. I didn't have plans for a room, because I never was a guy who thought that way. Don't ask me why." Fortunately, one of his relatives took care of that for him.

He was shipped overseas with Patton's Third Army, and when the war ended he rejoined his family, got a job in a major corporation, and rose to upper-level management. Mrs. Mitchell remembers, "He went to work, he came home and ate. I was with the kids. . . . I thought you'd be friends, and you'd do things together more so than it was."

They bought a house in the suburbs when the third of their five daughters was born. Despite the difficulties, Mrs. Mitchell said the best years were when the children were small, " 'Cause we were all the same age and we were all raising children. . . . It came in spurts. I was busy with the kids all the time. . . . I never had any free time . . . I really would have liked a career of my own so I would have something." Instead, she took part-time sales and clerical jobs three nights a week, which gave her clothing discounts for her five daughters' clothes.

When Mr. Mitchell was in his late forties, his company offered him a promotion that involved extensive travel overseas. "I wanted that job, but I wanted a wife to say, 'Go and do it, and good luck,' and I never got that from my wife. She said 'You're not leaving me here while you traipse . . . around the world'. . . . We didn't have a big dispute about it. . . . Again, that stupid feeling of mine whether I'm adequate all the time. It entered my mind." He still regrets not taking the job, and holds her responsible for the missed opportunity.

He retired after forty years with one company, and then returned to work because "I like it. . . . It's a psychological kind of thing. I'm waking up in the morning, getting dressed, shaving, comb[ing] my hair, putting a clean shirt on and going somewhere, and they appreciate me." Despite the fact that he has returned to work full-time, she says that after retirement he is always in the way and their relationship has become intolerable. He thinks occasionally they get in each other's way, and the marriage is about the same as it was before retirement.

They both say they are somewhat happy in the marriage. Otherwise, the Mitchells do not describe their marriage in the same way. They have few activities they share. He says, "We go in two directions now, because we don't even have the same taste in programs on TV. . . . I'm gonna watch . . . the ballgame, and she has no interest in that. . . . She doesn't like old movies. . . . She'd rather listen to some sob-story thing, . . . so she's in the den . . . and I'm in the other [room], and then I go to bed early."

Mrs. Mitchell's problems in the marriage have been finances, her husband's annoying habits, and his failure to help her with the five children and the household work. She sighs, "Work, that's all I do is work. That was one of the disappointments. . . . I don't even get to the movies. It's like I'm in prison. It's awful, but I just have to bear it, I guess. . . . I know I have to get rid of this house 'cause I can't take care of it anymore. So I'm waiting for everybody to take their belongings out. . . . It's just a nightmare thinking of all the work I have to do every day. . . . The house, it's too much work." She is currently caring for one of her grandchildren too. "I don't think older people should raise a child, it's not good for the children. They have to be with young parents." She says she and her husband, also fight over the grandchild, taking sides on what he should or should not do.

He says their problems are finances and chores around the house. He mimics his wife: " 'He never does anything here. I want him to paint the garage, I want you to do this.' And I refuse to be ordered to do something. I will do what I think I have to do. . . . Some men are very handy. I'm not the handiest guy. . . . When you call the repair guy it costs some money, now, so you do the things yourself. . . . I'm still a child of the Depression. . . . I like not to spend, because I don't like debt."

He thinks they both do annoying things and have bothersome characteristics, but does not see that as any problem in the marriage, because "That's true of any people living together." Of her constant complaints about him, he says "Women sometimes think they're martyrs, like, life has been so tough for them. . . . I sometimes don't understand women's paths when they argue, the pitch to exaggeration."

When they argue, she says, "It's always my fault. . . . He's got a very loud voice. . . . Then he loses his temper. . . . In a couple of hours he forgets about it." He agrees "We can argue, and we're stubborn people. . . . You have a little argument. . . . Before you know it, you're talking like nothing was going on." He doesn't like to argue, " 'Cause I saw it with my mother and father." On the survey he indicated that he "did what my spouse wanted" to resolve conflicts, and she checked "avoidance," "the passage of time," and "did what my spouse wanted." She says they sometimes resolve their conflicts, but he says they usually do. Without more honest communication it is difficult to know what the problems are, let alone solve them.

She says her love for him has changed over time. "It's like a seesaw, some days I hate him, some days I could kill him, like two animals living in a cage." He agrees that they "fight like cats and dogs" sometimes. What does she like about her husband? "Can't say he takes me out. Can't say he's good company. . . . Our entertainment is like nil. . . . He watches TV, watches sports or reads the newspaper, or reads books. That's his whole life. . . . What can I say? He's here to help me. . . . On the whole he's all right."

Neither is the other's best friend. She never tells him she loves him, and he rarely tells her. Sexual interest between them declined in the middle to later years and never resumed. She indicated the children as the only positive factor accounting for their long marriage, and he checked nothing. There was no particular time she was most or least happy, but he was happiest after the children were born. As to what is most rewarding after a lifetime together: "That we're alive!" she laughs, "I can't say I'm doing anything great tomorrow." Most rewarding to him now are his children and grandchildren, "Because I still think that's what life is, family. . . . You often wonder, . . . 'Should I have married? Why did I marry?' but you look at your kids and you look at what they do." Duty, responsibility, and lack of alternatives kept them in the marriage. On this, they both agree.

At one point, she thought they might divorce. "You think about it, but you never do it. It's like you want to kill somebody. . . . You always think of the extreme, opposite end of what you can do, but you never do it. You don't kill people, just like you don't get divorces." She compares herself to younger generations. "Kids nowadays just make up their mind and they do something," like her own divorced child. Asked how she would change her life she says, "There's nothing I can change now."

Mr. Mitchell says he never thought of divorce. "If you walk out, I don't know how you're possibly gonna handle the costs involved. . . . I could never run away from my responsibilities, which were her and the children. . . . I often said you gotta stay with things. I don't believe in quitting on things, . . . and then what are you changing for? Are you changing *for* something?"

Summary

Despite their many problems and low marital intimacy, Mr. Mitchell has a somewhat positive view of the marriage—more positive than her view. He likes her better than she likes him, he thinks they resolve their conflicts more than she does, and he expressed fewer complaints about her than she did about him. He believes that life is about family and thinks his children and grandchildren are the rewards of their marriage. He never thought of divorce, although he has sometimes wondered if he should have married.

Mrs. Mitchell says her life is a series of unfulfilled expectations. Her husband seldom took her out, was never home, never helped her with their children, is tightfisted with money, and is insensitive to her feelings. Even after retirement she is overworked, burdened with the responsibility of a big house and yard, and with the care of her divorced daughter's child. The best thing about her life right now is that she is alive. She has considered divorce, but would never do it, because of her religious beliefs and because of a lack of alternatives. Both are committed to the marriage, happy or not, and from her perspective, it is too late to change anything now.

Chapter Seven

Making a Marriage Last

*As we get older we're attached to each other, and
what else have we got, you might say.*—Mr. EC

Introduction

Interviewed couples compared their marriages to those of younger people,
particularly their own children, and described the factors that contribute to
lasting relationships. Questions focused on four areas: (1) why the divorce
rate is higher among younger generations; (2) why many of their children
divorced; (3) why their own marriage lasted for a lifetime, happy or not;
and (4) marital advice to younger generations.

Why So Much Divorce Now?

*We expected to work our way through it, but that's
not the way it works today.*—Mr. HE

Spouses were divided into two schools of thought on the higher divorce
rate: (1) the "at-fault" spouses, who think that younger people have particular problems or character flaws (i.e., they are too selfish, materialistic, un-
committed, or unconcerned) that prevent them from creating a long-term
relationship, and (2) the "times-have-changed" spouses who think that significant social changes have occurred that make long-term relationships
more difficult, if not impossible, to create and maintain. Among the sixty
interviewed couples, about 40 percent are in the "at-fault" category, and
about 60 percent think "times have changed," although some couples adopt
both points of view.

What do the "at-fault" spouses think is wrong with young people today?
They see the younger generation as being too materialistic, too selfish, too
lazy, with no work ethic or goals, and as having no values, morals, or sense

of responsibility and commitment. Most of the "at-fault" spouses began their own marriages with very little money and few material possessions. They see their children and grandchildren spending more money, faster, on credit, than they ever did.

While the older generation say they were happy with what they had, they often think their descendants want everything now and are unhappy if it does not happen that way. They describe today's youth as never being satisfied, as living well beyond their means, and as spending money they do not have. Having lived through the Depression, they take a very different view of debt and credit from the view held by younger people, including their own children.

> Mr. NN: "I feel that the young generation today sometimes feel like they've got it coming. Why do I have to struggle for all this?" Mrs. NN is unsympathetic: "I went through the Depression with the same kinds of problems that the kids have today, except I didn't have parents who had money."

> Mr. LE: "They're all spending as fast as they make it. . . . They complain. . . . Get up around my age, you start to get old fashioned, because you think of what you went through to get what you got. Today, it just gets thrown out the window."

> Mrs. CA: "They want what their parents have after all these years, but they don't think about how their parents started. . . . They want to fall into that right away. They get married, and [the wives] expect their husbands to provide this. . . . If he doesn't provide it, then they're upset, they're leaving."

> Mrs. AZ: "The main difference, as I see it, is in our day we had no money— weren't so independent as the girls are today. . . . Of course, our religion was a very strong reason, teaching us always to forgive and to love and to accept each person as they are, warts and all."

The "at-fault" couples told stories of family sacrifices that contrasted sharply with their descriptions of selfish Boomers, and of their own children. They see younger people as focused on their "own agendas" of personal fulfillment and satisfaction, inflexible and unwilling to make sacrifices for their families. Many said that today's young mothers, in their push to "have everything," work full-time and have less time for their family.

> Mr. LE: "There's no home life. That's the whole thing. . . . There's no sitting down at the table and eating, they've gotta watch the television. . . . These kids, what are they gonna look forward to in later life? They'll have nothing . . . . There's no togetherness, . . . no religion. . . . You have your dinnertime, you should all be together, you have things to discuss. . . . When they get

married they don't take their vows strong enough. It's just words. . . . They expect too much out of life. I have to laugh. They don't have this, they don't have that. We didn't have anything! We went through a Depression. . . . We found things to do for ourselves, but they don't! You had to struggle to get ahead!"

Mrs. PA: "It's not only 'I have to have it,' but 'I have to have it now.' We were raised in an era where you saved up all of your pennies, and when you had enough pennies, then you went to the store. You didn't go to the store first. First you saved up all of your pennies."

These spouses think that too many young people use sex as a leisure activity. Two-thirds of all interviewed spouses described a decline in values and morals from their generation. Few were willing to take a more relative perspective, to call present-day morals and values "different." Many said young people have too little self-respect and no respect for other people and things, including the institution of marriage and the meaning of a vow.

Mr. EL says, "How can you respect a gal if you go to bed with her on the second or third date?"

Mrs. RG told her niece, "I say, when you go to buy a pair of gloves, you'll try on your size, right? . . . But when you want to buy it, you're always gonna take that one off, and you're gonna take a fresh pair of gloves that nobody tried on."

Mr. RG: "We see certain things that happen, and we say, 'It seems the world has passed us by,' because the generations now, they don't think like we did . . . . Not that they're wrong. Maybe that's what the times require today. . . . We were brought up under different circumstances . . . moral values. . . . Basic values, respect for other people, consideration for other people. Where did it go?"

Many spouses point to our "throwaway culture" and give examples of this philosophy, from disposable diapers and disposable cameras to disposing of unwanted babies through abortion and disposing of unwanted spouses with divorce. A few spouses feel that young people use each other and then move on. Because it is a more "mobile" culture, stability has less value.

Mr. MR: "It's primarily because . . . of the flippant attitude that people take to marriage." Marriage becomes "a throwaway, another replaceable item."

Mr. LE: "It ain't like when you go out and buy a car and you don't like the way it runs, so you take it down and trade it in. You don't do that!"

Some "at-fault" spouses think the changes were partly their doing, because they taught both their sons and their daughters to pursue their goals in life. Some older wives express regret that they did not have the opportunities their daughters and granddaughters have. They saw the two sides of being selfish: you may get to have more of what you think you want (i.e., more accomplishments, more self-respect, more self-confidence, more independence), but it will be more difficult to create a lasting relationship. Many "at-fault" spouses conceded that mass media, television in particular, had created false and glamorous images of divorce, sex, and the "fast life." Finally, most of the "at-fault" spouses said the hippie, anti-Vietnam social movements of the 1960s changed social norms and values forever. Sometimes drugs were also linked to this transformation. Many older spouses felt threatened by the changes, as if all they believed in was being questioned.

> Mrs. MT says of the 1960s, "It was very unsettling . . . being in our generation. . . . All the things that we grew up believing were immutable were being challenged."
> Mr. MT agreed: "I think the sixties played a role . . . the sexual revolution, the idea of freedom to do what you wanted, to do your own thing, personal fulfillment. . . . I think that was true with our daughter."

The spouses who think "times have changed" see the same changes as the "at-fault" spouses, but they do not blame younger generations. They cite three social changes that make long-term marriage more difficult for younger generations: the decline of religion, socialization to different values and norms, and the increased educational and employment opportunities for women. First, the decline of religion and the rise of science and reason make logical "reasons" for divorce acceptable, and the traditional definition of marriage as a religiously sanctioned institution obsolete.

> Mrs. NA says, "I don't think we ever thought of divorce. . . . We went to church and they said 'till you die,' and that was the way it was."

> An unidentified spouse wrote on the survey, "In my day, when you married you made a commitment both to God and your spouse. There was no thought of not working problems out or seeking a divorce. (Of course, in those days divorces were hard to get and very expensive anyway.) You need to keep working with each other to improve your marriage and make it work and you always need God's help to do this. It makes it all worth while when you're older."

> Mrs. YE says, "It used to be a terrible word, divorce, . . . but today it almost seems like they made a contract that can be broken. They don't take their vows seriously."

Socialized to believe that divorce is an "unthinkable alternative," these couples believe it is better to stay in an unhappy marriage than to break up a family.

> Mr. WT remembers, "In our early days, I didn't know anybody who was divorced. People didn't get divorced, even if they were miserable; they lived their lives together, miserably."

> Mrs. HA: "When I was growing up, people were not divorced easily.... It had to be really something dreadful that did it. I always thought it would have to be a terrible thing to break up a home with children in it."

> Mr. ME comments on the changes he has seen since he married in 1930, "It was a shame to be divorced. Nowadays being divorced doesn't mean nothing!"

Now marriage is defined as a legal contract that may be broken with sufficient cause or desire. This makes divorce much easier and less stigmatizing.

Second, spouses who think times have changed said they socialized their children to different attitudes toward personal fulfillment and sacrifice. In seeking to give their children what they did not have, they created children very different from themselves. Not only are attitudes and values different, but they recognize that the lack of struggle meant their children did not learn how to work hard or why work is important. In centering their lives on their children, they raised self-centered children.

> Mrs. CN: "These problems are probably the fault of the parents.... It's permissiveness or giving too much. When you give too much to the children, they expect too much.... From the time they're little, they're used to too much."

> Mr. KP says, "They've had too much, and we the parents and grandparents are guilty of giving them too much."

> Mr. TN: "We had nothing.... We knew what to do without.... That's the problem with the generation today. We gave our kids too much because we didn't have nothing."
> Mrs. TN agrees: "Different times, different values, they just want, want, want.... Today, young people don't know how to give and take, share."

> About young people in general, Mrs. TM says, "They have to realize that you don't start out at the same level. You start out at the bottom and then you build your way ... but again, I think parents have something to do with that.... My granddaughter isn't getting the same basic training that her mother had. The parents are busy or working. They don't spend time with the kids, and they don't talk things over with the kids as much.... The kids nowadays don't do things for themselves. They have to be entertained.... A

lot of parents want to make it easier for the kids so they don't know how to face anything. My granddaughter doesn't know what the value of a dollar is. She gets money, she spends it. . . . This women's group I go to, we talk about our grandchildren and they're all the same. . . . They have every wish granted immediately. They don't know how to wait for things. . . . They want everything right away."

Mrs. WE: "It comes from the feeling of being constantly spoiled, having everything when you want it. . . . A lot of kids have just been handed too many things. . . . I tell my grandchildren, 'You don't start life being the president of the company. You start at an entry level, you work hard, . . . you learn.' Learn and accomplish . . . the same thing in a marriage."

Most of these "times-have-changed" spouses still look to the past, to their parents and grandparents, the Depression, and World War II to define what is of worth and value.

Mrs. EC, married in 1928, says, "It's hard for the young people to raise children today with the drugs. . . . We had maybe alcohol. . . . It seems so different from when we were growing up. You didn't have to lock your doors. . . . You don't have that good feeling about life. . . . The schools are not teaching the way we were taught. And the mothers are working. . . . I told my daughters, 'Stay home with your children till they're five years old and then, if you want to go to work, they've already got a start.' . . . But today's children have to work, you both have to get a job. In my day, you couldn't get a job." She remembers when nearly 800 people belonged to her lifelong church, and now the membership is about 60 people. Times have changed. "I was hoping it could go back, but I don't think it can go back. Something has to change, but I can't pinpoint it. I'd like to see it change for the children. I feel the children are being robbed."

In contrast, the interviewed couples think that many of the Boomers consciously chose not to emulate their parents and grandparents, whose marriages they defined as stifling personal growth.

Mr. EC: "Family values have changed. I don't think they get together like we used to years ago, or as we brought up our children. . . . I think children have their own ideas about what they want. And I don't think that they want to listen to what we say about it. . . . Even our great-grandchildren have minds of their own."

Mrs. TA: "They haven't got the patience to wait. . . . And I say to my kids, 'Well, look at me.' And they say, 'We don't want to be like you.' . . . They don't want to struggle. Let's put it that way. They want what they want. They're thinking too far into the future. . . . If we knew what was gonna be in the future, we probably wouldn't get married."

Mr. TI: "We're not really 'closers.' Our society does not feel that they have to finish a job. . . . That's a whole pattern in our society. It's an unfinished society. It's not a wild thing, then, that we get so many divorces, because you don't have to finish it. . . . We all do what is socially acceptable. It was *not* socially acceptable for people to get a divorce . . . it's socially acceptable *now.* . . . We may have wanted to be like our parents and stay together, you know, because it's a tradition. Now I feel like people think, 'I don't want to be like them. They're old and they're not "with it" anymore, and the things that they did in their generation were stupid and we're so much more advanced now.'"

The third change the spouses in this study discuss is increased educational and employment opportunities for women, which altered both the face of the work force and the character of home life. More women are educated and more women work outside the home, resulting in greater independence for women. Generally, the spouses want these changes for their daughters and granddaughters, but they also recognize the new family problems that are created. Now two careers compete with the family for time and attention. There are more opportunities to get in trouble, more alternative attractions to draw someone away from the marriage. The sexual revolution and birth control changed sexual behavior and fear of pregnancy.

Mrs. NA: "You can get jobs where things blend, but I think that has a lot to do with the divorce rates. . . . They want the good life."

Mrs. HA: "I think it's far more difficult for all the young people now to handle than it was in our generation. We were so concerned with making ends meet and surviving, that you didn't have time for all these other activities that would drive you apart. It was all in the home, and in your circle of friends."

Mrs. NN says, "Women today have a career so they *can* divorce. That's the difference, I think. . . . *You can!*"

Mrs. NG: "Women are better educated. . . . It's easier to get out of it. They've got the education. . . . I can remember my father saying, 'Girls don't go to school. They grow up and get married.'"
Mr. NG: "There's too much temptation going around."

Divorced Children of the Long-Term Married

They're living a whole different life than we ever did!—Mr. PG

Thirty-two of the sixty interviewed couples have at least one divorced child, so over half of them have seen firsthand how marriages and families come apart. Five of eight marriages (63 percent) with one spouse who was less happily married had one or more divorced children. All three couples in which both partners are less happily married have divorced children. Of the twenty-eight couples who are very happy together, only twelve have divorced children (43 percent). Of the remaining twenty-one couples, in which both partners are happy or one chose "very happy," while the other chose "happy," twelve (58 percent) have divorced children. This suggests that the quality of parents' marriage may play a role in whether or not their children divorce. Neither sons nor daughters were more likely to divorce.

Nearly all the interviewed couples say they expected to remain married and knew they had few alternatives. They think that today fewer people believe they have to finish what they have begun, and more believe they have the option not to finish. Divorce is now defined as a reasonable option. It is also more common for divorced children to move back home if they have to, and parents are sympathetic.

> In comparing the generations, Mr. TT said his parents would have told him, "You'd better get back! You have no room here!" if he left his wife. But what would Mr. TT do if his daughter divorced? "I would take her in, no doubt."

> One of the NGs' sons had a disastrous marriage. His wife had two children during their marriage, neither of which was his. When Mr. NG discovered the truth, "I thought my son was going to have a nervous breakdown. . . . Literally, we were sending money out there that he should go to a psychologist or something, because I thought the boy was going to fall apart."

> The ALs have one son who made an unhappy marriage. She remembers telling him, " 'You make your bed, you lie in it. You don't come back.' But I took him back. That's what happens with young people."

> Mrs. LA says of their divorced daughter, "She did all the pulling and all the supporting, and when he started to use drugs, she left."

> Mrs. MA: "My daughter was gonna straighten him out, but no way! You can't change a leopard's spots." They were married only seven months before the marriage ended.

> "The young people today," says Mrs. ME, "have one argument, they leave and go home to their mother, and their mother accepts them. . . . We went to a divorce party. The mother had a wedding cake with a bride and groom, and the groom had his head chopped off! . . . That's the happiest party the girl ever had!"

In only a few situations did spouses believe their own children caused the divorce. Reasons for their children's divorces included: marrying too young, infidelity, bad choice of partner (because of dissimilar backgrounds, unpleasant personality, or different religion), physical or psychological abuse, drug and/or alcohol abuse, and gambling.

Each of these long-married couples tried to make the divorce easier for their child. Unlike their own parents, they took the divorcing child, and sometimes grandchildren, into their homes. They helped financially or otherwise during and after the divorce. They sent money for counseling; provided sympathy; paid for educations, vacations, medical care, housing, and food; and performed services like cooking, laundry, and babysitting. What they say about divorce is not what they did about their own children's divorces. Their parental response is in stark contrast to their own parents' lack of support for them in troubled times, as will be discussed later. The shift in parental attitude on the part of these long-married couples enabled their children to divorce.

Some of the costs of divorce were hidden and hard to count. Most often, grandparents lost contact with their divorced sons' children, depriving both grandparents and grandchildren of an important family relationship. A few of the couples strived to keep their relationships with their former daughters-in-law open.

> The ERs' son divorced his wife to marry someone else. Mrs. ER: "We've loved her for thirteen years. . . . You can't turn that off. . . . In that first year . . . . We did everything for her. Helped her with the baby. . . . She had nobody else to do it. . . . Right now, we are 'in between,' we keep things together, but we aren't going to be around forever."

> Mr. KP told his former daughter-in-law, who lives nearby, " 'This is not gonna break our friendship'. . . . She said that when she and [our son] were divorced, 'Now, I have no family.' I said 'You have us. We're your family.' "

Explaining Their Marital Longevity

> *I still get a thrill when I walk in the house. It's still exciting.*—Mrs. NN

Most of the couples said they were married so long because they loved each other and had happy lives together. Ninety-three percent of the 1,152 surveyed spouses reported being very happy (56 percent) or happy (37 percent) in their marriages. Approximately 7 percent of spouses were less than happily married, and they most frequently indicated that the children held the marriage together. When they married, almost all spouses thought the marriage would last (99 percent).

Overall, intimacy levels are high, as would be expected among so many happily married couples (see Table 7.1). The positive factors that contribute to the success of their marriages are trust (82 percent), a loving relationship (81 percent), willingness to compromise (80 percent), mutual respect (72 percent), need for each other (70 percent), compatibility (66 percent), children (57 percent), and good communication (53 percent). The positive factor most often added by surveyed spouses was "sense of humor."

> Mrs. HE: "We see humor in the same things. And that gives you a unity that . . . you don't have with most other people." Her husband agrees: "Perhaps the constant humor between us tends to let us not take things so seriously. . . . But it's a big factor in the scheme of things."

Ninety-five percent of the surveyed spouses agreed with the statement "Fidelity is essential to a successful marriage." Ninety-four percent checked either "agree" or "strongly agree," for the statement "Marriage is a long-term commitment to one person," and 83 percent checked either "agree" or "strongly agree" for "Marriage is a sacred obligation." In fact, these surveyed spouses usually or always agreed on most important issues in life (see Table 7.2).

Nearly 25 percent of the 1,152 survey spouses wrote additional comments explaining the longevity and success of their marriages. Many believe that the key to lifelong marriage is willingness to give more than one receives, to think of one's spouse first. Couples in the follow-up interviews said the same thing. One or both partners must be willing to give more than he or she gets from the spouse, a position that may shift over time. Happier couples strike a balance between giving and receiving. As Cole has found, "In essence, high-quality marriages facilitate both partners in getting their needs met" (1984, p. 64).

> One surveyed husband wrote, "While my wife and I feel that we 'lucked out' in our choice of each other, we have over the years come to appreciate the important ingredients of a fulfilling union: they are very similar to a deep and lasting friendship, with the vital added element of lust! Throw in generous portions of mutual respect, signs of affection and giving the other person 'room' to develop as an individual, and you should have a recipe for a successful marriage. Like all recipes, practice makes perfect!"

A lifetime balance of giving and receiving is not always possible. In some long-term marriages, one partner continues to be willing and able to give more than he or she receives, an accepted and sometimes happy arrangement. In many less than happy marriages, one spouse feels that he or she continues to give more than is received, and is not happy about it. In other less happy marriages, neither partner gives much to or receives much

Table 7.1

Measures of Marital Intimacy (by Percentage of Spouses)

(A) I like my spouse as a person.

Always	Usually	Sometimes	Rarely	Never
61.5	35.8	2.7	0	0

(B) My spouse understands me.

Always	Usually	Sometimes	Rarely	Never
23	66	10	1	0

(C) My spouse is my best friend.

Yes	No
88	12

(D) How often do you confide in your spouse?

Always	Usually	Sometimes	Rarely	Never
44	47	7	2	0

(E) How often do you show affection to your spouse?

Every Day	Most Days	Sometimes	Rarely	Never
45	38	15	2	0

(F) How often do you tell your spouse you love him/her?

Every Day	Most Days	Sometimes	Rarely	Never
27	34	29	8	2

(G) How often do you laugh together with your spouse?

Every Day	Most Days	Sometimes	Rarely	Never
30	49	19	2	0

from the other, and both are dissatisfied. For the most part, these less happy spouses have remained in the marriage because of a sense of duty (to spouse, children, family, church, and/or the institution of marriage) or because they perceive a lack of alternatives.

Interviewed spouses frequently mentioned another factor contributing to the longevity of their marriages—that their own parents would not have supported them in a divorce or let them return home had they divorced. Their parents' attitude was frequently expressed as "You made your bed, now lie in it."

Table 7.2

Agreement on Eight Family Issues (by Percentage of Spouses)

(A) Family Finances

Always	Usually	Sometimes	Rarely	Never
46	46	7	1	0

(B) Recreational Activities

Always	Usually	Sometimes	Rarely	Never
21	56	18	4	1

(C) Religious Matters

Always	Usually	Sometimes	Rarely	Never
52	35	9	3	1

(D) Spouse's Career Decisions

Always	Usually	Sometimes	Rarely	Never
54	37	6	2	1

(E) Aims and Goals in Life

Always	Usually	Sometimes	Rarely	Never
43	47	8	2	0

(F) Division of Household Tasks

Always	Usually	Sometimes	Rarely	Never
34	45	16	3	2

(G) Sexual Activity

Always	Usually	Sometimes	Rarely	Never
22	51	18	7	2

(H) Amount of Time Spent Together

Always	Usually	Sometimes	Rarely	Never
46	47	6	1	0

Mrs. MA says, "I saw the way my sister was abused. . . . My sister was stuck. She came to my father, [he] said, 'You go back to your husband.' In those days. . . . I've got news for you!"

Mr. CI: "I went home. My father said to me, 'What are you doing here?' I

said, 'I had an argument.' He says, . . . 'You get outta here! Go back to the
house . . . where you belong. . . . You made your bed, now you're gonna
sleep in it. Go back!' "

Mrs. CI adds, "And he wasn't even allowed to sleep in his mother's
house."

Mrs. FL: "Where would I go? If I went to my mother, my mother would send
me back to my husband."

Mr. FL: "We had one big, big, serious fight . . . and she went to her mother.
Her mother closed the door in her face. She said, 'You have a fight with your
husband, this is not the place to come. We're not gonna protect you. You go
back.' And that's how it was in those days. Doesn't happen now."

Many spouses experienced several years of marriage that were difficult,
unhappy, and less than satisfying. Twenty-one percent of the spouses (24
percent of wives and 18 percent of husbands) at some point thought the marriage might fail, half the time, during the middle years. They coped with
serious problems such as death of children, alcoholism, family violence, bank-
ruptcy, chronic illness, and troublesome relatives. Interviewed spouses knew
divorced people, but from their perspective, "Divorce just wasn't done" and "It
wasn't an option" unless circumstances were severe. Not only were they taught
to stay in the marriage, but women lacked other alternatives. Several wives said
divorce was not possible, because they did not have the education or work
experience to support themselves and their children.

Husbands were also dependent on wives to provide them with a home, a
family life, and a social calendar. They remained in less than happy marriages because of their sense of responsibility to their wives and children;
because they had nowhere else to go; because they didn't want to leave
their children; and because they couldn't afford to divorce and to support
two households. In these cases men, too, were economically trapped.

The unhappily married couples had developed an interdependence of
sorts and had a lifetime of memories and experiences together. They knew
each other well, whether they liked what they knew or not. Finally, the
majority of interviewed spouses said their marital longevity depended, in
part, on their general lack of expectations. They contrast their hopes and
dreams with what they call the younger generation's expectations and sense
of entitlement.

Long-term marriages are not necessarily trouble-free or happy all the
time, but spouses saw their marriages as lifetime relationships, and so
remained committed, defining their troubles as obstacles that must be
overcome. Many said they enjoyed the satisfaction of weathering these
storms.

An unidentified surveyed wife wrote, "I believe we have both mellowed over the years, learned by experience, learned to appreciate each other without reservation—no longer wishing for changes—but able to enjoy each other totally. Perhaps (speaking for myself) being more secure in 'myself,' I feel that after fifty years, our marriage has come to a full flowering."

How to Make a Marriage Last: Advice from the Long Married

> *Many times you may have to do things you'd rather not do.*—Mr. EL

Most interviewed spouses stress sharing a common background, common interests, and common values with their spouses. They believe there are fewer disagreements, especially over raising the children, if both partners are from the same social class, religion, and ethnic group.

> Mr. RG: "I think if you take two people who have different backgrounds . . . it has to lead to conflict."

> Mr. CA: "You need a foundation, a base, and you have to have the same religious background. . . . Life is tough enough without creating things that you don't have to create."

> Mrs. NG: "Take your time. Look for good family background . . . in both the instances of the divorces in my children, both those people came from terrible backgrounds. . . . They had no idea of what marriage was about."

Nearly all interviewed spouses said marriages are more successful if the spouses have love, regard, and respect for each other. These feelings take time to develop. While this may seem obvious, many of these spouses thought young people confuse sexual desire with love and are too selfish to be respectful and considerate of others. Most of these couples knew each other a long time before marrying, at least a year, and often three or more years.

> Mrs. AL says, "I went with [him] five years. I knew all about him."

These long-married couples generally believe that love, respect, and regard in a relationship are easier to establish if one looks for a dependable, kind partner, not the "perfect" mate or "Prince Charming." Several spouses said that young people's expectations for a partner are unrealistic. If people's expectations are focused on money and superficial physical characteristics, they indicate, there is less chance of establishing a lasting relationship. Knowing a prospective spouse's character is especially important, they feel, because expecting a person to change after marriage is unrealistic.

> Mr. PG: "If you dislike something in the person you're going out with, don't expect to change it. If anything, it's gonna go in the opposite direction."

> Mrs. GR: "Look for somebody who's compassionate, who's caring, who's giving and understanding."

> Mrs. LA says, "Place more emphasis on the quality of the character."

Most of these spouses said that younger people do not define marriage as a lifelong commitment, so they are unwilling to stay married when their lives become difficult. They do not take their marriage vows seriously, because they do not have to.

> Mr. ER: "They didn't have to make the commitment that we made. . . . That runs right back to the religion. . . . There was no other choice."

> Mrs. AL: "They don't go into marriage with the proper attitude. . . . They go into marriage [thinking], 'If it works, it works. If it doesn't work, we'll get divorced.' Now in the old-fashioned way, when you get married, you stay married. You see, we were brought up that way. . . . There were households where these marriages didn't work out, but they stayed together."

> Mr. GR: "We don't have the commitment we had when I was a kid to our neighborhoods and to other people. . . . Today we are fragmented. When I was a kid, within an eight-block area all my cousins, uncles, aunts [were] living together. Today, [families are] spread thousands of miles apart. We don't have that close relationship that we used to have. So now we have to depend on our own resources, ourselves; and people are just not able to handle it."

> Mr. SE: "Some of the restraints are gone. . . . The social cohesion that held couples together, in terms of fear of pregnancy and the stigma of pregnancy if you weren't married. All of those are gone." His wife agrees: "Because divorce is easy, couples don't work at marriage. They just throw in the towel."

> Mrs. RG: "Funny thing is that every problem you overcome in a marriage, your marriage grows stronger. . . . So if these same young people took the time to solve the problem, their marriage would be that much stronger."

Usually, spouses stressed the importance of communicating openly, even when it is difficult. But honesty must be tempered with kindness and tact.

> Mr. EL gives his opinion on why there is more divorce now: "Pure and simple

because people don't talk to each other, during the courtship and after."

Mrs. TA: "I'm trying to think about my kids. . . . They haven't sat down and talked about what their problems were, or they just shrugged it off. . . . One of them would get huffy and just go out of the house and wouldn't discuss it. . . . They have to . . . share their thoughts, and always tell one another that you love them."

Mr. PA's advice is, "Communicate. . . . Read the body language. . . . Sometimes it's not what they say, but the way they say it is more important."

Mrs. HE: "Once tempers go, . . . the whole thing is finished . . . name calling or throwing things up to people. Those words, you can never take back."

Spouses must be able and willing to compromise and sacrifice, say the surveyed spouses, to give more than they take and to put the spouse first. They must be willing to share the load and work together, treating each other as they would like to be treated, taking turns having their way. Flexibility, tolerance, and negotiation skills all play a role.

Mr. GR: "I watch young people today. . . . They have their own agenda. You can't have your own agenda. You gotta have a joint agenda."

Mr. EL: "Whatever differences will arise, and they will, talk about them. Negotiate, give in here, ask your partner to give in there. . . . Try not to stay mad more than a day or so, because things are not always going to be perfect."

Mrs. MT: "Compromise, respect for each other's differences. . . . It's death on a relationship if you can't bend a little bit."

Mrs. KH: "You have to give more than you take. Don't get bogged down by unrealistic expectations, and never count on too much. This way you can't be easily disappointed. Take difficulties as they come, and expect that difficulties are simply a part of everyone's life."

Mrs. HE: "It's the ordinary things . . . the golden rule. . . . You don't snap their heads off, you don't throw things, you don't scream and cry. . . . Be patient. . . . Be willing to bend."

The idea that marriage is a fifty-fifty proposition was dismissed by most couples. You might work to achieve a more equitable balance overall, but it constantly shifts.

Mrs. EL: "When a marriage first starts out, it's not fifty-fifty and if anybody thinks it's gonna be fifty-fifty right then, . . . they're in for it. But if you just hang in there long enough, . . . it's all coming back."

Mrs. NG: "It's not fifty-fifty. No, no, to be realistic, you have to think, 'I'm ready to give 100 percent.' Hopefully, it'll work to a better division." Of course, the problem with this is when the other person is not ready to give 100 percent. Then the giver can hold up the relationship alone. "That's why my [divorced] daughter stuck in for twenty years, because she was ready to give 100 percent."

If both partners are satisfied with a less than equal exchange, the marriage can work. Mrs. TA says, "I give in a lot more than [he] does. . . . We're not a fifty-fifty basis, more like a sixty-forty, but it works out, even on a sixty-forty."

Mr. TI: "You've heard it said that marriage is fifty-fifty and that's the biggest bunch of bunk there ever was, because it's really ninety-ten or ninety-five–five, but if it's the same ninety-five–five in the same corner all the time, it gets very boring, so you switch off."

Some spouses combine all five points, highlighting the interplay of qualities that make marriage successful.

Mrs. CN: "Be able to communicate with each other, have respect for one another's viewpoints. . . . Always try to keep loving the person, no matter what they do, because if you're not perfect, you can't expect them to be perfect. . . . You have to give in sometimes, you can't always have your own way. . . . Just look at things with an open mind. If you think you're right, stick to it, but then . . . have flexibility."

Mrs. PA: "Learn to compromise. . . . After the first blush of romance is over and you get into the nitty-gritties of life, and things don't always go the way you'd like them to go. And you have to come out and meet the other guy halfway. If you don't, you're not gonna make it. You just will not make it. . . . Be kind to each other. . . . Learn to really listen."

Mrs. WE sums it up: "My first thing is mutual respect. . . . To understand the other person's point of view. . . . To be willing to work out the problems . . . not to give up without trying to make an effort . . . communication . . . perseverance. . . . Not to pick up your marbles and run away because nobody is playing the game the way you want to play it. . . . If you don't care for the person, then go on your way. . . . But if you feel strongly for each other, stay and try to work it out. . . . Don't be discouraged."

To create a successful marriage, these long-married couples advise: Find someone compatible, with a shared background, mutual love and respect.

Make a commitment and keep it, communicating, compromising, and sacrificing along the way.

Mrs. RG: "Marriage is like a business, you have to work at it all the time."

Summary

Spouses fall into two categories in explaining why the divorce rate is higher among younger generations: the "at-fault" couples who blame younger generations, generally, for being too materialistic, too selfish, too lazy, and too amoral to create and maintain lasting relationships, and those couples who think "times have changed." The spouses who think times have changed recognize that values and norms are different today, that parents socialized their children to these norms and values, in effect, creating a very different generation from themselves. These spouses attribute some of the difficulty of sustaining marriages to women's greater economic and educational options, at the same time that they generally favor these new roles.

Fifty-four percent of the interviewed couples have one or more divorced children, and the less happily married couples have a higher divorce rate among their children than do the happily married couples. These long-married couples usually excuse their own children's divorces. Unlike their own parents, they offer support and assistance to their divorcing children, making divorce a more attractive and available option than it was for them.

Over 90 percent of the surveyed couples are happily married, and the vast majority indicate relatively high levels of marital intimacy. They initially defined marriage as a lifetime commitment, and they were socialized to define divorce as a stigmatizing fate worse than an unhappy marriage and lacked parental support for divorce. Having defined marriage as a lifetime commitment, they had to work their way through life together, for better or worse. Those who are less happily married feel some commitment to their children, to the institution of marriage, and/or to the sacred vow they took. They also describe a lack of alternatives, inertia, and indecisiveness. Finally, the majority of interviewed spouses mention a lack of specific expectations about marriage.

Spouses have five suggestions for creating successful marriages: First, choose a spouse with a common background, interests, and values. Second, love and respect each other. Third, make the marriage commitment and keep it for better or worse. Fourth, communicate openly, but tactfully. Fifth, compromise, and be willing to sacrifice for each other. Over time, in a happier marriage, it will all balance out. If this giving and getting over time does not balance out, then the marriage is less likely to be happy. The Barnetts, profiled next, exemplify all the factors these spouses say create happy marriages.

Vignette: The Barnetts

We're like glue.—Mr. Barnett

The Barnetts are a middle-class couple, happily married just over fifty years. They met when they were fourteen years old through a club she and her girlfriends had organized. Mrs. Barnett says they didn't go out with each other at first. "He went with all my friends, . . . but the first time I met him, it was funny. I came home and I says, 'Mom, I met the fellow that I think I'm gonna marry.' "

After meeting him, she did not see him for over a year. On Memorial Day he came to see her. "He rings the bell, and I was so shocked. We took a walk and we've been walking since then. . . . It was different than today. We used to meet in . . . each other's house and play games and listen to records and dance and things like that, but we were in groups." While they were dating, he would come to Coney Island every weekend where she lived. "He used to take a bus and two trains and another bus. . . . He used to sleep on the boardwalk . . . so that he could see me Sunday morning . . . and when my mother heard, . . . she says, 'Are you crazy?' . . . She made him sleep over . . . with my brother."

She says she liked "everything about him. He was very gentle, he was very concerned. . . . Girls used to go crazy when they saw him. . . . He was always very attentive to me. . . . He was just the type that I always wanted. . . . From the time I met him, I thought about him." He says of her, "She had feelings, she had compassion. She was just a good person . . . never put anybody down. . . . I can't think of a negative thing to say."

Before marrying they pooled their savings. She had a part-time job and he was working too, so she kept a bankbook marked "his money" and "her money" because, she says, "If we don't get married, I'm giving him back all his money. . . . When we got married, we really didn't have anything, but we managed." They married in 1943 when she was nineteen and he was twenty-one. Sighing, Mrs. Barnett says, "It was a different time. It was during the Second World War. Everything was so different. . . . He was 1A. We just wanted to get married." His father died in December, and they married in February 1943, in the rabbi's house with about ten guests.

He went into service in June, serving three years. "He was in the Navy, and I followed him to California and stayed there for . . . two years . . . with him, and I became pregnant. . . . I was in the third month when he was shipped overseas. . . . Then he came home and my son was ten months old. . . . When he came home . . . I held the baby and . . . the minute he saw him he put his hand on his face and he says 'Dada.' He broke down and cried. It was as though he never left," she says. But it felt a little different to Mr. Barnett: "When I came home from the service we had to start literally from scratch. . . . I was making pennies. I always felt guilty [because] I couldn't support her the way I'd love to." His family's business was a casualty of the war. He had to work for others, something he has never liked. "I hated to work for people; it used to kill me. Not that I was a big shot. . . . It just irritates the hell out of me."

In their early years, they lived in a house belonging to her two aunts, who lived across the street. Her mother lived upstairs and they had the apartment downstairs. He recalls, "We didn't have to depend on anybody. . . . I used to get laid off a day or two. I used to try and hide out. I was so embarrassed for people to see I wasn't working that day. . . . I felt so inferior at the time. . . . I said, we have to get out of this hole . . . so we opened up this business." With his experience in upholstery and crafting of furniture, they became interior designers. "We struggled . . . but we never had to depend on anybody." Their store was in the same building where they lived, and that business lasted fifteen years.

They attribute their marital success to their consideration and concern for each other. She says, "The most important thing . . . you, me, and we. . . . We did everything to satisfy each other, but . . . we also knew what we wanted ourselves. . . . We talk, talk, talk. . . . We've never done anything without talking about it. . . . We don't let anything burn inside us." They share basic values, but she says, "We don't agree on everything. . . . I respect him for the way he thinks, and he respects me."

On the survey, they both indicated they were "very happy", and "always" liked each other. She feels he "always" understands her, and he feels she "usually" understands him. Both checked all positive factors, and she wrote "wanting to please each other." They both agree that marriage is a long-term commitment and that fidelity is essential to a successful marriage. Each is the other's best friend, and each indicated that his or her partner has grown more interesting over time. The Barnetts say they "always" confide in each other. She says she shows affection, says she loves him, and laughs with him every day, and he says he does most days. They continue to be sexually active.

Neither one checked any problems. She wrote, "I can't remember anything that we couldn't work out together." He wrote, "We always discussed and communicated." Like many of the spouses, she has an informal rule on conflict. He describes her rule: "She won't go to sleep until we straighten it out. . . . This I learned from her."

Neither ever thought the marriage might fail. She wrote, "Each phase we reached, we were happy." Asked whether their marriage turned out as they expected, he says, "There's nothing that you can expect. You're just hoping . . . that everything would be the way it should be." This lack of expectation included finances. In the interview she says, "We have never argued money. Money just wasn't that important to us, so long as we were together."

The main theme of this couple's life is togetherness. She says, "We always did things together. Whatever we did, we seemed to satisfy each other. He was always concerned about me and I was always concerned about him, so we were both sort of taken care of because of that. . . . We're always there for each other, no matter what. . . . It can't be just me . . . it's you, me, and we."

Her mother helped with the child care so the Barnetts could go out once in a while, but they went most places with their children. They took cross-country road trips with them, and later with their grandchildren. "We used to pack up the station wagon . . . foam rubber mattress in the back. . . . We've been a very close family," he says. She explains, "I was always involved with my children, in everything they did. It was an open house. If they had something to say, they were never afraid to ask anything. I was a working mother, but I was there for my children, too. They came first." Their children's families live within a couple of hours' drive, so they will not move to Florida, even though all their friends have done so.

The worst time in their lives, Mrs. Barnett wrote on the survey, was "Only when our son had his accident—but not with our marriage." Early in the interview, Mrs. Barnett said, "The only thing we do regret in all the years . . . when my son had his accident. He was hit by a car three weeks before his wedding." She picks up the story. "We [my son and I] were going to pick up my mother's dress. Our car stalled, . . . and my son says, 'There's going to be an accident if I don't push the car.'. . . [Another] car couldn't wait and crushed him against the car. . . . I was so afraid, when I called my husband, . . . to tell him what happened. If I told him . . . *he'd* have an accident too. I said my mother was in the hospital. I need[ed] him. And then when he got to the hospital, I told him."

He says, "I don't think we spoke to each other for six months. I didn't know what to say. We were depressed, cried. . . . I cry now. . . . That's the only thing I would change in my life." Mrs. Barnett says, "Every time we would try to talk, we would cry. . . . We weren't angry with each other. It was just that every time we'd try to say something, we'd just cry. . . . We just didn't know what to say." The son's legs were crushed between the cars, leaving him a paraplegic. They made sure their future daughter-in-law had plenty of time to make up her own mind and to be with their son. The son's fiancée decided to marry him, and they recently celebrated their twenty-fifth anniversary.

The modifying theme of their life is their son's accident. Their lives are divided into before the accident and after the accident. Mrs. Barnett says, "I always felt that God loved me very much, but then when my son had his accident, I said, 'What did I do wrong?' . . . He was always such a good boy. . . . I was very kosher. The children went to Hebrew School, my son was bar-mitzvahed." Not long after their son's accident, her mother died. "When my mother died, I seemed to have lost all interest in being that orthodox." They quit going to synagogue. They also gave up their business. She says, "We didn't have the patience for it after he had his accident. He [my husband] went to work for the federal government, and I went to work. . . . I taught myself bookkeeping."

Most rewarding to them now are their children and grandchildren. She says, "They're giving me such pleasure. . . . This is where I want to be." The most troublesome issues, she says, are "not feeling good, losing my brother, losing my niece." They are enjoying retirement. Both say they are much happier since retirement and are never in each other's way. He retired first, and she continued to work until he got tired of being alone all day and began to feel guilty. "I had money coming in. I had a pension, stocks and so on. She's out there working, I felt terrible; . . . so I used to get up in the morning at nine o'clock, I'd go shopping, . . . bring home all the food, . . . clean the house, I'd vacuum the whole house, polish."

Nowadays, they like to go to Atlantic City for fun. They take two college courses each term, and have many other leisure activities they enjoy. She has been very close to her two brothers, though one of them died not long before the interview. They are not close to his siblings. He says, "We meet at weddings and funerals." They have their children over for Passover and Thanksgiving, anniversaries, and other celebrations, but, he says, "They have their own lives too." Looking back on their lives together, he says, "She's been a good woman, and that's the most important thing. . . . She's the same person I married from the beginning." She says, "I did everything I wanted."

Their advice to youth today is to be abstinent and not to give so freely of themselves, although she admits if she were twenty-two now, maybe she would feel differently. "This is how I was brought up. . . . I don't know what I would do today." She worries about her grandchildren because of AIDS. "We had a lot of sex, . . . but it was just each other, and we pleased each other. . . . It was always something to look forward to with us. . . . It was always so special." Otherwise, they advise young people to be flexible. "That's the most important thing," he says.

About the same time as their son's accident, twenty-six years ago, they moved into their current home. During the move, Mr. Barnett came across all their wartime love letters. She says, "I had a carton of letters. . . . He cut up every letter and threw it out. He said, 'I'm not gonna let my children find these some day and see how horny I was!' " She remembers, "I used to get two and three letters a day." He laughs, "I'd send letters every chance I got. . . . There must have been 1,800, 2,000 letters in there!" She adds, "I would write three and four times a day too. They were really beautiful love letters." "Dirty!" he says. "Sensual!" she laughs.

Considering death, he says, "When we go, we're gonna go together. . . . I know it's gonna happen. . . . Still and all, I'd do what we're doing. . . . Everything we do is together, even to this very day. After all these years, we're like glue."

Summary

The Barnetts exemplify all the characteristics of a successful long-term marriage. They have known each other since their early teens, they share similar backgrounds, values, and religious training. They felt love and respect for each other that grew over time. They made the commitment to marry and work through their problems. They communicate with tact and concern for each other's feelings. Each is willing to compromise, to put the other first. Their otherwise very happy marriage has been disrupted only by their son's terrible accident, one of the few things they regret in the lives together. Still, they managed to overcome their tragedy and today define themselves as very happy.

Vignette: The Howards

In my head I'm still thirty-three.—Mr. Howard

The Howards met when they were counselors at a summer camp. She was seventeen, and he was twenty-one. "He and I went for a walk, and the moon was shining, and we were together alone, and something clicked between us." He says, "As we were walking together and our hands touched, it felt like a spark." She thought it was just a summer romance, but he did not. After summer camp was over, she went home with a bad case of poison ivy. One day, "The doorbell rings, and here I am with a face full of poison ivy and calamine lotion all over my face. . . ." He interrupts, laughing, "She looked like the bride of Frankenstein, and she was wearing a housedress!" But the spark between them was still there.

She says, "We continued to see one another, and his mother objected strenuously. For one thing, he had no job, which wasn't unusual, it was the late 1930s. . . . She not only objected to his seeing anyone, but she also didn't feel my family was of the caliber of his, the social level. I had immigrant parents." Mr. Howard interjects, "Socioeconomically, her family was poor and everything that goes with it. My family was middle class and American educated." She continues the story: "The next summer I went away to camp, and he stayed in the city, and I wrote to him under an assumed name. . . . After a while, his parents accepted that this was going to be a permanent relationship."

When asked what qualities drew them together, Mrs. Howard explains, "I don't think we analyzed qualities. I think there was almost a chemistry between us. Religion was the same and had it not been, that would have been a real factor. Educationally, we were on a similar level. . . . You feel a compatibility more than analyzing it. . . . I would marry someone certainly as intellectually stimulating as I felt I was. . . . I had to have somebody who was physically attractive. . . . He was romantic, he was a writer, a dreamer. . . . I think it's the creativity that really attracted me to him. . . . He wrote poetry to me." She was very young, and "very inexperienced. I had one other date before."

Mr. Howard says, "I don't think we analyzed it or thought about it. You grow into a situation, especially after three and a half years." He laughs, "She's one degree ahead of me and much smarter. . . . I just knew that [she] was a wonderful person, and that we had a lot of things in common that were important, and there was that chemistry there. . . . She was, and is a very caring, giving person, almost abnormally so."

They dated three and a half years before marrying, a very important fact to Mr. Howard. "We got to know each other really well without living together." She agrees, "You didn't have premarital relations in those days, at least it was not customary." He laughs, remembering, "But her father was worried about this unemployed young guy who was wooing his daughter. We were sitting on the sofa necking on a Saturday night, and I guess it was getting late. . . . About every hour or so he would walk by us to go to the bathroom . . . just patrolling."

The Howards differ on the reason they married when they did. Mrs. Howard, who describes herself as very practical, says, "Because I finished my education and we each had a job." He interjects, "The whole idea is because we were in love and we wanted to be together all the time, and we didn't want to wait any longer."

"But," she replies, "it was also a matter of money. . . . I got a job . . . and he was doing well in his business. . . . We were married in March 1940." Mrs. Howard's father had saved $300, and offered them the money or a wedding. She told him, "I'll take the wedding, because we'll always make money." They were given $150 in wedding presents, which they used to take a honeymoon. He remembers that they rented two floors of a prominent "marriage mill" of the time and had over a hundred guests, and they had a wonderful time.

From the first, they lived on their own. Mrs. Howard says, "When we first got married, all our furniture was secondhand. It didn't bother us." But when they got a new apartment, they bought new furniture. "Our policy was, we never bought anything that we couldn't afford. We never bought on the installment plan. We had to have the money in the bank before we bought anything."

Mrs. Howard recalls, "October 1942, we had our first child. And that was a marvelous occasion." He says, in a softer voice, "I lost her as a wife at that time. I shouldn't say that. I loved [my daughter], I used to write songs to her when she was in a cradle." She says, "It's so hard to think back. . . . It's a long time! I know we were very happy with our daughter. . . . We never had any problem with her." Mr. Howard worked in the city. She says, "Five and a half days a week . . . he didn't come home till after seven o'clock. I did not work at that time. I stayed at home. . . . He suffered from migraine headaches really bad. So that I would let him sleep Sunday mornings. He worked hard." Three years later, their son was born. When the children were aged two and five, Mr. Howard wanted to write a novel, but he began his own business instead. "I lost the money there, but I lost it more slowly," he laughs. Still she did not turn against him or give him trouble over money, which he thinks is remarkable.

Mr. Howard says, "I think if you know that you're deeply in love, nothing else seems to matter. Of course it does matter the day after you're married, if you discover there are incompatibilities which didn't show themselves when you were in the throes of that deep passion. Mrs. Howard explains, "I never thought that it would be anything else but a successful marriage. . . . If there were any problems I would make sure that they would not, in any way, cause a rift between us. In other words, if there were problems, and I'd have to swallow the problems, I would swallow them, because making a marriage successful was important to me."

They experienced conflict for a couple of years during the 1960s while their son was a teenager, but that passed. Mrs. Howard still deals with one problem: "There is one thing that's bothered me a lot. He was always late! No matter how late I wanted to be, he would always be later!" He acknowledged this: "But this was a character weakness on my part, which has improved a great deal, slowly." Both laugh.

She describes conflict resolution in their marriage: "If I had enough, I would scream and let him have it. When he really lost his temper . . . it was bad." That was not very often, she says, but "I remember one incident in which he just turned the table over." He laughs, remembering the table-turning scene: "I stood up, grabbed the ends of the table, turned it over in front of everybody, dishes, everything. The expression on my kids' faces. . . . So I walked out and drove around. . . . I came back very contrite. The kids have never forgotten that. That was not typical. Nothing like that ever happened before or since."

She agrees. "Our kids were funny. If we were having an argument, they would say, 'Fight, fight!'" She laughs, "'Cause we didn't do it that often. . . . We never went to sleep angry at one another. . . . We would wait until things cooled off. . . . We would yell and scream . . . until one of us would say, 'all right, look, let's just leave it now, and talk about it when we're cooled off.' What he would sometimes do is just get into the car and go for a ride."

She describes herself as "The great compromiser. . . . I think I may hold things in, but one of these days I'll blow. Maybe that's not such a good idea, but it's worked for us. . . . Sure you're gonna have some conflicts, you're gonna have some arguments. It's silly to think you're not. What kind of relationship would that be? But they're not serious enough to create any real problem. . . . Especially when you get to this point in life, whatever conflicts you've had you've pretty much resolved."

The only other big problem was illness. Mr. Howard developed heart problems in his middle fifties. He was fifty-seven when he cut back his work to three days a week, which continued for a couple of years. When he told her he wanted to retire, "I don't know to what extent the fact that he developed a heart problem triggered early retirement. . . . I swallowed hard. He had a good income. . . . I said well, if that's what you want to do, do it. And he did. I think he was fifty-nine. . . . He stayed home, and he wrote. He wrote every single day. I continued to work, and the first time he did the supper dishes, I swallowed hard. I let him do it." She laughs, recalling that he came from a very traditional background. "He's still pretty much that kind of person. . . . He gets waited on. He always has. I haven't been able to change that. He tries to be helpful. He'll give you the cleanest kitchen you ever want to see, but the rest of the house can go to hell."

Mr. Howard had an easy time retiring: "Men when they retire have had a great deal of authority. . . . And then one day . . . they wake up in the morning, they don't have to go anywhere, there's no work to do. They were somebody, and then the next morning he wakes up, he's unemployed. . . . His wife says, 'Did you take out the garbage?' So that's a trauma for a lot of men; their power, authority is gone, and there's nothing to replace it with . . . but I always wanted to do this novel thing, and get back to my poetry and painting and so on. . . . Women are never unemployed even if they don't have a job."

Like most other long-married couples, they, too, have long-term friendships and memberships. She describes their days now: "I have more time, and yet I seem to be so involved. I wonder where the day goes. See, we're both so busy. . . . We socialize more. . . . He's not as social minded as I am. He's very content to be home. I need people, so I'll always go out and seek people. He has become a much more social being than he ever was in his earlier years."

Discussing her husband's qualities, she says, "He's very loving, and it spills over. When someone loves you, then you'll tolerate little things that might bother you. He's involved in his activities, I'm involved in my activities. . . . We get together, we have things to talk about. . . . Fortunately we have enough money to do what we want to do. Basically, we've had a pleasant life. Sure, [he] lost his job periodically. I was working at the time, so we had enough to subsist on, you know, when the woman works, it makes a difference. It gave us the extra money for things that we needed or when he didn't work, but again, the money never seemed to create problems for us."

He says his love for her has "become more tender, more appreciative of her as a person, as a witness to all the great things she does. . . . She's turned me around in a lot of ways, and I'm very aware of that . . . learning from her, being encouraged and motivated by her. I keep it alive . . . by being very romantic and affectionate. . . . She's such a perfect mate. She meets me a lot more than halfway, and has given me the kind of emotional support and stability that has enabled me to do the things that are risky. . . . She has this deep common sense, that works not only for her, but for me too."

Their sexual relationship changed over time. Both married as virgins, and she says of him, "He was very understanding, he was always very gentle. . . . It took years for me to feel really free about sex. . . . He's a very sexually active person. . . . In recent years it's gone down for both of us. We still have sex, but you know people would say that once a week at your age is great!" she laughs. "There's still the desire to just lie next to one another.

When you're younger, no matter how busy you are, you find time for sex. Here you are older, with more time on your hands supposedly, and not doing it as often." He says their sexual relationship "changes in character, and becomes in a sense more meaningful."

Of life without his wife, "Naturally you think about those things. . . . I do dread it, because I think I would do poorly. She'd make a splendid widow, because she's so resourceful, so capable, so strong . . . a high-energy person . . . not many deep negative thoughts. . . . The woman is usually the social creature. She makes all the social arrangements, and in many cases the friends are truly hers, and when the wife dies . . . a man loses all the friends he thought were mutual friends. . . . You're a fifth wheel. But even more than that, she handles the finances, not that I couldn't do it, but I have no interest in it, so as a result I do it poorly. . . . And I would miss her terribly. I don't feel that I have quite the emotional resources she has to rise above it." He thinks people have a "need for companionship, even if you're not crazy about your companion, and as you get older you have fewer options, the only person who would be interested in you is another eighty-year old woman!"

Of life without him she says, "Sure, you can't help thinking about that. It would be difficult, but I would go on. See, I'm that kind of person. I wouldn't collapse. It would be very lonesome, but I would be capable of continuing. . . . A lot depends on the age at which certain things happen. See, if you're older you might not want the responsibility of a house any more. . . . I do all the money handling. . . . He took an allowance, whatever he needed, even now. . . . He says, 'Do I have any money in my wallet?' I said, 'If something happens to me, you're gonna be the reverse of the traditional situation.'"

She does not want to live with her children. "Never. . . . .I could if I wanted to, but I wouldn't want to. But you don't know what's gonna happen. . . . I would take care of him, no matter what. I just hope that whenever the time comes for either one of us, that it can happen quickly. . . . We have very loving children, which is a real asset."

Summary

The Howards, very happily married, cite all the keys to successful marriage: compatibility, love, respect, commitment, communication, compromise, and sacrifice. They have had few problems over the years, other than his annoying habit of being late, and those associated with raising their son during the '60s. Like many women who married in the 1940s, Mrs. Howard went back to work after the children were older. Unlike most women of her day, she had a professional career.

Mr. Howard retired early, partly because of health and partly because he had other interests he wished to pursue. Both remain active in the community, with long-time friendships and group memberships. Like most of the interviewed couples, right now their main concern is staying healthy. Overall, they are enjoying their golden years.

Chapter Eight

The Golden Years

I'd rather have my wife than ten Esther Williams!
—Mr. RA

Introduction

The later years of marriage bring new joys and challenges. Twenty-four percent of the survey couples chose "now" as the "happiest years" of the marriage. Only 6 percent said that "now" is the least happy time. This chapter, focused on interviewed couples, examines (1) marriage after retirement, (2) activities and friendships now, (3) relationships with adult children, (4) how the love and sexual relationships changed over time, and (5) the best and worst of their lives now. How the aging process affects these couples and their lives together is also highlighted. From the perspective of continuity theory, middle-aged and older adults have relatively stable ideas about themselves and the world, based on a lifetime of experience. Continuity theory predicts that people will attempt to maintain familiar friends, surroundings, interests, and activities throughout their lives.

Marriage after Retirement

At seventy-five, how can you make yourself important again?—Mr. NG

I highly recommend retirement. Live long enough to retire. It's the best way of life.—Mrs. SE

Retirement is a major adjustment for both husband and wife. When only one spouse has been working, there has been a territorial separation that disappears with retirement. Spouses who have been home alone have to adapt to the loss of some privacy, space, and freedom of movement. Spouses who worked outside the home have to adjust to the loss of a central, productive role. They usually have more free time, but they lack camaraderie and friendship with coworkers. If they were supervisors or managers, they may also have lost the power and prestige associated with their work roles. When the people in this study decided they wanted to retire, they adjusted more quickly. When they were forced to retire because of problems on the job, illness, or other people's plans, they had more problems adjusting. Several husbands mentioned a decline in job satisfaction and a "push" to retire when their work friends retired before them.

> Mr. NG says, "When I worked . . . I felt as though I was very important. . . . All of a sudden after twenty-eight years of working in the city, you're standing here, everyday, seven days a week, which is not good for both parties." So he went back to work for twelve more years. The last two months he has been ill and unable to work, so they've lost income. "She worries a little, but I think I worry about it more . . . because I was the provider with all the extra money. Now I'm not doing it anymore."
> Mrs. NG has had her own difficulties with his retirement. "When he first retired at sixty-two, I thought we'd kill each other. Anybody our age will tell you that. 'Get him out of the house!' The woman our age runs the house. And then the man's gonna come in there and tell you how to run it? . . . His whole life was Manhattan. The man becomes like a child, totally reliant on a woman. . . . After a couple of months he started taking all these little silly jobs," which seemed to help the situation.

> Mr. EG: "I was depressed for a month or so when I hit sixty. . . . I hadn't retired yet, but you could see it coming. . . . Friends that were older than me were already retired, and you began to lose these people. . . . I looked forward to retirement. I couldn't wait to get to sixty-five."

> Mrs. MT, a retired clinical social worker, says, "Mostly, I'm relieved. Seventy-three years old, that's enough already, . . . but I miss it too."

> Mr. CA is typical of many husbands interviewed: "I don't have a job now. I wish I had a job. I really do. Yeah, I would continue going to work. . . . I retired at seventy. But the reason I retired was so many . . . friends . . . retired, and the new group coming in, I didn't have any real rapport with them. And the job was no longer fun. . . . I'm 75 now, . . . and I guess I've been thinking about going back to work, doing something anyway."

Ten interviewed husbands and five wives missed the income, the work experience, and the sense of contribution, so they went back to work. Three husbands have never retired.

> Mrs. WT: "I'm not going to be employable very shortly, 'cause nobody

wants anybody my age. . . . Maybe I can fool them and they think I'm sixty, but they don't even want anybody that age anymore."

> Mr. WE, at age eighty-one, works as a security guard three days a week. "What would I do? Sit home . . . in front of the television? . . . It was getting monotonous for me to stay home and sit around . . . and you get lazy, you get old. . . . I saw the ad, I took a test, I got the job."

Some spouses adapted quickly to the slower pace of life, especially those who had blue-collar jobs, jobs they didn't enjoy, or jobs that were physically exhausting.

> Mr. PG: "I was worried about what I was gonna do. But I found out I didn't have to worry. I have been a lazy bum my whole life. . . . It's good if you have a hobby," he says. "It gets us away from each other."

> Mr. CN sees retirement as a great relief. Remembering his work life, he says, "It was a matter of going to work, come home, sleep, go to work, sleep. . . . It was just like, getting up ten after five, coming home at five minutes till four, dinner on the table right away." He concludes, "Most of my life I guess was working."

> Mr. EL: "We have to pinch ourselves to make sure we're not in heaven. . . . The availability of the time, relatively good health. . . . It's like a permanent vacation. I sometimes wonder how I ever found time to work. I love this life, just doing what you want to do, when you want to do it, and having money . . . . We're able to do so much together now." She attributes their situation to his good planning. "He thinks ahead. We have it very nice now."

The happier the marriage is overall, the less likely it is that partners are reported to be "in each other's way" after retirement. Among the surveyed couples, 60 percent said they rarely or never get in each other's way since retiring, and 33 percent reported occasionally being in each other's way.

> Nowadays, the YEs have some conflicts over personal space and time. He goes almost everywhere with her, which has limited her mobility and makes her nervous. She was a registered nurse and continues to volunteer at the hospital where she worked for over thirty years: "[He] doesn't care for that part. He just thinks it's terrible that I want that independence, but I just feel that I need it. . . . I enjoy it, but I also use it as a getting away."

> Mrs. ER sums up retirement: "There's a little too much togetherness."

Some couples wanted to spend every minute together, and there was no such thing as too much togetherness.

> The FTs spend their time "always together, everything, everything. . . . We don't go anyplace without each other." He explains, "We never had separate friends. We're together all the time. We stay by ourselves."

She agrees: "Outside we have friends, like in clubs, but it's not like we invite couples over and get involved. We don't get too close with other couples."

There are also a few spouses who are very independent of each other, and throughout their lives have had separate activities and interests. After retirement, their lives are no different in this respect.

Mrs. WT says, "There's not too much togetherness. . . . You can have a life together, but you have to have your own life."

Mrs. WE: "I enjoy reading and my husband doesn't at all. . . . I play golf and he doesn't. I'm a very outgoing social person, he's not. . . . He does his own thing, and I do mine."

The HEs golf, go out with friends, go to shows and concerts, go to New York City, and belong to various clubs. Mr. HE sees, in retirement, "no change in the relationship basically. I'm still just as busy now. . . . If I were to sit home here all day long I would be out of my cotton-picking mind. Sometimes [when] I come home at 9:30 at night, I'm not sure she missed me, even. But that's good, because that could be entirely different. . . . I guess there's an independence built into her, which is what I'm gratified about. . . . She is self-satisfying and she's self-entertaining, and she doesn't need me to be singing and dancing in front of her six hours a day. She's her own person. . . . When we get finished with whatever we're doing, we'll be here for a couple of hours every night, . . . reporting on what it is we've been through during the day or what has happened. Sitting in those two chairs talking. . . . It can't be healthy to be always involved together in everything you do. I want to do my own thing. And that's what I do, and that's what she does."

Forty-three percent of spouses said their marriage is better since retirement, and 53 percent said the marriage is about the same (for better or worse). The same factors that contribute to a happy marriage before retirement continue to be important. For the less happily married couples, the same problems that made the marriage unhappy before retirement persist into the later years. The STs are less happily married, with a number of unresolved conflicts, which have not improved since retirement.

Mrs. ST: "It's like a seesaw, some days I hate him, some days I could kill him, like two animals living in a cage. I think I'm a lost soul someplace. I'm in limbo."

Activities and Friendships in the Later Years

Activities and Organizations

We got a million things going in a lot of other places.—Mr. HE

It's become a lot quieter.—Mrs. SK

The majority of couples have successfully adapted to retirement by reorganizing their lives, finding new activities to replace those they lost, making new friends, and continuing to enjoy their lives together. Both spouses in ten interviewed couples said they keep their lives as busy as ever.

> Mr. HE: "She has always been a bookkeeper. . . . She does it for many of the organizations. . . . I just want you to have the understanding of how involved we are. . . . I'm up to my eyeballs in activity. . . . I've done very well in what I've received in this life, and much of what I do now is paying back a little bit of what I've been given."

For the rest of the spouses, life has slowed down. They reported a range of pleasurable pursuits, and said they are taking life at a more leisurely pace.

> Mrs. LA says, "Golf is our family sport. . . . He plays with me all the time."

> Mrs. AL says, "Sitting down on the couch and holding each other's hands and knowing we're together. That's what we want. We don't really have to go out. . . . People don't stimulate him. . . . He's very sociable once he gets started, but he doesn't go look for it, because he'd rather sit and read."
> Mr. AL agrees: "I find the company of books generally to be more fascinating than people. 'Cause there you can learn the best that's been thought and said. Whereas with other people, you socialize, but not necessarily with the best that's been thought and said, you follow me?"

> Mrs. CN says, "I read my Bible, he reads his *New York Times*."

Six couples seldom leave the house because of illness and disability. Spouses with no hobbies or few friends have more difficulty filling their time and often say they have nothing to look forward to.

> Mr. PA sums it up: "You feel sort of useless."

Other Enduring Relationships

> *She's been my friend since we were two years old.*
> —Mrs. NA

Another way of maintaining continuity in one's life is to keep the same friends, belong to the same organizations, and continue to live in the same home over a lifetime. Almost all of these long-married spouses have other long-term relationships and activities in their lives, which shed light on overall patterns of enduring behavior. Forty-eight of the sixty interviewed couples (80 percent) still have friends they have known for over thirty years. Over half of interview couples have had friends for over fifty years. In some cases, spouses had friends from childhood.

> Mr. CI: "When we make a friend, we stay with that. We don't drop [friends] .... Nobody ever dropped us yet."

Only four interviewed spouses said they do not have any close friends, new or old. The rest of the spouses have long-term friends, but some no longer see them because they have become too ill or moved away. Other friends have died.

> Mr. MA, at eighty, explains, "Close friends where we get together? No, those days are gone.... When you get old, our age, nobody wants to know you .... We're all on our own, more or less."

> Mrs. ER: "You don't realize that's going to happen. We used to be going out all the time with this one and that one, and all of a sudden, there's nobody."

> Mrs. NN: "We're going through a hard time, with people dying and getting permanently ill, so to speak."

Twenty-nine interviewed couples have participated in some group or organization for over twenty years, most often church- or synagogue-related, work-related, and community volunteer activities. Thirteen couples said they were not "joiners" at any time in their lives. A few spouses lost interest over time in longtime activities.

> Mr. HE explains, "Over the years we've belonged to so many organizations .... It really has gotten to a point where we're both a little bit bored with it now.... Before, when we were striving to move ahead ... we'd be at all of those things, but there's a reluctance now to get involved with them.... We'd just as soon stay home now and watch TV and read a book, or do something like that.... So we are less social." She laughs, "We're aging out or something."

> Mr. KR, married in 1933, says, "There's more to life than playing golf and gin. I think you have to keep on paying your dues. I was in the Scouts, and I'm still in, coming up on seventy years of service. I've been singing in the church choir seventy-seven years now this May.... I want to help, and I think I can make some small contribution."

Where to live, whether to move or stay put, is a dilemma for many of these couples. Seventeen of the sixty interview couples had lived in their current homes over thirty years, and five other couples had lived in their family homes over forty years. Three of the couples had moved frequently throughout their married lives because of the husbands' work, and their current homes were their retirement homes. When couples have relocated, it has usually been to smaller homes, easier maintenance situations, often senior retirement communities.

> The MTs sold their home ten years ago and moved into a condominium community. Mrs. MT says, "We don't have to worry about the roof leaking or getting the snow shoveled. . . . I miss the yard though. . . . Otherwise, it's much more comfortable for this stage of our lives."

Several spouses who have remained in their homes are considering moving, but the idea of cleaning out a house stuffed with thirty or more years of family belongings is daunting. Now that they are less able to care for their house and yard, they are also physically less able to handle a major move.

> The KRs are moving to a retirement community from their home, which her father built. They both have health problems, and it is difficult doing all the upkeep. Nevertheless, "I'm very ambivalent," says Mr. KR, "It's really no time to be making a move when I'm coming up on eighty-seven and she will be eighty-six this year."

> The EEs bought their current home in 1950, when the development was built. He did all the gardening and lawn care until last year, but says it's now "too time consuming and tiring. . . . You can't do the things you did when you were younger." So now a gardener does the yard, but "I still get up on the roof and clean out the leaves from the gutters." He is seventy-five.

Relocating after retirement could be tricky. A few couples moved to North Carolina or Florida, but were unhappy and returned to New York. Despite the advantages of condominium and age-segregated developments, nearly all the couples who live in senior housing say there is too much talk of sickness and death, and they miss the intergenerational component of regular communities.

> Mrs. WE: "Living in an environment like this, everybody's husband is dying. That's one of the things I don't like about it. . . . I'm surrounded by illness."

> The LSs' relocation to the South after retiring seriously divided the couple. She says, "I was not happy . . . and I made it known wherever I went. . . . It was very close to a split. I wasn't staying there one minute longer. . . . It was really backwater. . . . I didn't like the lifestyle. . . . It was drink and card games." They had planned to have their children visit them frequently. "We built a three-bedroom house, two baths, big house. We were always gonna have company. It wasn't like that. Their lives are so busy, they weren't coming down to us. Whenever anything went on in the family we just came up and visited. That was a big difference, . . . and then the real killer for me

was when he got sick. Most of the time I sat in the waiting room all by myself, and I figured this is never gonna happen to me again. I'm going back where I know people who'll be around when I need them." They moved back to Long Island. Although Mr. LS had loved his new life in the South, he says, "I think she was right. I'll say it now."

Mrs. LS had unfulfilled expectations. She did not like the lifestyle, and she communicated her feelings. The final stressor was his illness, and in this case, he did what his spouse wanted, because it was more important to her. They moved back to their network of social support, and both are satisfied with the decision.

Couples and Their Adult Children

> *You never finish with kids.*—Mr. EE

> *You bring them up, you educate them, you enjoy them, you take them all over, and then it's all over. They're gone.*—Mr. NA

Thirty-six of the interview couples (60 percent) have at least one child living close by (within two hours' drive) whom they see regularly. Several of them have more than one child on Long Island. Two of the interviewed couples have an adult child (both are sons) living with them. Twenty-four couples (40 percent) have daily contact with at least one of their children, including visiting and several telephone calls during the day. They celebrate family get-togethers on major holidays, either at their own homes or at the homes of the children. During the interviews, wives spent much more time discussing their children than did husbands.

> Mrs. CI says, "How could you live so far apart? How could you get together for the holidays? How could you have a birthday? . . . I've been blessed. My children are still around. They'd like to get out of New York because taxes are so high, but they say, 'We're not gonna leave mother.' "

> Mrs. WT says, "We see our children and our grandchildren, but life can't revolve around them because they have their own lives. . . . I go visit the kids, I can stay three or four hours, and I've had it. It's noisy. . . . There's too many dos and don'ts in the house . . . but I don't have to stay too long."

The most involved parents, those who interact regularly with children, providing financial and other forms of assistance, feel that their children will always be their responsibility. They have not given up caring for, helping, and loving their children, no matter what their ages. Just as their children are often described as the rewards of their long marriage, the children are also sometimes described as their greatest trouble or concern in the later years.

Mr. GR says, "We helped our kids out so that we have no more money."

The TMs have worried about one daughter ever since she was born: "They [our daughter and son-in-law] don't have a dime in the bank. . . . That showed up when they were little. She never had a nickel in her pocket." He says, "She doesn't have any more credit cards. We took them away from her." They have bailed her out financially several times over the last fifteen years.

Mr. EE: "There's an old saying: 'Small children, small trouble, big children, big trouble.'"

Mrs. KR: "He's always said if the kids need our help and we can help them, we'll do it."
    But Mr. KR warns, "If you get in the boat with me, I'll row with you, but I'm not rowing this boat alone. And they all subscribe to that. . . . I keep saying we're a product of our peculiar times. There was a bonding because nobody had anything, everybody had to stay alive, people had to work to-gether. . . . When you're in trouble, the best is generated."

In a few cases, the adult children provide help to the parents or work with the parents, and there are conflicts.

The ICs are somewhat dependent on their daughter, who lives nearby, be-cause Mr. IC is confined to a wheelchair and Mrs. IC does not drive. "*I'm* the child now, *she's* the mother."

Mr. FL says, of his relationship with his oldest son, "I love him very much, he's a great guy, he isn't a businessman. He and I are constantly on the warpath with each other because we're partners, and he is not a business man. He thinks he is and he's not. I won't entrust him with [the business], because he doesn't know the value of a dollar. . . . He knows nothing about business."

While many of the couples define parenting as a lifelong responsibility, many others "breathed a sigh of relief" when their children were grown up because, finally, they were no longer responsible for the children. Ten of sixty couples have much less contact with their children now because of geographic distance, and perhaps also because of less intimate relationships. Five of those ten couples scarcely mentioned their children.
    Family reunions played an important role in most spouses' lives when

they were young, but the tradition is fading away with increasing geographic mobility. People cannot afford the time or cost of frequent family get-togethers. One of the more significant differences between generations is the current lack of relationships with cousins, aunts, and uncles—the extended family. Many long-married spouses described themselves as a "dying breed."

> The FTs remember extended family gatherings when everyone lived close by, but now, "Everyone has their own families. . . . They go their own way. It's hard to bring them together now."

> Mrs. PA: "No, we don't have regular family reunions, no. . . . Just to get our kids together is a big trick." He continues with this train of thought: "Each one has his own interests, and they have their own family and they have to accommodate their children. . . . They start to get frantic if you even suggest something like that. 'I don't have the room, I don't have this, I don't have.' Oh, it's terrible. But as the children get older and are more involved in their own lives, it becomes more and more difficult. The last immediate family reunion we had was for our fiftieth wedding anniversary. Our children said, "What would you really like as a present?' and I said, 'To have our family together is what I'd really like.' . . . It's a lot of people. But the kids all came and we had a weekend together as a family. But, you know, it's very hard to do that."

How Love Changed Over Time

> *It's a different kind of love. It's a love of years and*
> *years and years.*—Mr. MA

Most interviewed couples said that over time their love changed, usually for the better. Sharing all their life experiences deepened and enriched their love. Many said that successfully overcoming hardship strengthened their relationship too. For many, raising a family changed their love from a couple-centered love to a family-centered love.

> Mrs. NA: "When I look back at us getting married, I thought we must have been nuts. . . . He was going into service. . . . I must have really loved him, even though love at that point isn't like it is as you grow through it. . . . Suddenly you realize what this person means to you. . . . If something happened, how would you face life without the other person?"

> Mr. AL says, "The feeling became deeper . . . because we went through a great deal of experiences together. . . . The bond has gotten stronger over the years, by having mutual experiences that you can recall."

Mrs. CA loves her husband more now, because, "When you're bringing up children, your interest was with the children . . . but now that we're alone you find that you depend on each other more."

Mr. CA experienced a similar change. "Not that I loved her less then, but I was so busy trying to make a living."

Mr. MA: "I appreciate her more than before. Before, you take her for granted. . . . Now, it's different in these twilight years. This is it for her and this is it for me. It's a different kind of love. It's a love of years, and years and years."

Mrs. NN: "In different times I have loved him in different ways."

Most couples said they grew together over time. Even very independent spouses developed a relationship of sharing and interdependence that altered the initial love of earlier years. Less happily married couples knew each other better and were interdependent in many ways after fifty or more years together, even if they did not love or like each other any better.

Mr. PA doesn't know whether he has felt love: "At times, yes, I've experienced it, but it was so elusive, and it's something you can't put your hands on and hold. . . . I think the only thing that keeps us going is a sense of humor, being able to laugh at yourself."

How Sexual Activity and Interest Changed Over Time

You can tell them it doesn't end at seventy!—Mrs. ER

It's gone and forgotten!—Mr. ME, age eighty-nine

Sixty-four percent of surveyed spouses reported a lessening in sexual interest over time, most often in the later years. Forty percent of interviewed couples are celibate. For the vast majority, sexual interest did not resume later: four out of five who lost sexual interest did not regain it. Even though the majority of spouses report a decline in sexual activity, there is no statistically significant relationship between current levels of sexual interest and activity, and marital happiness. Permanent declines in sexual activity during the early and middle years of marriage, however, are associated with lower levels of marital happiness and intimacy.

Almost all interviewed couples said their sexual activity fluctuated over time. Changes in sexual activity were reported at two different stages of the family life cycle: after the first few years of marriage, and in later years. Spouses remember how exciting and passionate sex had been in the early years, and how after a few years, the meaning and importance of sex changed, and other concerns and interests emerged—child rearing.

> Mrs. ER explains, "Well, when you're first married, it's you know, very, phew, steamy," she laughs, "but then it settles down, but we still love each other."

> Mrs. LA: "When you're new in your marriage and sex is a real big deal, and it's all so new. . . . Suddenly you're becoming sexually experienced, . . . but when that simmers down, the passion of the sex act itself is so beautiful and it's so meaningful and so it mellows. The whole sex act mellows beyond just the mere business of passion."

> Mrs. HE: "I think the intensity is less. . . . I don't see how it could not change in fifty years. . . . The excitement of the first years and the sexual part of that: . . . it's nice, but . . . it's not the important thing that carries you through all these years."

> Mrs. PA: "It changes because in the beginning it's very passionate, it's a hot love affair. You know you're very into the physical end of it. . . . And little by little it encompasses so much more. You start growing together, you start building things together, you have a family together, and so the kind of love changes. It has to change. . . . It can't stay the same. . . . You're no longer hep on swinging from the chandelier, but . . . there are other things that take over for it."

The more happily married and healthy spouses usually increased their sexual activity again after the children left home. Several spouses reported a renewed interest in and enjoyment of sexual activity when women reached menopause, and this continued into the later years.

> Mrs. CN: "I think after the menopause it was great, because then you don't have to worry about babies anymore." She is Catholic, and they never agreed on birth control.
> Her husband says, "We had one rhythm boy, second rhythm boy, third rhythm boy. . . ."

> Mr. ER laughs, remembering their youth, "We would look at our parents and we'd say 'They can't be doing it.' You know, with that gray hair, how can they possibly?' It's different when you get there."

When sex declines in later years, it seldom has anything to do with a problem in the relationship. Late life declines in sexuality are usually related to aging, health, and medication problems of one or both spouses.

> Mr. WD: "Let me tell you something here. What I did when I was twenty-five, thirty-five, or forty-five, at seventy you don't do it as often. . . . See, I

kid my sister-in-law, sex is always on her mind. . . . I say to her husband, 'Your sister, every week, five times a week.' She sits there, 'You hear this, you hear this!' And on the way home my wife says, 'Why do you say that to her? You know it kills her!' We laugh."

Mr. RG: "My sexual interest isn't as often, but it's just as good."

Differing sexual attitudes and practices did not cause many problems for these couples. Seventy-three percent of surveyed spouses said they always or usually agree on sexual activity, and only 10 percent said that sexual relations had created marital problems over the years.

> The TTs have somewhat differing views on their sex life together. She says, "It's not as frequent, but we're still sexual."
> Mr. TT says, "When we were first a very young couple, I guess . . . can't have enough sex. As the few years went by, . . . we decided it had to be mutual, otherwise forget it. . . . Now me, I would still go three or five times a week, but I can't. My wife would say, 'What are you crazy? You'll be worn out! You can't walk anymore!' . . . So you have to treat her gently. . . . We'll see, if it works, fine, if it doesn't work, we go to lunch. And that's the way it should be. It's gotta be mutual. That's the whole crux of everything."

When sex is no longer possible, the other positive factors continue, and perhaps, increase in importance. At least one-third of the couples had been celibate for several years due to illness and/or medications. The health conditions most often mentioned were prostate problems, vascular disorders, diabetes, and hysterectomies. Husbands more frequently expressed a sense of loss over declining sexual activity than did wives.

> Mr. YE had several prostate surgeries, and his wife says, "He has no drive at all physically, . . . and he is beside himself! But it doesn't bother me at all. . . . For him, it's been a terrible adjustment, because he was a very active man."

> Mr. WE says, "You can't do the things you used to do. . . . It's very difficult."

> Mr. TA is experiencing what he calls "an ebb in desire. . . . It's quite frustrating, because we had a very lively sex life."

> Mrs. EC: "Probably from the seventies on you kinda wean off of it. Some people do have sex . . . but at this age [she's eighty-four] forget it!" She laughs.

> Mrs. LE: "Well, because of his sickness . . . forget it." She laughs. "It doesn't bother me though. . . . I mean, what can the poor man do? . . . It's a shame you know, because he feels sorry for me, and I feel sorry for him, but what

can you do? That's life. There's nothin' you can do about it. I'd rather have him here with me than, God forbid, a heart attack."

Mrs. GE: "Well, after it peaked, it started to decline, and then, I guess, after my mastectomy it sort of wound up. . . . I don't know whether it's right or not, but I just didn't think I should expect him to be as loving, sexually loving, as he would have been. . . . Well, I don't know whether he's even able to at this point," she adds with a soft laugh.
    Mr. GE: "We don't have sex today, but . . . it doesn't materially change anything. I love my wife as much now as [when] we were sexually active. So sex doesn't play an important part. . . . Listen, we touch each other in other ways."

Most spouses thought declining sexual interest and activity, and the health problems that frequently caused it, were the inevitable results of aging, so they accommodated to the changes. Only two interviewed wives expressed sadness and concern over the lack of sexual activity in their marriages. Almost all of them said that, over time, the love and caring they felt for one another became more important than the physical act of sex. Most spouses said they remained intimate, expressing affection in a variety of ways.

The MRs are celibate because of health problems. "I think the longer you're married, and you're together and you're a family. . . . Love grows more, and sex sort of tapers. . . . It's not the same as when you were getting married or having children or doing things like that. . . . You get more involved with each other, but not on a sexual [level], like talking together. . . . Sex is sort of in the background." Mr. MR says, "Until we both got sick here it was reasonably [often], but since we've both been sick, it's been pretty inactive."

Mrs. MI: "We still have a very strong physical attraction to each other, which I guess will go right on until we're unconscious. . . . There's lots of other things you can do to amuse yourself besides have intercourse."

Looking Back at a Lifetime Together

The Rewards

I've known him all my life, practically.—Mrs. ME

This generation of spouses seldom lived on their own, alone, before they married. Most of them moved from their parents' homes (either before or after marriage) into their own homes. Married for at least half a century, they have spent almost all of their adult lives together. The MEs have known each other since 1928, the RAs and HAs since 1926—almost seventy years of togetherness. This length of relationship is unique, in part, because life expectancy has increased significantly. While most of these couples' parents were married for life, not that many lived long enough to be married for fifty or more years.

> Mrs. CA: "You can't imagine ever being separated. . . . You can't think that he lived with his parents, I lived with mine. You never associate that."

> Mrs. MT, who met her husband when she was fourteen, says, "Words we don't even have to say. . . . We exchange a look. . . . It isn't only the fifty-two years that we've been married, but all those years before. We have a whole life, really."

Most spouses described their relationships as improving over time. What seems most important to them now is the fullness of their lives. The happily married spouses said their relationships have blossomed, and they have grown in maturity and intimacy over time. They also mentioned good luck.

> Mrs. PA: "I think we did remarkably well. For two people who were married so young and no money, and neither one of us with a college degree. . . . We put three kids through college. . . . That's a very big accomplishment. We've paid off the house. It's a tiny house, but it's ours! And so we did very well."

> Mr. WT says, "As you grow older and you dispense with your responsibilities, the load gets lighter. We don't worry about the children any more. . . . The last ten to fifteen years have been the best years of our marriage, because . . . all the problems disappeared along the way. . . . We're enjoying life together now."

> Mrs. SK says that, currently, the most rewarding aspect of their lives is "that we have each other, because when you get to be as old as we are, most of your relatives are gone, your parents are certainly gone and anyone close to you . . . and we still have each other, which is fairly remarkable. . . . See, when we were your age, we couldn't anticipate being as old as we are now . . . couldn't imagine it!"

> Mrs. WE does not want to label one phase of her life as "the best," and she does not like to compare times of life. "Comparisons can be very destructive. . . . Every time of my life has been very rewarding in and of itself. . . . When my first son went away to college, I was devastated. . . . I was determined that I was not gonna be nostalgic or live in the past. . . . Every phase of my life has brought . . . a lot of different experiences." When they moved three years ago into a condominium, she says, "We threw out every bit of furniture we had, and we decided to start new. It was like an adventure! And that's been my

conscious decision and conscious attitude. . . . This is a wonderful time in our lives! We do what we want, we go where we want. We can do anything we want!"

More freedom after retirement was a major theme. Now these couples are able to do things for which they never had time or money when they were raising the children, working, or caring for their aging parents. As long as they remain relatively healthy, they can continue to enjoy these benefits.

At this point, Mrs. PA finds it most rewarding "that he and I can kind of pick up and do things just for us, without feeling the obligation, the *strong* obligation with the children. . . . There's just the two of you and you can just pick up and go."

One of the best aspects of these later years for several couples is less concern over money. Sixteen of the interviewed couples (27 percent) specifically mentioned that they are doing well, financially, in retirement. They are no longer struggling, and, instead, they have discretionary income to spend.

Mrs. MA says, "We're not supposed to save, we're supposed to spend."

Mr. HE: "I think the final years are made easier by the fact that there's money. I don't think that we would be in trouble without it, but it sure is a heck of a lot better this way. . . . When you can go where you want to go, or travel where you want to, or go out when you want to, it makes all this living together worthwhile. I think if we didn't have money. . .we'd probably argue about more things than we do now."

Mrs. NN: "Life is very good now, because we have the money to do things. I have a pension, he has a pension, so between us we're doing fine. . . .We're that group that young people resent."

Mr. DR sums it up: "I don't worry about spending a couple of bucks."

Troubles in the Later Years

> *I think laughter has a lot to do with staying upright.*—Mrs. SE

> *Many of our friends have already gone.*—Mr. HE

Finances, illness, and declining abilities are the problems most commonly faced by the interviewed couples. In contrast to many of the white-collar, corporate employees who had good salaries and pensions, many of the blue-collar workers never made much money when they were working, and after retirement they do not have pensions. They rely on savings and Social Security, and some have returned to work for additional income. Twenty-three percent of the interviewed couples expressed concern over their finances. Some see how the choices they made when they were younger led to less economically secure retirements than they might have had otherwise.

> Mrs. YE: "Neither one of us retired at the right time. . . . It's funny, throughout our lives we lived and spent. . . . We're sort of paying for it in our retirement. We didn't have a tremendous amount of savings, and we didn't have booming retirements and Social Security. . . . My husband . . . got a very good pension from the Navy . . . but we find that we should have thought about it a little bit more ten years before."

> When asked what was most troublesome at this point, both Mr. and Mrs. AE said "money." He was laid off after twenty-nine years, one year short of retirement, because the company abolished his department. All the children were still at home. He tells the story: "We had just bought the sailboat. . . . We cruised around all summer, and I was thinking, thinking. . . . I started to get my professional engineer's license, twenty-nine years out of school. . . . I went to work . . . at about one-third of the salary I had been paid. . . . We took all the money we could get out of the pension plan and spent it to keep our standard of living, rather than go ape. . . . You can't sit down and cry. You got yourself into it. Now get yourself out of it."
> She adds, "When we announced it to the kids, it was very calm, and . . . within the week all four had part-time jobs. We didn't ask them." Having spent their pension already, they are experiencing some financial constraints now.

> Mrs. NG says, "Our greatest fault is we did not plan for a retirement. . . . There's no plan going on in our life. . . . [He] would say, 'Let's see what happens.' . . . Nothing happens!"

One or both spouses in the majority of interviewed couples has at least one chronic health problem, not uncommon for their age (Atchley 1996). A few have had to give up favorite activities or friendships because of health constraints. Driving is frequently mentioned as a problem, mostly because of illness and changes in visual ability. Many of the couples said they no longer drive at night, because of vision problems, which are common among older adults (ibid.). Two of the wives interviewed have never learned to drive, so their freedom of movement is somewhat limited.

> Mrs. RG: "Seventy-four years old, do you think I'm gonna go learn to drive now?" "Luckily," he says, "we can walk to anything." She has also learned all the bus routes and commuter trains.

Mrs. AL: "I wonder what having fun really has to do with old age? . . . Last year, he had fainting spells and wasn't supposed to drive. I went through agony. We had the camper at the time with five shifts, and I was afraid to drive." Mrs. AL would like to go camping again, but says, "I think now we're too old. We can't do it alone. It's too dangerous."

Some spouses are experiencing life-threatening illnesses, causing additional uncertainty and fear. In these cases, there are more caregiving responsibilities, increased financial burdens, and the threat of death.

Mr. MA: "I went through the quadruple bypass, I went through a prostate operation, I went through a double hernia operation. I went through a cancer operation. And here I'm sitting to talk to you. God bless her! She takes care of me. I piss and moan and holler. She's always there. . . . I was tired of medication that I'm supposed to be on forever. . . . I got all my medication[s], I threw them down the toilet bowl. She was hollering and screaming. Flushed them. I'm gonna be eighty years old! I don't want to live to be 100! I want to enjoy my life now. . . . I drink my three beers a day, and at four o'clock I have my Absolut with orange juice. . . . It's the way I want to live!"

Mrs. MA is philosophical: "You're not put on this earth forever, nobody is. . . . That's why I enjoy everything. . . . If I died tomorrow, my husband would die right after me. . . . If he died first, it would kill me. I tell him, 'I need you, please, you gotta stay well.' . . . As strong as I am, he's my pillar."

Mrs. FL: "I truly feel that I'm here to take care of him, and even though everyone says you're your own person, you're really not. I'm really more dedicated to him than to myself. If I don't feel well, I don't tell him, because he will panic."

Mr. WE's health is troublesome, and his wife's sister recently died, reminding both WEs of their own mortality. Mrs. WE: "Our family is kinda getting down there. . . . We both had some major health problems. . . . As you get older, your options decrease. When you're younger, you always have another mountain that you can climb. As you get older, you find that there are less and less mountains you have the energy to climb and less opportunities for you to do it. I'm not saying that in any sadness. I'm just saying that as a fact. You learn to be happy and satisfied with what you have."

Mrs. HE: "We're both still very busy, . . . but we do know that we get tired easily, and we don't have too much patience. . . . We don't care to drive at night. . . . Some people are much worse off than we are. But you know that you're on the down side here." Her mother is ninety-four and her mother's sister is ninety-eight. "So I guess I could look forward to a fairly long life. . . . We take a few pills here and there, not a lot, to keep things under control. But it's happening. And we lose a friend here and a friend there, and a relative here. It gets a little bit depressing, sometimes, that facet of it."

Summary

Most interviewed couples have enjoyed the years after retirement, especially if they are healthy and have more disposable income. A few spouses are much less happy—wives who are overwhelmed by the husband's constant presence, husbands who do not know what to do with themselves after retiring, and the couples who have been less happily married throughout their lives. Some of the spouses have returned to work, mostly part-time, either because they enjoy the activity or need the money. They continue to enjoy the same long-time friends and leisure pursuits, as long as they are physically able, and many continue living in their family homes. Most spouses acknowledge that "nothing stays the same forever," but they struggle to maintain the familiar as long as possible.

> Mr. NN: "I find that, basically, I'm doing the same things I used to do for years. I'm just doing [them] a little slower."

Contrary to popular stereotypes, these couples are not isolated from their children and grandchildren. For all but ten of the interviewed couples, relationships with at least one or more of their children remain close and active. For most spouses, love and respect have grown and developed over time. They speak of the enriching experiences they have shared, the challenges they have overcome together, and the respect and intimacy that developed as they raised children. They, literally, created a lifetime together.

By the later years, approximately 40 percent of the interviewed couples are celibate. Most celibacy is related to health problems, beyond the spouses' control. Good communication, a sense of humor, trust, and respect eased the transition. Celibacy is not significantly related to marital happiness, unless celibacy began in the early to middle years.

The greatest rewards of a lifelong marriage are still being together and having their children and grandchildren. Unhappily married couples, of course, are more likely to say their children and grandchildren are the reward, and not the marriage itself. Nevertheless, whether the couples are happily or unhappily married, their lifetime marriage is central to lifetime continuity.

> Mrs. TI: "It's worth it in the long run if you can see it through, because when you finally do all your growing and everything, and you can look at each other. It's so precious now. . . . We sort of created each other."

Most troublesome right now are health problems. Coping with and adapting to the fear, uncertainty, limitations, and costs of illness create major concerns in interviewed couples' lives. Most studies suggest that married people live longer (Atchley 1996). The couple can act as mutual caregivers as long as they are together, so that husbands, typically, will remain in the home as long as possible, cared for by their wives. Of course, when the husband dies, the mutual caregiving ends, and the wife is left without support and day-to-day assistance. Several wives in this study, well aware of this eventuality, express concern.

Vignette: The Johnsons

We just sorta went along and managed.
—Mrs. Johnson

The Johnsons live in a house nearly a hundred years old, which was built by Mrs. Johnson's grandfather. Mrs. Johnson grew up there and lived there until she was sixteen, when her father was murdered while on vacation. Twenty-three years ago the Johnsons returned to live in the house, when her mother died and left it to them. Mrs. Johnson says, "I really didn't want to come back here in a way. . . . All the family had been here and everything . . . . I've never been sorry, but sometimes it's hard to see all the changes. . . . It's not as nice as it used to be."

The couple met by accident when he came to Long Island to a party with a mutual friend. He told his friend that night, "I'm gonna marry her!" Mrs. Johnson says, "I don't know how he knew so fast. I wasn't that sure! . . . I was very interested. . . . I remember thinking 'Gee, he's a little bit different from anybody I know.' . . . He has always been a complete extrovert." At first they dated in New York while she was working, but then she moved back to Long Island to live with her mother and he visited on weekends. Even though he was not very close to his parents, he gave whatever he earned to his mother, so when they married they had no real savings. "[His parents] were very much in need of money during the Depression and [were] in trouble, and . . . so he just left high school and went to work. . . . They were very different times from these," she says.

Once they met, they stopped dating others. He says, "I just liked *her*. Pretty girl. . . . I never did any fooling around with any dames . . ." before or after marriage. She says, "I guess it was a whole different world than it is today. . . . He was a very good-looking young man and full of personality, and we had a lot of friends in common . . . laughed at the same things, liked the same things. . . . He's a very dependable person, and I think it offsets my disposition. . . . I was certainly a very romantic soul, looking for love and romance."

Three years after they began dating, they married during the hurricane of 1938, when she was twenty-five and he was twenty-four. They had a traditional church wedding in the same church where their own daughters would later marry, and where some of their grandchildren would be christened. His parents were driving from New Jersey, but, lost in the storm, they didn't arrive until after the wedding. They had a reception dinner for thirty and took a honeymoon in upstate New York. About marriage she says, "We didn't think about it. We just figured we'd live together and be married and that's it."

Like most young couples of the time, they struggled financially at first. He held down two or three jobs at a time. Mrs. Johnson worked occasionally throughout the marriage to buy extras, to help make ends meet. They loved babies, and enjoyed having them, but did not think about saving for college. They could hardly save anything as it was. One year when the children were little, they could not afford any Christmas presents. Their first daughter was born one year after they married, the second three years later, and their third daughter (who was not intentional) came a decade after that.

Both agree the last daughter is quite different from her sisters, partly in temperament and partly because she grew up in the turbulent sixties. Mr. Johnson says, "She's a party girl. She grew up in the sixties when everything was very bad. . . . The other two were completely different. No big problems at all. But I guess the time they grew up was a different time." Mrs. Johnson often found herself defending the youngest daughter, not telling her husband everything, because she felt he was too harsh with her. While Mrs. Johnson describes the daughter as "high spirited," Mr. Johnson says, "I couldn't stand her conduct." Mrs. Johnson confirms this. "He was very severe with her, and then I would try to ease it off." The third daughter had a bad first marriage, but she has remarried, and now has children and lives nearby. Another of the three daughters also lives on Long Island, close enough for regular contact.

About her children, Mrs. Johnson says, "It's very gratifying when you put in all those years of sacrifice. You don't realize you're doing it at the time, and when it comes back to you so much, then you're very grateful. Of course, they're all busy and all have their own lives, which is understandable, and we are alone a lot more than we used to be. But when we need them, we can count on them, which is great. . . . We're a close family and we do get together when we can, but it isn't as often, maybe, as we'd like it to be."

Over the years the Johnsons' biggest problem was having her mother living with them. Mrs. Johnson felt responsible for her mother, who spent approximately thirty years living with the Johnsons, off and on. "My brothers didn't take as much responsibility as they might have . . . busy with their own lives. . . . I think girls are much more dedicated to their parents. . . . Nobody's mother should live with a young couple and children. . . . She tried very hard to be independent. She had never worked. . . . She devoted the rest of her life to us and clung to us and just never met anybody else. Again, a woman who came from another generation, just a whole different world. . . . Yet in the end, she was very good to us. . . . My allegiance to my mother overpowered what should have been for my husband."

From Mrs. Johnson's perspective they always resolved their conflicts, while he says they usually did. There was no particular time when either thought the marriage might end. Both were happiest before and after the children were born, and she was least happy after the children left home.

Both say they are very happy in the marriage. She says, "There were quite a few periods that were pretty hard, pretty bad, but then, the good ones offset them." They both have tempers, and he says, "We raise hell with one another. . . . It's bickering really, is what it amounts to. There's never been anything really serious." His good and bad points? He has a terrible temper, but he's very good with illness or problems, she says; "I knew I could count on him." Each is the other's best friend, and they usually confide in each other. Most days they show affection and say "I love you" to each other. Sex has declined in later years because of health problems.

They both agree that a loving relationship, good communication, trust, and compatibility are positive factors that contribute to their long marriage. He adds to those factors willingness to compromise, need for each other, and children. Both strongly agree that marriage is a long-term commitment, and both agree (she, strongly) that marriage is a sacred obligation and that fidelity is essential to a successful marriage.

They think today's young marrieds lack the commitment to make a marriage work. They believe promiscuity before and after marriage is one of the reasons for the high divorce rate. "We might have wanted to [live together first], but we didn't do it," he says. Mrs. Johnson regrets not going to college, so they made sure their own daughters finished college. She says, "My mother was pretty inexperienced. . . . In her day girls didn't go to college."

Mrs. Johnson is also well aware of the differences in opportunities and values between her generation and her daughters' generation. "I just accepted all this. Girls today work and have interesting jobs. . . . Today I would have done something about it. But I was very submissive always."

She can't imagine her daughters "putting up with the things that I did! They just wouldn't do it! . . . Today women are . . . doing all these great things. . . . [My two older daughters] are both much more independent in their thinking than I ever was. . . . Wives! They should have a life of their own and that's important. Now that it's too late, I know that," she laughs. "Much too late. But I wouldn't have done it any differently anyway. When you have little children, and they're dependent on you, you just do what you have to do."

Nowadays the Johnsons have few social ties beyond their children. He is not close to his sister. His only good friend died about twenty years ago, and he has few social activities. "I'm not a joiner," he says. They have two friends from their youth; these are friendships that have been rekindled since the Johnsons returned to the old neighborhood. Mrs. Johnson says, "[My friend] and I didn't see one another for years, and it's only now in our old age that we do. And with our other friend, it's the same way, he took different directions, . . . but now we see more of one another, because we're both older . . . and in the same place." Once again, propinquity plays a role in developing social relationships.

When Mr. Johnson retired in 1978, he was restless, so he went to real estate school and then worked in real estate for about four years. Now she complains that he can sit all day in his chair and read or watch television. He used to carve ducks in the basement, but lately has given that up too. He says, "I'm bored stiff . . . I was thinking last night, that today when I got up, I oughta have something to aim at. And that's what you need. If you retire *you should have something!*"

Mrs. Johnson also has very few activities or outside contacts now. They are home together much of their time. They go out to dinner and visit friends and family. Money is not a problem. He says, "We have enough income to be fairly comfortable . . . but I don't think we're the last of the big-time spenders." For health reasons, they cannot travel as much as they did in the past. He says, "We're tied together all the time. Sometimes we get teed off with one another." This has been more the case this winter, because she fell and injured her shoulder and so cannot go out or drive alone. She is more dependent on him than ever. He helps her dress and bathe each day. Like so many caregivers, he has injured himself taking care of her. Since he retired, he does more work around the house. Besides being responsible for the yard work and household repairs, he mops the floor and vacuums; he began doing this even before she hurt herself. "She won't do it, so I do it," he says.

They laugh wryly about aging. Mr. Johnson: "We get the business all the time 'Gee, you look great!' Yeah, yeah, fine, but they don't know how we feel!" She says, "Nobody ages without difficulties.... Everything wears out." He used to swim, but he smoked for years and now has breathing problems. He nods and comments, "This summer I have this darned lawn to take care of, and I'm getting to the point I'm not sure I'm gonna be able to do it too long because I find I wear out fast. I have a slight case of emphysema.... I've never had any serious illnesses at all, and to all of a sudden ... [to] be incapacitated at all bugs the hell out of me."

He says of himself, "For most of my life, nothing ever bothered me. Slaphappy in a sense, but I don't think anything bothers me much even now, except that I'd like to do more than I'm able to do." She realizes she is not a relaxed person and is given to worrying too much: "I've always been a worrier ... but I guess what you are, you can't change.... I'm the way I am, and I've grown to accept that, too. For a long time I thought, 'Oh I wish I were different' ... and now I think, 'Well, to heck with it. I'm me and that's it.'"

Mrs. Johnson does not think you ever know everything about your spouse: "In later years I've discovered that he and I are very different, and even earlier in our marriage, I found that we were.... I think the attraction that we had for one another overwhelmed that, so that when we were younger, I didn't really think about it.... Later I grew more conscious of it." They do share most values and basic attitudes toward life. "It hasn't been perfect or peaceful, in any way, that's for sure. And for one reason, we're very different personalities. Which I didn't realize when we were young. Two of the most unlikely people in the world to ever get together.... I was very close to my family, and [he] was not.... And our dispositions are very different. We couldn't be more different, really. We have tastes in common, we both like reading, and the theater, and travel, and things like that, but fundamentally we're terribly different, and I don't know whether that's good or bad."

Describing how their love changed over time, she says, "Young love is quite different from older love and affection.... It's bound to be. I wish it could stay that way forever, but it doesn't.... I think there's a permanence about so many years together that's very important.... I know I can depend on him for almost any help that I need, and I think he knows it with me too.... It only comes from many years together, and hardships and struggles and everything." He says, "We loved one another very much, and that lasted.... After a good many years, things get to be kind of by rote, ... but if you maintain interest and concern, that has a lot to do with it.... I love her just as much as when we were married. You take for granted a lot of things after a while, which you shouldn't do. I think both people do that. But I wouldn't know what to do if I didn't have her." Five years ago, he adds, "She got caught with cancer.... She's clean now."

She says what is most rewarding to them now is "that we have each other.... We both try to be grateful for that, because alone it would be pretty bad." They have no idea what will happen when one of them dies. Mr. Johnson says, "She wouldn't know what to do, I wouldn't know what to do.... We wouldn't live with any of the girls, either of us." They are sure about that. She says, "After my experience with my mother, I don't ever want to feel that I would live with one of them and mess up their marriage.... When we came back here, we didn't think in twenty or twenty-five years we'd be older, and it would all be more difficult to maintain here.... It's the kind of place that I don't think really I could successfully live in alone.... Sometimes you just have to go with the flow, so that's what we're doing, ... but it was the same way with our marriage.... I don't know what's gonna happen.... Here we are in an older life, in an old house, with all kinds of difficulties, and ... I guess we'll have to cope with it. I try not to think about it, but late at night or early in the morning I often do."

Summary

The Johnsons overcame different backgrounds and contrasting personalities to create a happy, lifelong marriage. They love and respect each other, share some interests, and are committed to each other. They communicate, compromise, and sacrifice for each other.

Nowadays, life is a lot quieter for the Johnsons. Two of their children live nearby, and they have renewed some old friendships. They want more activity in their lives, but they are somewhat limited by health problems. At this point in their lives they are thankful to have each other, and they hope for the best. But late at night, in their 100-year-old house, she worries about what the future holds.

Chapter Nine

Till Death Do Us Part

Thank God, we have each other, how long we don't know.—Mrs. KP

Introduction

Simply to have lived so long together is an achievement. All the interviewed spouses were at least sixty-seven when they participated. In the United States in 1991, 21 percent of men and 49 percent of women aged sixty-five to seventy-four were widowed. After age seventy-five, 34 percent of men and 76 percent of women were widowed (Atchley 1996, p. 35). Because men have a shorter life expectancy than women do, and men tend to marry women younger than themselves, the majority of men are married until death. The others are usually widowed later in life than are women. The average duration of widowhood varies by sex, from 14.3 years for women to 6.6 years for men (Kart, Metress, and Metress 1988).

No matter how long a couple have been married, particularly if the relationship has been happy, widowhood is a time of loneliness, disorientation, anxiety, and uncertainty. A widow or widower has lost a friend, a lover, a supporter, a built-in companion, and a partner in life. A lifetime continuity has been permanently disrupted. Holmes and Rahe (1967) define loss of a spouse as life's most stressful event. Coping with the loss requires many major life adjustments, such as finding new activities and companions, perhaps relocating, and taking on unfamiliar domestic roles. In this chapter the lifetime spouses who participated in this study describe their views of widowhood.

Four Perspectives on Widowhood

Somebody has to go first.—Mr. KH

Interviewed spouses represent four orientations to future widowhood, although both partners in a marriage do not always take the same ap-

176

proach. First, a very few spouses avoid the topic of death and widow-hood, refusing to discuss it or to make preparations. They recognize the inevitability of death, but avoid thinking about or discussing it. Second, a few "solo" spouses already live somewhat separate lives and can imagine surviving without their partners. They do not think that widowhood will be devastating. Third, a much larger category of more "realistic" spouses recognize their mortality and would be "devastated" by the loss of their partner. Most say they have the skills to survive, but are not sure whether they would have the will to survive. Fourth, about one-sixth of spouses acknowledge that death and widowhood are inevitable, but they define the loss of each other as "inconceivable" and "intolerable." They do not think they would survive the loss. Many of these spouses hope they will, some-how, go together.

Nearly all the less happy couples interviewed are solo in their orientation to widowhood. They already lead somewhat separate day-to-day lives and can fairly readily envision a life for themselves after the spouse has died. More often than happily married spouses, they discuss the possibility of remarrying or at least finding a "friend," an escort. Many of the less happy spouses have considered divorce, and thus have some experience in imagin-ing life without their marriage, without the partner. The one exception was one of the least happy couples interviewed, the Raglins, who are profiled at the beginning of this book. Neither spouse wants to be alone, considering it better to be unhappily married than alone.

Death-Denying Spouses

> I don't like to plan ahead for unpleasant
> eventualities.—Mrs. KH

Fourteen interviewed spouses (three couples, seven individual husbands, and one individual wife) refused to discuss death of the self or the mate. These death-denying spouses said they do not want to think about the possibility; they do not want to be morbid; they cannot see the use in thinking about such things; or they hope they die first and quickly, so they never have to consider the possibilities. These partners diverted the conver-sation; focused on some small aspect of change; or simply refused to say anything about their wishes, plans, fears, or thoughts. During interviews, some husbands focused on trivial issues, like missing their wives' cooking or some financial issue, but would not address widowhood directly. Some-times one partner's inability to discuss or make plans for death or widow-hood becomes a source of conflict in the marriage. As the numbers cited above show, more husbands than wives fit into the denying category of partners.

> Mr. GE: "Oh boy, don't even mention it. Don't even mention it. I don't want to think of it. I can't." He is near tears and refuses to discuss the topic further.

> Mr. LA: "I try to avoid that. I don't think we can predict what the psychological impact would be."

> Mr. EC, age eighty-six, says, "No, I haven't really thought about it, to tell you the truth. No, no, I'll deal with that if, *if* the time comes. . . . I never expected to live this long."

> Mrs. EE: "I try not to think about it. Why should I be morbid? Life goes on."

> Mr. DR: "I don't want to think about it. I don't think about it. When the time comes, I'll deal with it. But I really don't think about it. First of all, statistics say I'm gonna go first anyway."

> Mr. HE is in partial denial. He has thought briefly about death and widowhood, but he tries not to think about it and changes the subject soon after it is introduced in the interview. "I turn it off and get away from it, and don't spend a lot of time thinking about it. . . . The first thing that becomes a problem, she's my financial agent. . . . She's in perfect control of everything. . . . I would probably have to stop everything I'm doing now, contributing to other people . . . to stay home and try and put all of this together. It would probably take me months or years, . . . but for my own survival, I would probably have to spend all of my time on that."

It is fairly uncommon to avoid all discussion of death and widowhood, because, by this age, couples have witnessed family and friends die and become widowed, and many of them have already experienced a serious illness, forcing them to face their mortality.

Solo Spouses

> *I have my own golf partners, so I'd be OK that way.*—Mrs. WT

Eleven spouses (five couples and one individual wife) all less happily married, said they already lead relatively separate lives and do not anticipate many problems in adjusting to potential widowhood. They have accepted the inevitable possibility that one of them will be left alone, but that possibility is not especially disturbing to them.

Mrs. NG, whose husband has been ill for a few months, asks rhetorically, "What would I do without him? I haven't given it serious thought. . . . I *am* the dominant figure in this marriage. . . . I think I would survive."

Mr. NG: "It would be sad for a while after she died, and . . . I think probably I might move to Florida." (This is something Mrs. NG absolutely refuses to do, despite her husband's strong wishes to do so.)

Mr. WT: "It wouldn't be very interesting. . . . I think I might become reclusive. I don't think I would look for a woman. . . . It wouldn't bother me that much. I mean, I would miss her of course, but I really don't think I'd become a social butterfly."

Mrs. WT: "I don't want to be blasé, but it's 'que sera.' . . . Everybody is mortal. . . . I figure whatever's gonna happen is gonna happen," she laughs. "I wouldn't get married again, but if I could have a relationship, that's OK, too. I mean, you have to face the fact that it may happen! Remarrying causes too many complications, because the thing is, if you have a relationship, fine you stay together, somebody gets sick, you can break it up. Once you're married, it's not that easy. . . . I definitely do not think I would want to be alone . . . but of course, the numbers are against you. If something happens to your husband, you don't find anybody because men are not interested in a seventy-year-old woman."

These spouses have led somewhat independent lives for years, with their own activities and their own friends, sometimes their own bedrooms and areas of the house. They can see themselves adapting to the loss and going on with their lives. Their level of acknowledged interdependence is relatively low, and most of them are in fair to good health.

Realistic Spouses

I feel a little more comfortable with the eventuality.—Mr. MT

Thirty-two couples, plus four individual husbands and four individual wives (seventy-two spouses altogether) are "realistic" about the possibility of losing their spouses, and expressed some acceptance of future death and widowhood. They recognize their mortality, but nearly all of them feel losing the other would be devastating. While they might survive, they will not do so happily. Usually they have discussed death and widowhood with their partners. It was typical of these spouses to say they are grateful for the time they have already had together, and they feel lucky to have lived so long and to have had such good lives together.

Mrs. MT: "It will probably be dreadful. . . . It's impossible to imagine how I would react or how he would react. . . . I think it will be very difficult, whichever one of us goes first. We kind of go on the assumption that he will, not only because statistically, men tend to die, but because he's had such a fancy medical history. I think we're both rather resilient. . . . We'll manage somehow or other. We've been through so many things. He had the first bypass operation, . . . and then he had the second one. We sort of talked about the possibility that he might not live through the operation. Our general conclusion was [that] we were lucky that we had what we had, and if we were more lucky, we would have more."

For the most part, these more realistic partners take a practical approach, preparing wills and health care proxies, buying long-term care insurance and life insurance, buying their cemetery plots, and distributing much of their property to children and grandchildren.

The KRs have planned for their deaths. He says, "Everything is tagged . . . the kids have all walked the house. . . . It's all part of my game, being wise in time, we used to say in the bank."

Mr. EG says, "I'm ready to go tomorrow. I don't want to live forever. . . . We have just completed living wills. Neither one wants to be resuscitated. We don't want to be on machinery. When it's time to go, pull the plug." If his wife dies first, "I would want to stay here, at least for a year. I understand from what I've read, don't make any decisions for a year."

They have mentally rehearsed future loss through experiencing their friends' and families' widowhood. Although they think the survivor can manage, they know he or she will be lonely and will have a difficult time.

Mrs. HE: "I see the progression, this is how our lives go. And I see it with our neighbors and I see it with my friends. And so you have to be ready for it. It's inevitable. You can only hope that, like my mother, your problem is not too bad and your mind is clear."

Ten percent of the interviewed couples are taking care of very ill partners. These caregiver spouses, from a practical standpoint, often hope their partner dies first, because they fear the dependent partner could not survive without them.

Mr. TR: "She's limited in what she can do. I have to do more around here than I would otherwise, . . . and that's all right. . . . I think, gee, if anything happened. . . . I just have to keep going on, keep strong."

Mr. HA almost lost his wife in 1992. "I wouldn't want to be here alone. I can handle this alone, if God will decide which of us should go first. It'd be better and more favorable if [my wife] did. She couldn't handle the house and things."

If they can survive the loss, they know it will be with the help of social supports, usually their children.

> Mr. AL says, of his life at this point, "You know that you're in the declining period of your life, and you're hopeful that if you have to go, you'll go without pain and without some of those consequences. And I imagine there must be a sense of desolation, particularly if you've had a good relationship, but after all, that's what this life is all about I suppose, right? There's no guarantees, and it's full of uncertainty after that, after death. It'll be a very lonely life for a while, but that's what families are for. So I imagine I'll get support. And I hope she does too. I'm sure she will. . . . It's just the children will accommodate us if we have to. In fact, they've already offered that, but as long as we can be independent, that's the way it's gonna be. . . . We just hope for good health."

In general, healthier spouses thought they could have a meaningful, if not as happy, life after being widowed. Most spouses anticipate having their social supports continue in their lives. People who have helpful children nearby, friends and activities they enjoy, financial stability, and a place in the community usually feel more comfortable contemplating widowhood than do those who lack such support.

While these spouses have not yet experienced widowhood, the couples who have talked about life without each other, who have taught each other how to manage alone, and who have made some plans and preparations for widowhood express less fear and more acceptance of the inevitable. Other research has demonstrated that spouses who made plans and preparations for the eventuality of death adapted better (Atchley1996).

Inseparable Spouses

> *We're gonna hold hands and walk off into the sunset.*
> —Mrs. TR

Nine couples and five wives consider themselves "inseparable." They have recognized the inevitable, but have great difficulty imagining a life without the partner. They do not believe they could survive the loss. Many of these spouses say they want to die together, or will die soon after their partner does. They cannot imagine how they could function on a daily basis without the other person. Sometimes the need or dependence is physical, but more often it is the social, emotional tie that is critical to them. They talked about the unique, irreplaceable character of the spouse and marriage. They described how a lifetime together has forged them into "one." These spouses stated emphatically that they would never remarry. They plan not to survive long enough to start a new life. Fear, anxiety, worry, dread, and misery at the thought of losing each other permeate their comments. Without their lifetime partners, they see themselves as lost souls, bereft, unable to manage, without a will to live.

> Mr. FT: "God forbid, because we're too close. If one of us goes, forget it."
> Mrs. FT: "Either one of us, I don't think the other'd last."

> Mrs. KP: "We've already decided that we're going to have a plane or boat accident and go together."

> Mrs. DR: "This may sound awful, but I hope we die together. . . . I think it would be harder for my husband if I die first."

> Mrs. ME says, "Living together for so many years, we're like one. Over sixty-eight years, that's a long time. I never went with anybody else after I went with him. . . . The day he dies, I die too. Who's going to take care of me? . . . He tells me the same thing. What is he gonna do? He is very dependent on me, and now I'm dependent on him."

> Mr. NA: "I don't think I'd hang around too long. I think I'd just let myself go. If she wasn't around, I'd say to hell with it. The children are all set up. They've all got their lives to live, and . . . I'm not gonna be a burden to them."
> Mrs. NA: "I would be without my right arm. You realize what this person means to you. If something happened, how would you face life without the other person. . . . You need somebody to be there. And it must be awful not to have anybody. . . . Suddenly, you're in your seventies. Your life is slipping fast away. Your children, they're on their own, your friends start to go. It's awful. I always say life is meant for two people. If there's only one of you, you feel alone."

For these couples, it is the love and companionship of a lifetime relationship that shapes their will and desire to die with their partner. Fifteen of the sixty interviewed couples (both husband and wife) said that now is the happiest time of their marriage, and nine of those fifteen could not conceive of their lives without the partner.

> Mrs. AL says, "Oh, I can't imagine myself without him! I told him if he dies first I'm gonna throw myself in the grave."

> Mrs. ER: "We want to go together [in a] common automobile accident . . . if it's possible, because I hate the thought. . . . We see what's happened to the other half. We have such a commitment, where in the heck would you start?" She continues, "I'd be lost. We really hate the thought of being alone."

Interdependence of Spouses

I'd be miserable. I don't know what I'd do.—Mrs. IL

Couples who have lived together fifty or more years have had the opportunity to develop a unique level and style of interdependency. The RGs and the GRs illustrate the intertwining of two partners, the interdependence they define as being one. Each of these husbands encourages and supports his wife's independence so that she can survive without him. But neither the husbands nor the wives in these two couples are very optimistic that they *would* survive without each other.

> Mr. RG says, "I'd be lost. I try to tell her not to be lost, because I think a woman survives better than a man. [Women] take care of themselves better. If a man is left alone, I think he's left at odds. A woman sort of serves as an anchor for him. I know I depend on her for a great many things. And if, God forbid, she ever precedes me in death, it'll be a terrible, terrible thing for me. I don't think I'll be able to live much longer after her. Yet, I know that when I go, I want her to live long, and I want her to have a good life. In fact, I made arrangements so she'll get half my pension for the rest of her life too, in addition to our Social Security and our investments. She'll be very comfortable. But I won't be OK without her, I know I won't. Unfortunately, as much as I would like to be independent, she's a mainstay.... And in addition to the fact that I love her very much, I depend on her in a practical way, yeah. I think that's how it is. And like I tell her, I say to her many times, 'It's better for me to go first.' That's my preference. I realize that everything has to come to an end at one time or another, but in the meantime we're enjoying ourselves."
>
> Mrs. RG agrees: "He says he's going first, ... but I hope ... I don't wait too long. I want to go with him, because I feel it will be lonely, very quiet."
>
> Mr. RG sums it up: "We love each other, we're for each other, and this is the way we're gonna be until God decides to separate us."
>
> Mr. GR manages a little humor: "I'm dragging her along with me because I'm not gonna break somebody else in. I'm idiosyncratic. It would be devastating. I don't know if I could survive it."
>
> Mrs. GR says, "He makes me independent. When I go to my daughters, he'll sometimes insist that I go by myself, so that I should drive myself, so I don't rely on him.... He has made sure I maintained my independence. I know women who are widows who don't drive, and it's disastrous. I think my life without him would be null and void because I am so much a part of him, and he's so much a part of me. My kids would not let me be alone, but it would be lonely."

Describing life without the other as "null and void" is common among husbands and wives. Their distinction between being lonely and being alone is very clear: other people will be with you, but the spouse is irreplaceable. After two people have shared half a century of life together, no one else may be alive who has known them so long, who lived through and remembers the same events. No one else may remember them as they were at different stages of life. The adversity and crises they faced and overcame were bonding influences, as these spouses repeatedly mention. A few of them talk about how inconceivable becoming intimate with another person would be.

> Mrs. FL: "We sometimes talk about it. I could never imagine being without him. I am not a loner. Recently my husband said 'Oh honey, if anything happens to me, I'd like you to meet a guy.' . . . I cannot imagine myself with another man."

> Mr. NG: "I don't think I'd ever get married again, even though I'm seventy-five, although you hear of people that do get married. . . . Six months later, they're seeing someone all of a sudden. . . . I'm sure they're getting a little sexy. . . . I don't think I could do that, because I would think of all the nice relationships I've had with my wife, and I don't think it would be fair to this person. . . . Making love to them if I could, and I'd be thinking of my wife. In the middle of it, I'd probably stop, you know, and say, 'I can't, I can't go on.'"

> Mrs. GR: "I would never want another man. Nothing could measure up. . . . You get an old man, and you never know what you're letting yourself in for."

> Mrs. CN: "I can't ever visualize myself getting married again. I have four or five widow friends, and none of them wants to get married again."

> Mrs. WE is very emotional thinking of the possibility of losing her husband. "My feeling about being alone, I guess goes back to the insecurities of childhood. He's been such an influence on my life, the thought of living without him. . . . I cannot think about. . . . I had breast cancer and I survived. My husband had malignant melanoma and he survived. We've been through a war together, we've been through the kids, we've been through so much, that at this point there isn't anything else but each other. As much as our children are important to us, they'll never be a substitute. They'll never be a substitute for him, they'll never be a substitute for me. We are survivors!"

As Atchley (1996) has discussed, there is a pulling together of a couple over the years. Spouses who spend a lifetime together, making so many mutual decisions, sharing so many experiences, tend to grow together, happily or not.

Potential Widowhood: His and Hers

> *I think if the man is left alone, it's harder.*—Mrs. EG

Interviewed husbands and wives show some gender differences in attitudes toward death and widowhood. Men more often avoid the topic of widowhood, and are usually the ones who will not make future plans like wills, or health care proxies. Not only is it evident in the interviews that men more often avoid the topics, but their wives also note the difficulty this presents to them. Women express more open concern over their futures as widows, perhaps because they know, statistically, they are more likely to experience it. Mrs. PA, married to an "avoider," has few plans and many worries. Mrs. EG, married to a "realistic" husband, feels more prepared.

> Mrs. PA says, "The most difficult thing I have to deal with, and what I have the most trouble with, is that he is the kind of man who cannot face his mortality, so he never wants to plan for the eventuality of his death. . . . He just will not face those things. He doesn't want to hear about it. We didn't have wills until not all that long ago because he wouldn't make a will." She wanted him to decide whether he wanted burial or cremation. "Six years later, he's still thinking about it, because he doesn't want to make a decision. . . . I think of the eventuality of his death, and statistically, he's gonna go before I will, so that's very hard."

> Mrs. EG: "If I had some close girl friends and some people to help me through the mounds of paper and what to do next. My husband has that written down, what to do, when to mail, such good order." She says her daughter and son-in-law would definitely help too. "I would hope I would live here, and enjoy the house. I think I would have a lot of company. I think that would help me, because I like people. . . . I just hope I can get along. I hope I keep my senses, and not like this friend of mine with Alzheimer's. If I get sick, I'd like to get sick and die real quick. I don't want to linger."

On the positive side, because Mr. EG has played the role of good provider all his life, Mrs. EG will be financially stable if he dies first, and he has even purchased long-term care insurance for both of them.

There are other significant gender differences in widowhood beyond the fact that women are more likely to experience it and for a longer period of time. When women are widowed, they are also likely to experience changes in their financial situation. The average standard of living for wives dropped 18 percent after the husband died, and 10 percent of women who had been above the poverty line fell below poverty level when their husband died (Bound, Duncan, Laren, and Oleinick 1991). Thus, in addition to losing their most important social support, widows tend to have less money. This further constricts their social lives and even their health care options, another cause for worry and depression.

Several spouses worry about their mates' lack of familiarity with managing money or household tasks. The usual division of labor is that husbands keep up the checkbook and do the family bookkeeping, but this is not a universal pattern. Some husbands have had their wives establish their own credit cards, and have taught them to keep the books and write the checks.

Some wives have taught their husbands basic housekeeping and cooking skills. These spouses are preparing their partners to be independent, teaching them unfamiliar tasks that will be necessary in widowhood.

> Mr. NN says, "I changed the credit cards to her name. I said, 'If anything should happen, you don't have any credit.'"

> Mr. KR: "So I used to go around lecturing wives of corporate executives, [telling them], 'Get your husband to loosen up, what do you know about his affairs?' . . . Here am I telling other people what to do virtually all my life . . . and then I come home and Baby [his wife] says, 'No, that's my job.'" She does not want to know about the finances and left it up to him.

> Mr. AL: "I think if she survives me, she's gonna have a tough time because she's not knowledgeable and she doesn't seem to be particularly interested. She doesn't want to even hear of it. I don't know whether that's simple ignorance or whether she just doesn't want to contemplate the possibility. . . . I have arranged for somebody to educate her. . . . She won't express any particular interest in financial matters that I'm handling, so I do it all. . . . I try to explain to her, but she's not cooperative."

A few husbands recognized the problem but did nothing about it.

> Mr. FL, a devoted businessman who has still not retired, says, "This has been in my mind over the last couple of years. . . . I was thinking of talking to her about it. I can't get myself to do that. It's traumatic to me every time I think of her if I should pass away. She can't even think without me. . . . I would shiver to think of her running around without direction, and all the sharks, if you have a couple of bucks, how easy it is for them to extract it. I don't know how she would handle it, and unfortunately, I don't have anybody that I could even have to administer my estate. . . . These things bother me."

Mr. FL's inability to discuss potential death and widowhood has prevented him from preparing his wife to be more independent. From the perspective of continuity theory, Mr. FL is relying on the coping strategy he has used throughout his marriage: he avoids difficult issues, will not discuss them, and from his perspective, they have gone away.

Widowers are often less prepared than widows to arrange social occasions for themselves. One reason may be that wives are usually the ones responsible for making the social contacts, setting the social calendar, making the phone calls to children. When the wife dies, the husband is unfamiliar with these activities and may not know how to reach out. Others might interpret this as disinterest on his part and avoid him (Atchley 1996). Widowers actually get less social support than do widows (Longino and Lipman 1981).

> Of life without his wife, Mr. WD says, "A woman knows how to cope a little better than a man. If I have to, I can shop, I can cook, you know what I

mean? I can clean. . . . I've done it all my life . . . because we helped each other. But as far as the bookkeeping or the house with the bills, I'm up the creek. I'm at the stage I wouldn't know what to do without her. I mean just making a meal for yourself and sitting here like a jerk all day, what do you do with yourself?"

Where to Live?

Relocating

> *I have everything here that's familiar to me.*
> —Mrs. PA

Approximately one-third of the couples who are still living in the family home said they have considered moving, most often because of the difficulty of keeping a large house alone. They have lived much of their lives in one home, in one town, so that all of their significant ties are in a single place. Moving means leaving behind their social convoy, the social supports of a lifetime. Living near their children is a possibility for some, but many fear they would become dependent in a new location, since they would not know anyone other than their children. Learning to drive in a new area, finding new doctors, making new friends, and adjusting to different housing are too many sudden breaks from a familiar world. The majority of spouses said they prefer to remain in familiar surroundings.

> Mrs. HE has a plan for her widowhood. "I know what I would do, which is to stay exactly where I am right now and continue in the women's organizations that I belong to as long as I possibly can." She feels comfortable and safe in the small community where the HEs have lived for over twenty years. "If I started to have health problems, I would have to move. I would have to be near my daughter. I wouldn't want to live with her. But I would have to be near her . . . the same as my mother now."
>
> Mrs. PA: "My youngest daughter . . . has pleaded with us to move nearer to her. I don't really know what I would do. . . . Probably I would sell the house, and take an apartment near her, . . . but who knows?" When her daughter asks her, "Why do you stay on Long Island? You have nothing to keep you there," she answers, "I have forty years of my life here!"
>
> Mr. FL, who has not retired, plans to cloister himself in his business if his wife dies first: "I'd probably move my bed into [the office]; that's it. That would be life at this point."
>
> Mr. LA is more concerned about the burdens of a final illness. "I say maybe what we should do is sell our house. It's time to move into a retirement home. That's anathema to my wife. She doesn't want to do that, maybe never. . . . When one of us becomes terminally ill, the other is bound to have

to take care of him, because to have outside care for a terminally ill person is very expensive. Whereas if you make a contract with one of these live-in situations, a modern home for the aged, you sign away all your life assets and they take care of you for life. . . . That means that you're not asking that other person to take care of you when you become a burden. We haven't got to that stage. . . . If there's anything where we have a difference of opinion, that would be it."

Mrs. LA illustrates that difference of opinion: "I know what I won't do. I won't go into any retirement home. I abhor nursing homes. I think they're a blight on society."

Mr. TM: "I could go and live with my daughter, she's got room for me, but I wouldn't want to do it. Most of my friends who've lost wives are staying right there. I have several good friends, they haven't moved anywhere, they stayed right where they are. I've thought about that. . . . I would probably stay right here."

"Staying put" provides stability and predictability, a sense of belonging, and a greater sense of control. An unspoken aspect of relocation is temporary loss of control. Everything has to be relearned. Every potential friend must be met and tested over time. For the majority of the spouses, it is easier and more rewarding, as long as their health lasts, not to move.

Living with Children?

I would never want to be a burden to my children.

—Mrs. CN

While children remain important in these older couples' lives, almost none of them wants to move to a child's house after a spouse's death. Most would not mind living *near,* but not *with,* a child, most often a daughter. Only four spouses, two husbands and two wives, said they would live with one of their children if they were widowed. Sometimes their own expectations are shaped by the experiences of caring for their parents.

Mr. WE says, about the prospect of losing his wife, "I'm not gonna get married again. What am I gonna do? I'm eighty-one years old! Who's gonna take care of everything? She takes care of the financial things. . . . I wouldn't stay here. My daughter wouldn't let me stay here. . . . My son wouldn't let me stay either by myself . . . but for now we don't want to move up there [to where my daughter lives]. But if something happens . . . my wife would go up there."

Mrs. EC: "You don't depend on your children, if you can help it."

Mrs. NN says, "I worry about what will happen if I'm left. I don't want to go live with my children. I don't think it's fair to them." Her mother came to live with the NNs when she was widowed. Mrs. NN continues, "[My mother] died here, and because my mother was here, I know how helpless I became, . . . I think I'll just stay here."

Mrs. RG: "My daughter says, 'Ma, you and Daddy will never have to go into a home, . . . 'cause I saw the way you were with your parents.' . . . I don't want to live with my children, but I'm so afraid that my home's gonna be empty. . . . I won't have anybody to talk to, and so I'm frightened."

Mrs. WT: "I don't think parents belong with children. . . . I mean, we were just lucky that our parents died young enough so that we didn't have to take care of them." She laughs. "I hope I can do the same thing for my kids. My mother and father just died, and the same thing with his. I think it's a blessing."

Issues of independence, control of one's domain, and privacy were also important to both husbands and wives interviewed. While other research has demonstrated that men are, typically, not as close to their children as women are, and are less able to move into their children's homes after widowhood (Atchley 1996), this was not evident in these interviews. As many husbands as wives thought they would be welcome in an offspring's home. Welcome or not, almost none of the husbands and wives wished to live with their children.

Mr. NG: "Probably my daughter would say, 'Come on,' now that she's divorced, 'Come and live with me, Dad.' No, because I wouldn't be the master of the house anymore!" and he bangs the arm of his chair with each word. "We'd never live with the children!"

Mr. MA would never live with his children either: "Privacy at my age is everything because I don't do things normal any more. . . . Believe me, for elderly men it's a serious problem, believe me!" Asked if he would have a social life as a widow, he replied, "In all our life, never did I go to a party or to an invite without my wife. Never!"

Mrs. NG: "I wouldn't ever want to. Children really don't want . . . a parent to move in with them. It's not good. To be close, yes, the way we are right now, you know forty-five, fifty minutes away from each other is fine. Somebody's in trouble, you can get there; . . . for the fun, you can get there. . . . They wouldn't say it, but I know it wouldn't work. . . . I adored my mother. She was the craziest, [most] fun loving, happ[iest] woman in the world, but we couldn't live together. If I move near the children, I'm dependent on them, and vice versa. No, I've got a good life here."

Mrs. ER: "I don't want to move in with my children."

Mr. ER adds, "That's one we agree on too. The thought of going into one of their houses . . . what a mess."

Summary

Interviewed spouses can be grouped in four categories in their approach to widowhood: 12 percent of the spouses avoid the topic; 9 percent live relatively separate lives already and think they can adapt; 60 percent are realistic, but question whether they would have the will to live after such a loss; and 19 percent are inseparable and cannot imagine surviving without each other.

DiGiulio (1989), Brubaker (1985), and Lopata (1973) described the stages of coping with widowhood, from grief and shock to acceptance and the beginning of a new life, which can take years. It is no wonder that the majority of these long-married spouses regard potential widowhood as their greatest threat. After losing a lifetime partner at the end of one's life, what "new life" is there, and how much time is left to build it? A hypothesis for future testing is whether age at widowhood, number of years married, and marital happiness can predict illness and premature death among the widowed.

Spouses who have talked about the possibility of widowhood and made some preparations, who are relatively healthy, who have friends and children close by, and who have productive activities outside the marital relationship to keep them busy are more likely to think they would be able to adapt to widowhood than are those who lack these supports. Gelfand and Barresi's research had similar results (1987). Unfortunately, by the ages achieved by the couples in this study, social supports are also disappearing. Their brothers, sisters, and friends die or move away, and their children are involved in their own lives. Surviving widowhood is, in part, a function of flexibility and adaptability. Spouses must be able and willing to cope, which depends on how they define the loss.

As Mr. KH says, "I would have to make up my mind that life must go on."

Another hypothesis for future study is whether spouses who avoid the topic of death and widowhood, who have made no preparations, and who are relatively rigid in other attitudes and behavior experience more difficulty in adjusting to widowhood.

Despite the overwhelming importance of children and grandchildren in the lives of most of the couples in this study, almost none of the spouses would want to live with their children should they become widowed. Two-thirds of the interviewed couples preferred not to relocate, expressing the tendency for people to maintain continuity in their lives, especially in the later years (Atchley 1996).

The long-married spouses are, to varying degrees, interdependent. Most spouses said they need each other in many ways, both practically and emotionally. Whether a couple are happily married or not, one's lifelong partner is irreplaceable. No one else has experienced what the spouses have known and done together, and that shared life, happy or not, ends forever with the death of the partner.

Conclusion

The Long Island Long-Term Marriage Survey makes five significant contributions to research on marital success and longevity. First, this research did not discover a simple recipe for marital longevity. Instead, creating successful, enduring marriages involves the complex interplay of personal and social factors. All the surveyed couples are married for a lifetime, but they are not all happy.

The happier couples said they are still married because they love each other, and enjoy each other's company. They have created a life together, which they cherish. Usually they share similar backgrounds and values. They have compatible interests; they love and respect each other; they are committed to each other and to the marriage; and they communicate and compromise, and are willing to sacrifice for each other. Not all the happily married couples surveyed have all these characteristics, but having at least a majority of them is crucial to creating marital success. Lauer and Lauer (1986) found much the same pattern in their study of successful enduring marriages.

When all these positive factors are not present, but couples remain married, it is usually because of a sense of commitment, religious beliefs, and/or lack of alternatives (including parental support). These marriages have been unhappy because one or both partners have unmet expectations; because they lack communication, love, and respect; and/or because they are unwilling to compromise or sacrifice. After fifty or more years of marriage, the spouses have accommodated to their differences, usually by investing their energy in other directions.

Most of the couples, happily married or not, share similar religious, ethnic, and social class backgrounds. Not all of these couples grew up in stable, happy families, and over half of them have divorced children, so role models are not the only answer to creating successful marriages, although they may help. Less happily married couples among those interviewed have more divorced children than do the happily married couples.

Beyond these personal factors, the larger society plays a role. Values, norms, beliefs, and social institutions need to be supportive of long-term marriage. All the spouses in the study grew up during the Depression, and over three-quarters of the interviewed spouses discussed at length how growing up in that time taught them to value hard work, thrift, and perseverance. Interviewed spouses repeatedly said that experiencing the Depression and the war created a sense of uncertainty in their lives that led to hopes rather than expectations. Most interviewed spouses said these early experiences helped them to create successful lifetime marriages. Elder (1974) has suggested that persons who overcome much adversity develop coping skills they can use the rest of their lives.

The spouses said that they were socialized to believe in lifetime marriage, most often defined as a sacred commitment, and that divorce was difficult and stigmatizing. Women often lacked the education and work experience to support themselves and their children. These spouses had fewer acceptable options and consequently less role strain when they were young married couples than do present-day young couples.

The majority of the surveyed couples think many aspects of today's society are detrimental to the formation of lasting relationships. By over-emphasizing personal fulfillment, individual independence, and sexuality, society discourages the development of values encouraging compromise and sacrifice, sharing and interdependence, and fidelity. Change is positively valued nowadays, not stability and permanence. Marriage is now defined as a legal contract, rather than a sacred institution, making divorce acceptable and available. There are far more acceptable options for both men and women now, so roles are unclear. Nearly all the interviewed spouses discussed these changes in values and norms over time in the larger society and how they affect couples' abilities to create successful lifetime marriages today.

Second, these couples are "long-term" people. Nearly all the interviewed couples had kept friends and maintained group memberships for thirty or more years. Many had lived in the same home for decades. Most of them have regular contact with one or more children who live in the area, so they have family continuity too. This social convoy becomes more important as the spouses age, and each loss makes adaptation more difficult.

The keys or guidelines offered by these couples for creating successful lifelong marriages can be applied to other relationships as well: those with friends, other family members, employees and employers, customers, and businesses. Lifelong relationships are more likely when the participants share common backgrounds and values, are compatible in interests, care about and respect each other, commit to each other, communicate, and compromise, and are flexible enough to give to the other person.

Third, this research raises many interesting questions about marital happiness over the lifespan. Nearly all the less happily married interviewed couples had struggled with the same problems all their lives together. Marital happiness began to decline early and remained low for the duration. Happily married couples did not love each other less at any point in the marriage, but the time and attention they gave to the marital relationship varied, depending on other demands. When one or both partners had little time to devote to the relationship, it suffered—when mothers were overwhelmed with domestic responsibilities and husbands were overworked breadwinners. So it is not a surprise that marital happiness appears to be lower in the middle child-rearing years. When the conflicting role demands lessen—when the children grow up, and the workers retire—there is more time to focus on each other. A corresponding increase in marital happiness may occur if the couple have other factors working for them—commitment, communication, love, respect, compatibility, compromise, and so on. After fifty or more years together, these spouses have grown together, whether happily or not. Most say their love has grown over time, and 60 percent are still sexually active.

Fourth, both survey and interview data show that husbands and wives do not have the same experience of their marriage. Husbands have more positive views of their wives and their marriages. Interviewed wives presented more complex descriptions of their marriages and their spouses, discussing both the positive and the negative aspects. Husbands typically focused on the positive qualities of their wives and relationships, downplaying problems. Husbands less often reported declines in sexual interest and reported a higher level of conflict resolution than did wives. Yet these differences are only a matter of degree. When husbands say it "always" worked out or they "always" like their wives, those wives say it "usually" worked out, or they "usually" like their spouse.

The family roles that men and women play also create different experiences of marriage. Men, socialized to be the breadwinners, were away from home most of the time, knew less about and spent less time with their children, and left most of the day-to-day decision making to their wives. The wives were socialized to be traditional housewives, at least while their children were young. However, wives who married during the war years were more likely than Depression-era wives to return to work later. The majority of working mothers scheduled their jobs around their child-care responsibilities. Only a few wives had careers, or hired professionals to care for their children while they worked. Families always came first for wives. Theoretically, family came first for husbands, too, but that meant supporting the family, not necessarily being with the family.

Fifth, the interviewed couples offered a revealing portrait of change in attitudes toward divorce over time. On the one hand, they were not encouraged or allowed to return to their parents' homes should they have marital problems. They said they married for life, made a sacred vow, and meant to keep it. The happily married couples, especially, provided good role models for their children. But this older generation of couples enabled the younger generation to divorce. As parents, they socialized their children to different values and norms regarding sacrifice and individual fulfillment, and they did not apply the same standards to their children that they did to themselves.

This change in attitudes is not necessarily bad. The couples in this study took care of their children and helped them when they were in trouble; what parent would not do that if he or she could? They want their children to do well, to follow their dreams. They are generally pleased with the expanded opportunities their daughters and granddaughters have. Yet these changes have helped to create the high rate of divorce since the 1970s in the United States. Whether or not couples today can follow all the guidelines to marital success depends on the supports available in the larger social and historical context.

Appendix A

Long Island Long-Term Marriage Questionnaire

1. For which of the following reasons did you marry? (Check all applicable.)

   ____a commitment to my future spouse   ____family pressures
   ____love for my future spouse   ____financial reasons
   ____the time was right to marry   ____pregnancy
   ____duty, obligation to others   ____arranged marriage
   ____to have children
   ____to become a citizen
   other reasons_____

2. When you married did you think your marriage would last?
   ____yes ____no

3. Did you marry within your religion? ____yes   ____no
   If you did not, did this cause problems? ____yes   ____no

4. I like my spouse as a person
   ___always ___usually ___sometimes ___rarely ___never

5. My spouse understands me
   ___always ___usually ___sometimes ___rarely ___never

6. Overall, my marriage has been
   ___very happy ___happy ___somewhat happy ___unhappy
   ___very unhappy

7. If you think your marriage has been moderately to very unhappy what held your marriage together? (Check all applicable.)
____children   ____finances   ____family pressures
____afraid of alternatives to marriage
____indecisiveness   ____other_____

(If not applicable, skip to No. 8.)

8. What are the positive factors that account for your long marriage? (Check all applicable.)

____loving relationship   ____compatibility
____willingness to compromise   ____need for each other
____trust   ____mutual respect
____good communication   ____children
          ____other_____

9. Marriage is a long-term commitment to one person.
___strongly agree ___agree ___neutral ___disagree ___strongly disagree

10. Marriage is a sacred obligation.
___strongly agree ___agree ___neutral ___disagree ___strongly disagree

11. Do you consider fidelity essential to a successful marriage?
___yes ___no

12. My spouse is my best friend. ____yes ____no

13. My spouse has grown more interesting over time. ____yes ____no

14. How often do you confide in your spouse?
____always ____usually ____sometimes ____rarely ____never

15. How often do you show affection to your spouse?
____always ____usually ____sometimes ____rarely ____never

16. How often do you tell your spouse you love him or her?
____every day ____most days ____sometimes ____rarely ____never

17. How often do you laugh together with your spouse?
____every day ____most days ____sometimes ____rarely ____never

18. Did you experience a lessening of sexual interest over time?
_____yes _____no

19. If you did experience a lessening of sexual interest, when did it occur?
_____early in the marriage _____midway _____in later years

20. If you experienced a lessening of sexual interest, did it resume later?
_____yes _____no

21. If you and your spouse are both retired, do you get in each other's way?
_____always _____often _____occasionally _____seldom _____never

22. Since retirement, has your relationship with your spouse been
_____much happier _____better _____about the same _____unhappy
_____intolerable

23. Over the years, how often did you and your mate agree upon the
following issues?
Family finances
_____always _____usually _____sometimes _____rarely _____never
Recreational activities
_____always _____usually _____sometimes _____rarely _____never
Religious matters
_____always _____usually _____sometimes _____rarely _____never
Spouse's career decisions
_____always _____usually _____sometimes _____rarely _____never
Aims and goals in life
_____always _____usually _____sometimes _____rarely _____never
Division of household tasks
_____always _____usually _____sometimes _____rarely _____never
Sexual activity
_____always _____usually _____sometimes _____rarely _____never
Amount of time spent together
_____always _____usually _____sometimes _____rarely _____never

24. Over the years, what issues created problems for you as a couple?
(Check all applicable.)
_____finances   _____wife working
_____husband not working   _____infidelity

___raising the children   ___sexual relations
___ill health   ___relatives
___spouse's annoying habits
___other_____

25. Over the years, how did you overcome problems and conflicts in your marriage? (Check all applicable.)
___we communicated honestly   ___we compromised
___we avoided discussing problems ___passage of time
___I did what my spouse wanted   ___counseling
___my spouse did what I wanted   ___temporary separation
___other_____

26. My spouse and I have been able to resolve our conflicts.
___always ___usually ___sometimes ___rarely ___never

27. Was there ever a time when you thought your marriage would not last?
___yes ___no

28. If there was a time when you thought your marriage would not last, indicate when:
___early in the marriage ___midway ___later years

29. During the years of your marriage, when were you the happiest?
___before children born ___after children born
___after children left home ___right now ___no particular time

30. During the years of your marriage, when were you the least happy?
___before children born ___after children born
___after children left home ___right now ___no particular time

Please answer the following questions about yourself.
   Your sex: ___female ___male
   In what year did you marry? _____
   How old were you when you married?_____
   Do you have children? ___yes ___no ___number of children
   Your educational level:
   ___eighth grade ___less than high school ___high school
   ___college ___postgraduate or advanced degree

What is your current joint yearly income?

___under $20,000   ___$20,000–29,000   ___$30,000   ___39,000

___$40,000–49,000 ___$50,000 or more

Race or Ethnic Identity: _____

Religious affiliation:
___Catholic   ___Jewish   ___Protestant ___ Muslim ___other
___none

Occupation: _____

If you are willing to participate in the interview portion of this study, please indicate your name, address, and telephone number. You will be contacted by the researcher for an interview at a time convenient to you.

Name _____

Address (Street) _____

(City)_____ (State)_____

(Zip Code)_____ (Telephone) _____

Appendix B

Long Island Long-Term Marriage Survey: Interview Questions

Getting Married

How did you meet your spouse?

How long did you know your spouse before you decided to marry him or her?

How long did you date?

Why did you marry your spouse at the time that you did?

Why did you choose this person to marry?

If you had to do it all over again, would you marry the same person?
    Would you marry someone else?
    Would you remain single?
    Explain.

Describe your wedding.

When you married, were you financially stable and secure?

Was your marriage actively supported by family and friends?

Having Children

How old were you (how far into the marriage) when you had your first child?
    Was it a boy or girl?
    The next children?

How did your marriage change when you had children?
    Time together? Leisure? Money? Other?

What were the biggest problems during the child-rearing years?

What were the best parts of having children?

Marital Quality and Expectations

Thinking back to yourself as a young person
> Explain your expectations of marriage then.
> Explain the ways your marriage was nothing like you expected.
> Explain the ways in which your marriage was much as you expected.

When you married, what were the most important qualities that you wanted in a spouse?
> Does your partner have these qualities? Explain.

Right now, at this stage of life, what do you think are the most important qualities you want in a spouse?
> Does your partner have these qualities?

Overall, what was the best period of time in your marriage? What were you doing then?

Overall, what was the most difficult time in your marriage? What were you doing then?

Right now, what are the most rewarding aspects of your marriage?

Right now, what are the most troublesome aspects of your marriage?

What advice would you give to younger people who are marrying today? (What can you explain to them to help them create successful relationships?)

Why do you think the divorce rate has been so high for so many years? Have values changed? If so, how?

You and Your Family

Were your parents married until death?

Do you think your parents had a happy marriage or not? Explain.

Do you have brothers and sisters?

Did your brothers and sisters have long marriages too? Explain.

Is there anyone with whom you have been friends for fifty or more years? Who?

Have you belonged to any groups, clubs, religious, or other organizations for a long time?
  Which groups? How long?

How frequently do you have or attend family reunions?
  When was the last one you attended?

Do your children have long-term marriages? Explain.

Describing Your Marriage

Overall, what do you think are the most important reasons your marriage lasted? (If you had to instruct young people on the reasons for the longevity of your marriage, what would you tell them?)

Were any of the following reasons an important factor in keeping your marriage together for fifty or more years?
  Religious beliefs?
  Social stigma of divorce?
  Limited financial resources?
  An absence of alternatives?
  Perseverance in the face of adversity?

Do you enjoy spending time with your spouse?

What kinds of activities do you enjoy doing with your spouse?

Have you kept your own identity through the years of your marriage?

Do you have personal time to yourself?

Do you have your own friends, separate from your spouse?

Do you have your own space in the house, a room, a study?

Do you think having time and space to yourself has been important to the maintenance of your marriage? Explain.

How did World War II affect your marriage?

Did you (your spouse) work outside the home during the marriage?
  When did you (your spouse) work and for how long?
  If your wife worked, was this acceptable to you? Explain.

Over the years, did you experience a change in the way you loved your spouse? Explain.
  Did these feelings change or go away?

Over the years, did the sexual interest and activity between you and your spouse change? If so, how?

How have your lives changed since retirement?
    Do you have more time together now?
    Are you enjoying your time together now?
    Are there any problems that came with retirement?

Have you thought what your life would be like if you should lose your spouse? What do you think you would do?

Conflict and Conflict Resolution

Over the years what problems arose in your marriage?

How did you handle these problems?

When you want to talk over a problem, do you (your spouse) open up and discuss the problem? Explain.

Do you (your partner) withdraw from discussions of problems or try to avoid discussion of them? Explain.

Do you feel comfortable telling your spouse what is bothering you? Explain.

Do you and your spouse argue in similar ways?
    Different ways?
    Explain what happens during your arguments.

How do you resolve conflicts?

Do you and your spouse share similar values? Explain.

Has a value difference caused a problem in your marriage? Explain.

After you married were you ever tempted to or did you have a sexual relationship with a person other than your spouse?
    If so, when in your marriage did this occur? Explain.
    How was this resolved?

Did you ever consider separation or divorce?
    If so,when in your marriage did this occur? Explain.
    What brought you back together?

Bibliography

Ade-Ridder, Linda. 1989. "Quality of Marriage" In *Lifestyles of the Elderly: Diversity in Relationships, Health, and Caregiving,* ed. Linda Ade-Ridder and Charles Hennon, 37–48. New York: Human Sciences Press.

———. 1990. "Sexuality and Marital Quality among Older Married Couples." In *Family Relationships in Later Life,* ed. T.H. Brubaker, 48–67. 2d ed. Newbury Park, CA: Sage.

Ade-Ridder, Linda, and Timothy Brubaker. 1983. "The Quality of Long-Term Marriages." In *Family Relationships in Later Life,* ed. T.H. Brubaker, 21–30. Beverly Hills, CA: Sage.

Atchley, Robert. 1992. "Retirement and Marital Satisfaction." In *Families and Retirement,* ed. M. Szinovacz, D.J. Ekerdt, and B.H. Vinick, 145–158. Newbury Park, CA: Sage.

———. 1994. "Is There Life Between Life Course Transitions?" Paper presented at the Annual Meeting of the Gerontological Society of America, Atlanta, November 1994.

———. 1996. *Social Forces and Aging,* 8th ed. Belmont, CA: Wadsworth.

Baumeister, Roy, Todd Heatherton, and Dianne Tice. 1994. *Losing Control: How and Why People Fail at Self-Regulation.* New York: Academic Press.

Berger, Peter, and Hansfried Kellner. 1992. "Marriage and the Social Construction of Reality." In *Marriage and Family in a Changing Society,* ed. James Henslin, 165–174. 4th ed. New York: Free Press.

Berger, Peter, and Thomas Luckmann. 1966. *The Social Construction of Reality.* New York: Doubleday.

Blood, Robert, and Donald Wolfe. 1960. *Husbands and Wives.* New York: Macmillan.

Bound, John, Greg Duncan, Deborah Laren, and Lewis Oleinick. 1991. "Poverty Dynamics in Widowhood." *Journal of Gerontology* 46, no. 3 (May): S115–124.

Brossard, James. 1932. "Residential Propinquity as a Factor in Mate Selection." *American Journal of Sociology* 38: 219–224.

Brubaker, Timothy. 1985. *Later Life Families.* Beverly Hills, CA: Sage.

Byrd, Mark, and Trudy Bruess. 1992. "Perceptions of Sociological and Psychological Age Norms by Young, Middle-aged and Elderly New Zealanders." *International Journal of Aging and Human Development* 34, no. 2: 145–163.

Clark, A.L., and P. Wallin. 1965. "Women's Sexual Responsiveness and the Duration and Quality of Their Marriage." *American Journal of Sociology* 71: 187–196.

Cole, Charles. 1984. "Marital Quality in Later Life." In *Independent Aging: Family and Social Systems Perspectives,* ed. W. Quinn and G. Hughston, 72–90. Rockville, MD: Aspen Systems.

Cooley, Charles H. 1922. *Human Nature and the Social Order.* New York: Scribner's.

DiGiulio, Robert. 1989. *Beyond Widowhood.* New York: Free Press.

Elder, Glen, Jr. 1974. *Children of the Great Depression: Social Change in Life Experience.* Chicago: University of Chicago Press.

Field, Dorothy, and Sylvia Weishaus. 1984. "Marriage over Half a Century: A Longitudinal Study." In *Changing Lives,* ed. Martin Bloom, 269–273. Columbia: University of South Carolina Press.

Gelfand, Donald, and Charles Barresi. 1987. *Ethnic Dimensions of Aging.* New York: Springer.

Gordon, Lois, and Alan Gordon. 1987. *American Chronicle: Six Decades in American Life.* New York: Atheneum.

Gove, Walter. 1972. "The Relationship between Sex Roles, Marital Status, and Mental Illness." *Social Forces* 51: 34–44.

Hansson, Robert O., and Jacqueline Remanded. 1987. "Relationships and Aging Family: A Social Psychological Analysis." In *Family Processes and Problems: Social Psychological Aspects,* ed. Stuart Oskamp. Beverly Hills, CA: Sage.

Herman, Steven. 1994. "Marital Satisfaction in the Elderly." *Gerontology and Geriatrics Education* 14, no. 4: 69–79.

Herz, F. 1980. "The Impact of Death and Serious Illness on the Family Life Cycle." In *The Family Life Cycle: A Framework for Family Therapy,* ed. E. Carter and M. McGoldrick, 223–240. New York: Gardner Press.

Hill, Reuben. 1958. "Generic Features of Families under Stress." *Social Casework* 39 (February/March): 139–150.

Holmes, Thomas, and R. Rahe. 1967. "The Social Readjustment Rating Scale." *Journal of Psychosomatic Research* 11: 213–218.

Judd, Eleanor. 1990. "Intermarriage and the Maintenance of Religio-Ethnic Identity: A Case Study: The Denver Jewish Community." *Journal of Comparative Family Studies* 21: 251–268.

Kahn, Robert, and Toni Antonucci. 1981. "Convoys of Social Support: A Life-Course Approach." In *Aging: Social Change,* ed. Sara B. Kiesler et al., 383–405. New York: Academic Press.

Kart, Cary, Eileen Metress, and Seamus Metress. 1988. *Aging, Health, and Society.* Boston: Jones and Bartlett.

Kaufman, Sharon. 1986. *The Ageless Self: Sources of Meaning in Late Life.* Madison: University of Wisconsin Press.

Klein, David, and James White. 1996. *Family Theories: An Introduction.* Thousand Oaks, CA: Sage.

Krantz, Les. 1993. *America by the Numbers.* New York: Houghton Mifflin.

Lauer, Robert, and Jeanette Lauer. 1986. "Factors in Long-Term Marriage." *Journal of Family Issues* 7, no. 4: 382–390.

Lauer, Robert, Jeanette Lauer, and Sarah Kerr. 1990. "The Long-Term Marriage: Perceptions of Stability and Satisfaction." *International Journal of Aging and Human Development* 31, no. 3: 189–195.

Locke, H.J., and K.M. Wallace. 1959. "Short Marital Adjustment and Prediction Tests: Their Reliability and Validity." *Marriage and Family Living* 21: 251–255.

Longino, Charles, and Aaron Lipman. 1981. "Married and Spouseless Men and

Women in Planned Retirement Communities: Support Network Differentials." *Journal of Marriage and the Family* 43: 169–177.

Lopata, Helen. 1973. *Widowhood in an American City.* Cambridge, MA: Schenkman.

Macionis, John. 1997. *Sociology.* Upper Saddle River, NJ: Prentice-Hall.

McCubbin, Hamilton. 1979. "Integrating Coping Behavior in Family Stress Theory." *Journal of Marriage and the Family* 41 (August): 237–244.

McCubbin, Hamilton, and Joan Patterson. 1983. "Family Stress and Adaptation to Crisis: A Double ABCX Model of Family Behavior." In *Family Studies Review Yearbook,* vol. 1, ed. David H. Olson and Brent Miller, 87–106. Newbury Park, CA: Sage.

Medley, M. 1977. "Marital Adjustment in the Post-Retirement Years." *Family Coordinator* 26: 5–11.

Mintz, Steven, and Susan Kellogg. 1988. *Domestic Revolutions.* New York: Free Press.

Neugarten, Bernice, and Gunhild Hagestad. 1976. "Age and the Life Course." In *Handbook of Aging and the Social Sciences,* ed. Robert Binstock and Ethel Shanas, 35–55. New York: Van Nostrand Reinhold.

Newman, Katherine. 1988. *Falling from Grace: The Experience of Downward Mobility in the American Middle Class.* New York: Free Press.

Nordstrom, Bruce. 1986. "Why Men Get Married: More and Less Traditional Men Compared." In *Men in Families,* ed. Robert Lewis and Robert Salt, 31–53. Beverly Hills, CA: Sage.

Parron, Eugenia. 1982. "Golden Wedding Couples: Lessons in Marital Longevity." *Generations* 7, no. 2: 14–16.

Rindfuss, Ronald. 1991. "The Young Adult Years: Diversity, Structural Change and Fertility." *Demography* 28, no. 4: 493–512.

Roberts, W.L. 1979–1980. "Significant Elements in the Relationships of Long-Married Couples." *International Journal of Aging and Human Development* 10: 265–272.

Rowe, G., and W. Meredith. 1982. "Quality in Marital Relationships after Twenty-Five Years." *Family Perspective* 16: 149–155.

Schiff, H. 1977. *The Bereaved Parent.* New York: Crown Publishers.

Schwartz, Mary Ann, and Barbara Marliene Scott. 1994. *Marriages and Families: Diversity and Change.* Englewood Cliffs, NJ: Prentice-Hall.

Smith, J., J. Mercy, and J. Conn. 1988. "Marital Status and the Risk of Suicide." *American Journal of Public Health* 78, no. 1: 78–80.

Spanier, Graham, and Erik Filsinger. 1983. "The Dyadic Adjustment Scale." In *Marriage and Family Assessment: A Sourcebook for Family Therapy,* ed. E. Filsinger, 155–168. Beverly Hills, CA: Sage.

Spanier, Graham, R. Lewis, and C. Cole. 1975. "Marital Adjustment over the Family Life Cycle: The Issue of Curvilinearity." *Journal of Marriage and the Family* 37 (May): 263–275.

Sporakowski, M., and G. Houghston. 1978. "Prescriptions for Happy Marriage: Adjustments and Satisfactions of Couples Married Fifty or More Years." *Family Coordinator* 27 (October): 321–327.

Stinnett, N., L. Carter, and J. Montgomery. 1970. "Marital Need Satisfaction of Older Husbands and Wives." *Journal of Marriage and the Family* 32: 428–434.

Stinnett, Nick, Linda Carter, and James Montgomery. 1972. "Older Persons' Perceptions of Their Marriages." *Journal of Marriage and the Family* 34: 665–670.

Stinnett, Nick, and K. Sauer. 1977. "Relationship Characteristics of Strong Families." *Family Perspective* 11: 3–11.

Swenson, C., R.W. Eskew, and K.A. Kohlhepp. 1981. "Stage of the Family Life Cycle, Ego Development, and the Marriage Relationship." *Journal of Marriage and the Family* 43: 841–853.

————. 1989. "Five Factors in Long-Term Marriages." In *Lifestyles of the Elderly: Diversity in Relationships, Health, and Caregiving,* ed. L. Ade-Ridder and C.B. Hennon. New York: Human Sciences Press, pp. 71–79.

Tietz, W., L. McSherry, and B. Britt. 1977. "Family Sequelae After a Child's Death Due to Cancer." *American Journal of Psychotherapy* 31, no. 3: 417–425.

U.S. Bureau of the Census. 1992. "Marital Status and Living Arrangements: March, 1991." *Current Population Reports,* Series P-20. No. 461. Washington, DC: U.S. Government Printing Office.

Waller, Willard. 1937. "The Rating and Dating Complex." *American Sociological Review* 2: 727–735.

Waller, Willard, and Reuben Hill. 1951. *The Family: A Dynamic Interpretation.* New York: Dryden Press.

Wallerstein, Judith, and Sandra Blakeslee. 1995. *The Good Marriage.* Boston: Houghton Mifflin.

Walsh, F. 1980. "The Family in Later Life." In *The Family Life Cycle: A Framework for Family Therapy,* ed. E.A. Carter and M. McGoldrick. New York: Gardner Press.

Index

About the Author

Finnegan Alford-Cooper earned her Ph.D. in Anthropology at the University of Pittsburgh in 1979. She was associate professor of sociology at East Central University in Oklahoma and at Southampton College of Long Island University in New York, before joining the faculty at Stetson University in DeLand, Florida, in 1996. Her areas of interest are in gerontology, particularly family relations in later life; gender roles; and sociology of health. She has published several articles on different aspects of family relations.